MUSIC IN OPERA

MUSIC IN OPERA
A Historical Anthology

ELAINE BRODY

Professor of Music
New York University

PRENTICE-HALL, INC., Englewood Cliffs, New Jersey

TO MARTIN BERNSTEIN

Printed in the United States of America

13-608109-6

Library of Congress Catalog Card No.: 70-118317

Current printing (last digit):
10 9 8 7 6 5 4 3 2 1

PRENTICE-HALL INTERNATIONAL, INC., London
PRENTICE-HALL OF AUSTRALIA, PTY. LTD., Sydney
PRENTICE-HALL OF CANADA, LTD., Toronto
PRENTICE-HALL OF INDIA PRIVATE LIMITED, New Delhi
PRENTICE-HALL OF JAPAN, INC., Tokyo

Foreword

A successful book publisher was once heard to say: "Slap the title 'Anthology' on any conglomeration of poems, essays or short stories and it's bound to sell." This hard-boiled remark suggests three debatable corollaries. The first—a base untruth—is that the anthologist's life is easy; secondly, there are purchasers who may never open the volume but like to display it on their shelves; third, other buyers, mildly interested in the subject and piously hoping to "get to it one day," subconsciously enjoy being able to profit inexpensively from someone else's collecting zeal and expertise.

Because some truth resides in the foregoing, it has become a fashionable sport of critics today to denigrate the anthology and the anthologist. The word *non-book* has become the epithet with which any compilation may be disparaged. The most outrageous example of how this game is played may be found in a book review written by W. H. Auden, a great poet and librettist who really should know better. The first sentence of his review reads: "An unbook, unwritten by, it would seem, an anal madman." And he further describes the compiler's efforts as "such senseless industry . . . unburdened by the slightest mental effort."[1] The reader of the present "unbook" may be startled to learn that the "volume which Auden sought to destroy with a wave of his waspish wand"[2] was *Mozart: A Documentary Biography* written by the late Otto Erich Deutsch, one of this century's pioneering musical scholars. Few books—or non-books—published in recent years have been of greater usefulness to musicians and students, to musicologists and biographers, to all friends of Mozart. A fourth—and undebatable—corollary may be added to the three above: No matter how painstaking his labors, how useful and comprehensive his compilation, the anthologist's job is a thankless one; and in addition to the conventional attributes of a good author, such as scholarship, imagination, and writing ability, he must also possess dauntlessness, omniscience, and a thick skin.

Anthologies of music have been less subject to a la mode attack than prose or poetry; fortunately, peevish poets have greater difficulty in reading musical notation than they do verse. Music anthologies abound in many areas: folksongs, pop songs, hymn tunes, hit tunes, "Anthology for Musical Analysis," "French horn solos of medium difficulty from the standard orchestral repertory," etc. Many have a clearly defined didactic purpose growing out of classroom experience. Others are of limited or negative value and serve only to prove the book publisher's cynical adage cited above. Historical anthologies fall into a special category, however, for they are harder to "slap together." Not only must primary sources often be tracked down and transcribed, but the very title *Historical* always seems to engender editorial responsibility. Three generations of fledgling musicologists in Germany cut their teeth on Riemann's *Musikgeschichte in Beispielen* and Schering's *Geschichte der Musik in Beispielen.* In the United States, it would be difficult to conceive of teaching music history courses during the two decades

---

[1] *The New York Review of Books,* V, No. 1 (5 August 1965): 12.

[2] From a letter to the editor of *The New York Review of Books* by the infuriated author of this foreword. Never printed!

following World War II without the Davison-Apel *Historical Anthology of Music* or the Parrish-Ohl *Masterpieces of Music Before 1750* and *A Treasury of Early Music*. A score of general historical anthologies have been published to date,[3] and several others are on the way including the vast collection entitled *Das Musikwerk* of which some thirty of a projected fifty specialized volumes have already appeared.[4]

In the field of opera, there has existed hitherto only a single serious historical compilation; it is limited to ten well-chosen excerpts covering the period 1600-1823.[5] There is good reason for the "compleat anthologist" to shy away. The field of opera is immense. An anthology thereof would have to embrace an area equal to that of the spoken drama from Shakespeare to Ionesco but with such added inconveniences as the several unchartered segments of operatic history, the numerous major sources destroyed, and the forgotten improvisational traditions, both musical and theatrical. Furthermore, although a five-hour opera and play are of equal length in the theatre, it takes ten or twenty times as many pages to print the piano-vocal score of the former as it does the text of the latter. The complete operatic example is often very lengthy by itself. Snippets are useless and even a collection of arias alone would project an utterly inadequate portrait of the genre. To depict opera properly—as music drama—full scenes and various types of full scenes must be included. The anthologist must also contend with many voices, sometimes confusingly simultaneous in ensembles and choruses, with many instruments, many languages, ridiculous plots that survive only because of the music with which they are clothed, and curious stage directions that make sense only because of their musical setting.

By effectively anthologizing music in opera within the covers of one volume, Professor Brody has achieved the seemingly impossible. The excerpts are carefully chosen and fulsomely presented; the commentaries are succinct and the translations apt. The latter are ideally placed, that is, *prior to* rather than following or cluttering up the music; and they are linked to the score pages by a novel method of superscripted measure number.

Opera buff and music lover will be pleased to browse through the pages of this volume. For those who will be taking or teaching a course in the history of opera, life will henceforth be infinitely more agreeable with "Brody" on hand.

Barry S. Brook

[3] In addition to those already cited, mention may be made of Johannes Wolf, *Sing- und Spielmusik aus älterer Zeit;* Harold Gleason, *Examples of Music Before 1400;* Karl Geiringer, *Music of the Bach Family;* Jaroslav Pohanka, *Dějiny ceské hudby v príkladech;* W.T. Marroco and H. Gleason, *Music in America.*

[4] Professor Walter Gerboth of Brooklyn College and Joseph Boonin are preparing an *Index of Historical Anthologies of Music* to be published in the Index Series of the Music Library Association. In addition to separately published anthologies, it will also index complete musical examples in the standard histories of music. This will be an invaluable finding list for both teacher and student and permit ready confrontation of two or more versions of the same piece.

[5] Anna Amalie Abert, *Die Oper von den Anfängen bis zum Beginn des 19. Jahrhunderts* in the series *Das Musikwerk;* a second fascicule, *Die Oper II* by W. Pfannkuch, is projected.

Preface

Music in Opera should interest lovers of music and lovers of opera. Traditionally the two groups have maintained their isolation with opera considered "too highbrow for the masses, yet too lowbrow for the classes." Hopefully, this book will convince the music lover of the significance of opera as the source of much instrumental music he loves and respects, and awaken the operagoer to the variety and diversity of music to be found within his favorite genre. Certainly singers and instrumentalists, who, by the very nature of their profession, must spend considerable time perfecting their individual specialities, will gain greater perspective of their collective contribution to the totality of opera.

Music in Opera grew out of my efforts to collect material for a course in the history of opera. Histories of opera, synopses of plots, and countless back issues of *Opera News* did not substitute for the scores themselves. Although records helped, and nothing could compete with attendance at live performances in the opera house, we really could not begin to understand the complex organism we call opera without recourse to the music. Because it is both difficult and costly to acquire even a small collection of scores, I decided to compile this anthology, which, with its close to one hundred excerpts, should provide a bird's-eye view of the monuments of operatic history.

Excerpts are arranged in historical sequence, beginning with the first attempts of the Florentine Camerata and continuing through the equally experimental offerings of twentieth-century composers. Each of the rubrics includes a list of the cities in which the various operas received their first performances. At suitable places in the commentary, charts and diagrams amplify the material of the text. Although *Music in Opera* is not a history of opera, the introductory material of each chapter provides a historical framework from which the interested reader can proceed to further investigations, while the reader with less time or inclination will find he can acquire the essential background for understanding the trends in the growth of opera.

Each excerpt has its own commentary; the emphasis varies from piece to piece. I have tried to show the different ways in which composers have treated music in opera through the past three hundred and fifty years. The reader will discover how musical forms developed within the context of the opera; how arias are different from recitatives; how the composer uses music to set the scene, to further the drama, to heighten the expression of the text. The historical sequence of the examples displays the gradual increase in the indication of dynamics, performance instructions, stage directions, and instrumentation.

Many factors determined the selection of a work. First, all operas from which we have taken excerpts are, in the opinion of the editor, monuments in the history of the genre; second, all excerpts selected are available on records; third, all examples exhibit one or more formal musical characteristics that warrant closer examination; fourth, all pieces are sufficiently short to be included in their entirety. This is not a collection of arias. Our excerpts are yards, not swatches, cut from the fabric of opera in order to help us to understand the way in which the operatic musician organizes his composition. For the earlier operas, the burning question remained: performing edition or scholarly edition. Decisions of this nature are among the most difficult to make. I tried to select wisely and carefully; and in an effort to bring this work to conclusion, I determined to wed practicality to scholarship.

I have had the advice and assistance of colleagues and friends too numerous to mention. However, I should like to acknowledge my gratitude to Professor Martin Bernstein for his initial encouragement and his constant assistance in musical and literary matters whenever and wherever I called upon him. Murray Ralph, my research assistant, made frequent and regular trips to the library, collecting scores and duplicating necessary materials so that I could remain at my typewriter and write. He read the entire manuscript and offered hosts of suggestions. My colleague, Joel Lazar, also read the manuscript and made countless recommendations, particularly in the chapter on contemporary music which he understands so well. Floyd Grave assisted with the mechanical details as the deadline grew close. My husband, David Silverberg, provided the constant support and encouragement without which no author can ever complete a book.

Elaine Brody

Contents

XV
EARLY TRENDS IN TWENTIETH-CENTURY OPERA
PARIS, BERLIN, PRAGUE,
BOSTON, LONDON, MILAN, WASHINGTON
(c. 1900-1960), 467

List of Musical Examples

List of Abbreviations

Only a few abbreviations appear in the text. Most items can be identified by consulting the bibliography at the back of the book. Those books or periodicals which have not been included in the bibliography, but which have been mentioned in the commentary, appear below.

AAA Amalie Abert's "The Opera" in *Anthology of Music* (Köln, 1962).

HAM Davison and Apel's *Historical Anthology of Music* (Cambridge, Mass., 1946).

JAMS *Journal of the American Musicological Society.*

MA Emanuel Winternitz's *Musical Autographs,* 2 vols. (Princeton, 1955).

MoM Parrish and Ohl's *Masterpieces of Music Before 1750* (New York, 1951).

SHO Grout's *Short History of Opera* (see Bibliography).

SR Strunk's *Source Readings* (see Bibliography).

TEM Parrish's *A Treasury of Early Music* (New York, 1958).

Measure numbers placed at the upper left hand corner of each system indicate the numbers of the measure within the excerpt. Each excerpt is numbered separately. Numbers in superscript placed at the upper left hand corner of a word, i.e. ^{111}king, indicate that that sentence (in the translation) begins in measure number 111 of the musical example. Superscripts should help the reader find his way back and forth from the translation to the original language of the score. A superscript with another number, i.e. $^{111-2}$informs the reader that the second stanza also begins at measure 111.

MUSIC IN OPERA

I

Early Baroque Opera

Florence, Mantua, Rome

(c. 1600-1640)

In 1600, Jacopo Peri, a member of the Camerata, wrote and presented *Euridice* as part of the wedding festivities celebrated at Florence in honor of Henri IV, King of France, and Marie de Medici. The composer himself sang the role of Orfeo. *Le Musiche . . . sopra L'Euridice,* as it appears on the title page of the printed score (1610), is the earliest opera for which both music and text are extant. *Euridice* consists of a prologue and six scenes; it is not divided into acts. The action is carried on by solo voices in the then new Florentine theater style, *stile rappresentativo,* a hyperemotional recitation of the words that followed the natural rhythms, accents, and inflections of the language (see Ex. 1). Except perhaps for the strophic aria, there are few self-contained musical forms in the opera. Although Peri uses choral *ritornelli,* or refrains, to unify the more extended scenes, he has not achieved any structural unity of the kind we shall notice in Monteverdi's works. A few accompanying instruments, principally lutes and harpsichords, were played behind the scenes. To us, however, their music is somewhat of a mystery because the score contains only a sparsely figured bass-line placed below the melody of the solo part. These figures, a musical shorthand for the keyboard player, indicate the sequence of chords to be used as accompaniment, not the actual figuration itself. (The tradition of placing the vocal part immediately above the thoroughbass, as the accompaniment was called, lasted through the time of Handel. See MA, plates 17,40,48).

Although *Orfeo* (1607) appeared only a few years after Peri's *Euridice,* several of its features attest to Monteverdi's markedly superior gifts as a musician. For example, he effectively combines pastoral scenes and madrigalesque choruses, theatrical and compositional techniques of the Renaissance, with the new emotional style, the expressive monody of the Baroque. Monteverdi begins to differentiate between lyrical and declamatory recitative, monody, strophic aria, and strophic variation (see Exx. 3-A and 3-B). He indicates specific instrumentation at particular sections of the drama, and finally, he seems to have an overall musical plan for the five acts of *Orfeo.* Despite his concern for the music, however, Monteverdi insisted that the words be the master, not the servant, of the music. (L'orazione sia padrone dell'armonia e non serva.)

After the beginning of opera in Florence and Mantua, new and more lavish productions appeared in Rome where, owing to the presence of the Papal choir, choral operas on religious subjects became popular. One of these operas, *Il San Alessio* (1632) by Steffano Landi (c. 1590-c. 1655), contains a second act introductory piece, a *sinfonia.* The tripartite sectionalization of this sinfonia, or Italian overture, anticipates the number and the sequence of movements in the classical symphony of the eighteenth century (see HAM, 208). The following excerpts from operas produced at Florence and Mantua illustrate several different musical forms and styles that began to crystallize at the opening of the seventeenth century. Unfortunately, we have not been able to include material from any operas staged in Rome.

1

1. STILE RAPPRESENTATIVO

Euridice (1600)

The Messenger Scene, ii

Rinuccini   Jacopo Peri (1561-1633)

In his preface to *Euridice,* Peri describes his attempt to find a proper declamatory style for the new drama: "I judged that the ancient Greeks and Romans (who, in the opinion of many, sang their tragedies throughout . . .) had used a harmony surpassing that of ordinary speech, but falling so far below the melody of song as to take an intermediate form" (SR, p.374). It is this kind of melodic speech that we find in the following example. Peri uses a stepwise melody that derives its shape and rhythm from the text, while the continuo (thoroughbass) provides a rather static accompaniment that moves slowly through a succession of keys. Notice the frequent cadences (mm. 12-13, 16-17, 21-22, 30-31). The editor's embellishment that highlights the word *onda* (wave) at measure 30 seems entirely in line with contemporary performance practice. Remember that only the bass line and the vocal part are Peri's work. The editor has realized (filled in) the balance of the accompaniment. This excerpt reveals another feature of classical drama that reappears in the Renaissance pastorals: the messenger scene designed to inform the audience of proceedings offstage (compare Ex. 3-A).

Translation

In that graceful, tiny grove, where, among the laurel trees the spring flows slowly among the flowers, the lovely bride frolicked with her friends. [19] In the meadow, some picked violets and plucked roses from among the sharp thorns to make wreaths for her hair; others leaned against the flowered banks, singing gently to the sound of the murmuring wave.

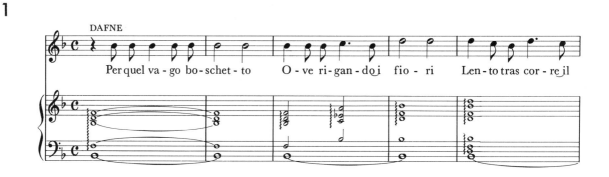

2. INSTRUMENTAL MUSIC IN OPERA
Orfeo (1607)

Toccata, Ritornello, Prologue

Striggio   Claudio Monteverdi (1567-1643)

Instrumental pieces in *Orfeo* include the opening toccata, a fanfare of Venetian origin, various ritornelli (instrumental interludes or refrains) that serve to connect separate stanzas of an aria, and a few seemingly independent *sinfonie*. Recurrent ritornelli unify material within an act (see SHO, p.52). Furthermore, in Acts II and IV, Monteverdi reintroduces the ritornello that preceded the prologue in a manner that interrelates the five acts of the opera. In the original performance instructions (see Sandberger facsimile), the composer requests that the toccata be played three times by all the instruments before the curtain rises, "making it a tone higher, desiring to play the trumpets with mutes." (Mutes raised the pitch of the trumpets a whole tone, so the toccata sounded in D.) The toccata is probably the oldest extant overture. La Musica announces the subject in the prologue. (In early operas and ballets, one or more narrators representing deities or virtues would brief the audience in a prologue before the first act.)

Translation

From my beloved Permessus I come before you, heroes renown'd, off-spring revered of princes, whose glorious achievements[30] fame's voice far vaunting, falls short of truth because the theme's too lofty.

Measures 17-24 recur after each of the four stanzas sung by La Musica.

Toccata [for 5 Trumpets; to be played before the curtain rises]

G. Francesco Malipiero, ed., Monteverdi's *Orfeo* (J. & W. Chester, Ltd., London, 1923.)

3. SEPARATION AND DIFFERENTIATION
OF ARIA AND RECITATIVE
Orfeo (1607)

A. Scene from Act II

Just as it did in the dramas of ancient Greece, the chorus here comments on the action at the opening and closing of the scene. A ritornello (mm. 8-11) introduces Orfeo's tuneful strophic aria and recurs between each of the four stanzas (here abridged). Orfeo rejoices (the presence of nymphs and shepherds emphasizes the joyful atmosphere) until the messenger brings him the news of Euridice's death (mm. 44-81; see commentary for Ex. 1). Monteverdi contrasts lyrical (mm. 31-43) and declamatory (mm. 45-50) styles of recitative and offers an example of monody in Orfeo's "Tu sei morta" (m. 127 ff.). The closing chorus unifies the scene and calls attention to the tragedy by its repetition of the messenger's text, "Ahi caso acerbo" (m. 149 ff.). Notice also the shepherd's repetition of this phrase (compare m. 45 with mm. 112 and 149).

Translation

Chorus of Nymphs and Shepherds: Thus, Orfeo, make worthy of the sound of the lyre these plains, where moves the aura of Sabean scent.

Orfeo: Do you remember O shady woods, my long and cruel torments, when the stones, moved to pity, answered to my lamentations? . . . [23]Because of you, beautiful Euridice, I bless my torments. Pleasure after pain is sweeter; after misfortune happiness is greater.

Shepherd: Look, O look, Orfeo, for all around wood and field are full of laughter; [38]continue with the gilded plectrum to sweeten the air in such a happy day.

Messenger: [44]Alas, bitter fortune, alas impious and cruel fate, alas injurious stars, alas greedy sky.

Shepherd: What mournful sound perturbs the happy day?

Messenger: Thus miserable must I, while Orfeo with his music consoles the sky, pierce his heart with these words of mine?

Shepherd: [58]This is gentle Silvia, sweetest companion of beautiful Euridice: Oh, how sorrowful does she appear! Now what happens? Alas, supreme Gods, do not turn from us your benign gaze.

Messenger: Shepherd, stop your song, for all our happiness has changed to grief.

Orfeo: [70]Whence do you come? Where are you going? What news do you bring, O nymph?

Messenger: To you, Orfeo, I come, unhappy messenger of an unhappier and more fatal accident. Your lovely Euridice . . .

Orfeo: Alas, what do I hear?

Messenger: [80]Your beloved bride is dead.
Orfeo: Alas!
Messenger: In a flowered field with her other companions, she was gathering flowers to make a garland for her locks; [89]when an insidious snake, hiding in ambush midst the grass, bit her foot with a poisonous tooth. Then behold! suddenly her pretty face grew pale and in her eyes those beams with which she put the sun to shame disappeared. [97]Then, full of alarm and grief, we all surrounded her, attempting to revive the spirits, which had abandoned her, with cool water and powerful songs, but nothing was of any use, alas miserable me, for opening a little her languid eyes and calling you, Orfeo, after a deep sigh [107]she died in my very arms, and I stood full of pity and fear within my heart.

Second Shepherd: [111]Alas, bitter fortune, alas, impious and cruel fate, alas injurious stars, alas greedy sky.

First Shepherd: At the grievous news wretched he becomes like silent stone that cannot grieve because of too much grief. [121]Alas, well would he have a heart of Tiger or of Bear who does not feel compassion of your grief deprived of all your happiness, O miserable lover.

Orfeo: You have died, O my life, and I draw breath? You have departed from me never to come back again, and I remain? [135]No, for if songs possess any power, I shall go safely to the profoundest depths, and, softening the heart of the King of Shadows, I shall take you back with me to see the stars: [141]or, if bitter destiny deny me this, I'll then remain with you in company of Death. Farewell Earth, farewell Sky and Sun, farewell.

Chorus of Nymphs and Shepherds: Alas, bitter fortune, alas, impious and cruel fate, alas injurious stars, alas greedy sky.

ORFEO

Sol per te bel - la Eu - ri - di - ce, sol per te bel - la Eu - ri -

di - ce be - ne - di - co il mio tor - men - to, do - po il duol vi è più con - ten - to do - po il mal vi è più fe -

il - ce. Sol per te bel - la Eu - ri - di - ce, sol per te__ bel - la Eu - ri - di - ce.

PASTORE

Mi - ra deh mi - ra Orfeo che d'o - gni in - tor - no ri - de il bo - sco e

ri___ de il pra - to. Se - gui pur col plet - tr'au - ra - to d'ad - dol - cir

10

l'al___tre sue com-pa - gne gi - va co-glien-do fio - ri per
far - ne una ghir-lan-da a le sue chio-me, quand'an-gue in-si-dio- so ch'e - ra fra l'er-be a-sco-so, le punse un
piè___con ve-le - no-so den-te. Ed ec - co im man-ti-nen-te sco-lo - rir-si il bel vi - so
e ne suoi lu - mi spa rir que' lam - pi ond'el-la al sol___ fea scor - no al-
l'hor noi tut-ti sbi-got-ti- te e me-ste le fum-mo intor-no ri-chia-mar tentando li spirti in lei smarriti con l'on-da

13

fre-sca e con pos-sen-ti car-mi, ma nul-la val-se, ahi las-sa ch'ella i lan-gui-di

lu-mi al-quan-to a-pren-do e te chia-man-do Orfe-o, Or-fe-o

Do-po un gra-ve so-spi-ro, spi-rò fra que ste bar-ccia ed io ri-ma-

si pie-na il cor di pie-ta-de e di spa-ven-to.

PASTORE

Ahi ca so a-cer-bo ahi

fat'em-pio e crude-le, Ahi stel-le in-giu-rio-se, ahi ciel a-va-ro.

14

15

mai più non tor-na-re ed io ri-man - go, no, no,___ che se i ver - si alcu - na co - sa pon - no,

n'an-drò si - cu - ro a' più pro-fon - di abis - si e in - te - ne - ri - to il

cor___ del Re de l'om-bre me-co trar-rot - ti a ri-ve-der le stel - le, O se ciò neghe-

ram-mi empio de-sti - no, ri-mar-ró te-co in com-pag-nia. di mor - te

ad-dio ter - ra, ad-dio cie - lo e So - le, ad-di - o.

* Inconsistency in time signature appears in edition cited.

G. Francesco Malipiero, ed., Monteverdi's *Orfeo* (J. & W. Chester, Ltd., London, 1923).

B. "Possente spirto" from Act III

"Possente spirto," Orfeo's virtuoso aria, is in the form of a strophic variation. A recurrent bass line unifies the stanzas by remaining practically the same throughout all but the fourth of six stanzas (mm. 66-69, three measures more than appear in our excerpt). Until the middle of this fourth stanza, Monteverdi writes out two versions of the solo: one simple and one adorned. Scholars have speculated about these two versions. Some suggest that Monteverdi provided an alternative should there be no virtuoso singer available; others assert that the ornamented melody offered one possible manner of embellishment, but not necessarily one that should be followed at each performance.[1]

Monteverdi himself stipulated the various accompanying instruments for each successive stanza: two violins for the first; two cornetti[2] for the second; a double harp for the third; two violins and a *basso da braccio* (cello) for the fourth; three *viole da braccio* and a *contrabasso da viola* for the fifth; only the thoroughbass for the sixth. When the vocal line is particularly brilliant, the instrumental accompaniment exhibits corresponding virtuosity.

Translation

Orfeo: Powerful spirit, most dreadful of Gods, failing whose aid, to pass yonder shore, spirit from body severed, vainly essayed. [16]I live no more, whose breath of life is taken. My bride beloved, my heart no more dwells in me, and without heart, how can I be living? [28]To you I turn my steps through air of blindness, for wherever you are, [33]wherever in Hades such wondrous beauty a paradise createth. [47]Lo, Orfeo, I, who do seek to trace my Euridice's footsteps amid these sands of darkness which, ere this day, [58]no mortal foot hath trodden. O glorious lustrous eyes, eyes so serene, a single glance from you restores my life: [64]ah, who would deny me solace for my sorrow?

3-B

ORFEO [sings his solo to the sound of a chamber organ and a Bass lute]

Pos - sen - te spir - to

Pos - sen - te spir - to

Violino

Violino

[1]See Robert Donington, "Monteverdi's First Opera" in *The Monteverdi Companion,* ed. Denis Arnold and Nigel Fortune (New York: W. W. Norton, 1968).

[2]A *cornett* is an obsolete woodwind instrument sounded by a cupped mouthpiece. Widely used in the sixteenth and seventeenth centuries, it was still used by Gluck in his *Orfeo* (see Ex. 12). The cornett (pl. *cornetti*) should not be confused with the present-day cornet.

20

- co.

- co.

Ritornello

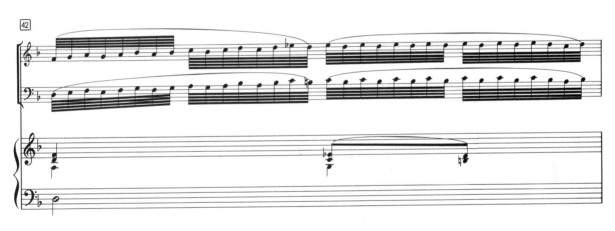

27

61 Here the fourth variation concludes and Monteverdi discontinues the ornamental version.

lu - ci mie   lu - ci se - re - ne,   s'un vo - stro sguar - do   può tor - nar-mi in

64

vi - ta,   ahi chi nie - ga il con - for - to a   le ___ mie pe - ne, ___

G. Francesco Malipiero, ed., Monteverdi's *Orfeo* (J. & W. Chester, Ltd., London, 1923).

4. CHORAL MUSIC IN OPERA

Orfeo (1607)

Scene from Act I

Besides commenting on the action, the chorus in *Orfeo* has two other functions. Its members, who are dressed in rustic costumes, contribute to the pastoral setting the composer required; the chorus members also double as dancers. In the following example, Monteverdi opens with a dancing chorus in the imitative texture of a Renaissance madrigal. At measure 9 he changes to a block chordal style for careful declamation of the text. Malipiero has indicated that the second stanza of the chordal section be repeated after the ritornello. The original manuscript does not state the precise sequence for this repeat. However, both the chorus (mm. 1-15) and the ritornello recur later in the first act, probably for the purpose of unification.

Translation

Chorus of nymphs and shepherds

Leave the mountains, leave the fountains, O nymphs so gay and charming,
O'er green turf skipping in wonted tripping, the wanton foot bestirring.
[91] The sun amazing in wonder gazing, more lovely in your motion than stars entrancing to Luna
   dancing in night's dark purple ocean.
[92] With flower'd caresses adorn their tresses whom death alone can sever.
Thus shall the fire of their desire fierce burn, and bless forever.

29

4

BALLETTO (to be sung by chorus and played by 5 Vlas. , 3 Bass lutes, 2 Hpschds. ,
1 Double harp, 1 Double bass, and 1 small recorder)

30

G. Francesco Malipiero, ed., Monteverdi's *Orfeo* (J. & W. Chester, Ltd., London, 1923).

II

Middle Baroque Opera

Venice, Vienna, London, Paris

(c. 1640-1680)

The first public opera house opened in Venice in 1637. This event accounted for a change in both the quantity and the quality of opera. The newer operas were not occasional pieces to be presented once before an aristocratic audience. They attracted a wider public and, if successful, achieved several performances. Before the end of the century, almost four hundred operas had been produced in seventeen theaters in Venice itself, and probably as many more by Venetian composers in other cities (see SHO, p. 79). Librettos changed, too. Mythology, formerly the exclusive source for these dramas, gave way to history, and plots with historical themes abounded. Recitatives decreased in number as composers began to concentrate on the aria as an alternative to the monotonous recitative and as the best means of lyrical expression at moments of extreme passion. Along with the expansion and elaboration of the aria came the phenomenon of the virtuoso singer who, delighting in the plaudits of the crowd, often indulged in vocal acrobatics at the expense of the action. As the music of opera assumed greater importance, it was left to the composer to seek a balance between the text and the music. Monteverdi attained this goal in *L'incoronazione di Poppea* (1642), his last opera, in which he treated a historical subject, compressed the action into three acts instead of five, and achieved a degree of musical characterization unequalled before Mozart (see Exx. 5-A, 5-B, 5-C).

Later in the century, the more spectacular operas of Monteverdi's pupil Cavalli (1602-1676) showed a tendency to cater to public taste. Their frequent performances outside of Venice, in other Italian cities and in Paris, attest to their popularity. *Egisto* (1643) and *Serse* (1654) both appeared in the French capital a few years after their initial Italian performances, *Serse* with ballets by Lully. By mid-century, in the operas of Cesti (1623-1669), Cavalli's younger contemporary, arias began to outnumber recitatives and to sound appreciably different from them. Furthermore, the arias now assumed distinguishable forms: strophic, through-composed, and strophic variation, the last appearing most frequently in laments (Ex. 7-F; see also SHO, p. 76).

Although opera originated in Italy, it had begun to take root in France by the mid-seventeenth century, and in the last decades of this century in England and in Germany as well. Differences in French and Italian operas of this period reflect the sociological differences between the two peoples. In France, a flourishing ballet fostered the growth of opera. The tastes of a strong monarch, Louis XIV, surrounded by a court extending from Paris to Versailles, favored the development of a national opera rather than the regional types (religious and comic) found in various Italian musical centers. Lully, an expatriate Italian, arrived in Paris as a youth and by astute business management soon made himself virtually musical director of France. In charge of the royal Paris Opera, he became a significant figure in the growth of the orchestra as an entity. Lully selected his players carefully, trained them, well, and thus established the foundation for one of the best-known orchestras of the eighteenth century. The string section of Lully's orchestra was still divided into five parts. (The idea for five-part string sections probably started in the sixteenth century, when choral music was generally written in five parts, and instruments, if they participated in performance, doubled a specific vocal line.) Flutes and oboes usually performed in pastoral scenes, with bassoons and harpsichord supplying the continuo; trumpets and drums joined the players in more jubilant passages. Owing to the classical influence of contemporary French dramatists—Corneille (1606-1684), Racine (1639-1699), and Molière (1622-1673), the last of whom collaborated with him on several operas—Lully sought to further the importance of the drama in the total scheme of opera. Towards this end, he insisted that his singers attend rehearsals at the French theaters to familiarize themselves with the gestures and the declamation of the actors; he wrote his operas in five acts; and he observed the classical unities. Lully adapted recitative to the inflections of the French language and employed the orchestra to accompany specific recitatives in order to heighten their dramatic effect. He began to use the shorter *air*, less elaborate than the Italian aria, and occasionally, in the interest of the drama, he interrupted a long *arioso* (a song that is midway between an aria and a recitative) with sections in recitative. Several other conventions accrued to French opera as the result of its close association with the theater and the ballet: the stately French overture (see Ex. 6-A), the vivid portrayals of nature scenes, and the numerous stylized dances and processionals (see Ex. 11).

Seventeenth-century English opera originated in the earlier *masque,* a more static dramatic entertainment than the contemporary French and Italian opera. Although replete with scenery and costumes, interpolated songs, and instrumental pieces, the masques had relatively little action. With the resumption of stage presentations after the return of the monarchy in 1660, the dramatic works of Henry Purcell (c. 1659-1695) emerged as the most significant English contribution to the development of opera. In *Dido and Aeneas,* his only opera that is sung throughout (the others are plays with incidental music and spoken dialogue), Purcell returned to classical mythology for his subject, showed his French training with his use of storm scenes, added an English witches' and sailors' chorus (danced as well as sung), and set a very inferior text to remarkably fine music. Despite the poor text, Purcell succeeded in writing unusual figurations for his recitatives, created several beautiful arias over a ground bass (Exx. 7-E and 7-F), and left us superb examples of text underlay for the inflexible English language. He derived his rhythms and accents from the words in a manner that became the model for Handel and also for Sir Arthur Sullivan two centuries later. Purcell's writing for strings was more advanced and more idiomatic than Lully's, but he contributed little to the growth of the orchestra.

5. VOCAL TYPES IN ITALIAN OPERA

L'incoronazione di Poppea (1642)

A. Act I, scene iv

Busenello   Claudio Monteverdi

In this scene between Poppea and her nurse Arnalta, Monteverdi paints two constrasting musical portraits: the self-assured, confident, willful Poppea, and her older, more mature, wiser nurse, Arnalta, whose advice she refuses to heed. Monteverdi underlines Poppea's arrogance with short notes and syllabic text setting (mm. 26-33). Arnalta's admonitions are in longer notes (mm. 61-66), and only after Poppea's persistent "No, no, non temo" and "Per me guerreggia" does she retort with "Ben sei pazza." Monteverdi achieves unity without sacrificing variety. The scene is unified by the ritornello (mm. 1-8) that recurs (in mm. 12-18 and 54-60) and also by textual repetition (cf. mm. 26 and 67, 36 and 85). For variety, the composer has altered the music of the repeated text.

Translation

Poppea: Hope, you come caressing my heart, flattering my spirit, and in my fancy, surround me with a royal mantle. [26]I have no fear. Love and Fortune fight for me.

Arnalta: Ah my daughter, let us hope you are not courting disaster.

Poppea: I have no fear . . .

Arnalta: [74]Empress Ottavia knows of your love for Nerone, so I am afraid, I fear every day for your life.

Poppea: Love and Fortune fight for me . . .

Arnalta: [103]You are surely mad if you believe that a blind boy and a bald woman can keep you safe and sound.

36

Spe-ran - za, _____ tu mi va-i il ge-nio lu - sin - gan -

do. E mi cir-con-di, intan - to, Di re-gio si, ma ___ im-ma-gi - na - rio man -

to. No, no, non te-mo, no, no, non te-mo, no, di no-ia al - cu - na, no, no, non

te - mo, no, no, no non te - mo, non te - mo, no, no, no non te - mo, non te - mo, no, no,

no, di no-ia al-cu - na Per me guer - reg - gia, guer-

reg - gia, per me guer-reg-gia, guer-reg - gia, per me guer-

reg-gia, guer-reg - gia A-mor, guer-reg-gia A - mor, e la For - tu - na, e

la For - tu - na.

ARNALTA

Ahi, fi - glia, fi - glia,

vo-glia il cie - lo Che que-sti ab-brac-cia men - ti Non sia-no un gior-no i pre-ci-pi - zi

No, no, no, no,no, no, no, no, non te - mo,_____

tuo - i.

no, no, no, non te - mo, no, no, no, non te - mo, no, di no-ia al - cu - na.

ARNALTA

L'im-pe - ra - tri - ce Ot - ta - via ha pe-ne - tra - ti Di Ne-ron gli a - mo - ri, On - de

Monteverdi's *L'incoronazione di Poppea,* edited by Giacomo Benvenuti (1937). By permission of Edizioni Suvini-Zerboni, Milano.

B. Valletto's Song, Act II, scene iv

In the second act, Monteverdi inserted a short comic intermezzo in which a young page boy describes his puzzling palpitations (mm. 1-8) when in the presence of the maid Damigella. (Notice that the characters' names indicate their social station, valet and maid.) We might regard this song as an example of modified strophic form, with the two stanzas separated by a ritornello (mm. 17-21) that also concludes the piece. (The term *ritornello* now begins to be used for any instrumental interlude in an aria.) Valletto's question should be compared with Cherubino's "Non so più" from the first act of Mozart's *Le Nozze di Figaro*.

Translation

Valletto: I feel a certain—I don't know what—that bites me and delights me. [5] Tell me what it is, lovely damsel. I should do, I should say, [13] but I don't know what I want. [22] If I am with you, my heart beats so, and when you leave I feel so silly. I am always thinking and dreaming of [29] your breast. I should do, I should say . . .

5-B

Monteverdi's *L'incoronazione di Poppea,* edited by Giacomo Benvenuti (1937). By permission of Edizioni Suvini-Zerboni, Milano.

C. Final Duet, Act III, scene ix

With the magnificent final love duet sung by Nerone and Poppea, Monteverdi set a standard of excellence unmatched by several generations of opera composers who succeeded him. The form of the duet is ternary: a da capo aria (ABBA; the middle section appears in mm. 37-66), further unified by the recurrent basso ostinato, a four-bar melody in triple meter that characterizes the A section. (See Schrade's *Monteverdi,* p. 366 ff., for an excellent analysis of this piece.) The balance between the voices, the spacing of the imitation, and the flow of the melodic lines demonstrate the talents of a master craftsman.

Translation

Poppea and Nerone: Let me but gaze on you, delight in you, hold you and enfold you. [17]No more anguish, no more death, O my life, O my treasure. [37]I am yours, you are mine, my hope, tell me so, my idol. You are my joy, my heart, my life. [66]Let me but gaze on you . . .

5-C

Monteverdi's *L'incoronazione di Poppea*, edited by Giacomo Benvenuti (1937). By permission of Edizioni Suvini-Zerboni, Milano.

6. INSTRUMENTAL AND
VOCAL MUSIC IN FRENCH OPERA

Alceste (1674)

A. Overture

Quinault   Jean-Baptiste Lully (1632-1687)

The French overture, of which the following example is typical, evolved from numerous sources, among them the instrumental *canzona* and the Venetian fanfare (see Ex. 2). Lully firmly established the musical form of this genre. It begins with a slow introduction, in duple meter, which is generally homophonic in texture and proceeds in dotted rhythms. The second section is faster, characterized by polyphonic texture with free imitation between the parts. The second part is often followed by a return to the stately pace of the introduction (as in our example) without, however, any thematic resemblance to it. Usually the entire second section (mm. 25-54) is repeated. Later composers, among them Purcell and Handel, made frequent use of the French overture to introduce their operas and oratorios.

In $\frac{6}{4}$ in the original.

Lentement

Lully's *Alceste*, ed. by Theodore d. l. Lajarte (Theodore Michaelis; represented by Broude Brothers Ltd., 1967).

Alceste

B. "Scène infernale," Act IV, scene i

Lully's significant contribution to French opera lies in his treatment of recitative. He shaped his recitative to have it follow the changing dramatic inflections and pauses of the text. He learned this technique from observing actors in the French theater. Because of its extremely precise fidelity to the text, French recitative of this epoch usually contains numerous meter changes. These changes are not as complicated as they look in the score; they simply correspond to the declamation and accents of the narration or dialogue (see m. 57 ff.). Lully introduced the arioso style of melodic writing, a vocal style midway between aria and recitative, thus reducing the difference between recitative and melodic passages for solo voice that was so marked in Italian opera. Compare, for example, the passages in the dialogue between Charon and the shade (mm. 57-66) with the aria-like section that precedes it.

Translation

Charon: Sooner or later everyone must cross in my boat, young or old, as it pleases the Fates. Shepherd and king, we treat them both without ceremony.

You who wish to cross, come, wandering spirits; forward, mournful shades, and pay the tribute that I levy or else turn back and wander on these gloomy banks.

Chorus: Pass me, Charon, pass me.

Charon: First you must satisfy me; I must be paid for such hard work.

Chorus: Pass me, Charon, pass me.

Charon: Pay, pass, pay, pass . . . Wait; you have no money; off with you.

Rebuffed Shade: A shade takes so little room.

Charon: Either pay or turn your steps elsewhere.

Shade: Mercy! For pity's sake don't turn me back.

Charon: There's no pity here and Charon grants no mercy.

Shade: Alas!

6 - B   (This scene portrays the dismal shores of the river Acheron.)

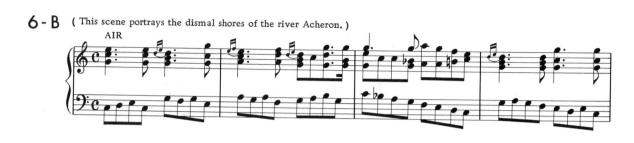

CARON   rowing his boat

Il faut pas-ser tôt ou tard, Il faut pas-ser dans ma bar - que; Il faut pas-

ser tôt ou tard, Il faut pas - ser dans ma bar - que. On y

vient jeune ou viei-llard, Ain-si qu'il plait à la Par - que. On y re-çoit, sans é-

gard, Le ber-ger et le mo - nar-que; On y re - çoit, sans é - gard, Le ber-

ger et le mo - nar - que. Il faut pas - ser tôt ou tard Il faut pas - ser dans ma

bar - que; Il faut pas - ser tôt ou tard Il faut pas - ser dans ma bar -

que.

Vous qui vou-lez pas - ser, ve - nez, mâ-nes er - rants, Ve - nez, A-van-

54

S.

pas.

Hé - las!

C.

La pi-tié n'est point i - cy   bas,   Et Ca - ron ne fait point de grâ - ce.

Lully's *Alceste,* ed. by Theodore d. l. Lajarte (Theodore Michaelis; represented by Broude Brothers Ltd., 1967).

7. INSTRUMENTAL AND VOCAL MUSIC IN ENGLISH OPERA

Dido and Aeneas (1689)

A. Overture

Tate   Henry Purcell (c. 1659-1695)

Purcell studied with a pupil of Lully, whose influence we notice in this French overture (compare Ex. 6-A), in the numerous dances and incidental music, and in the outdoor scenes, many of which are set through music (see the Witches' Cave). Observe the binary form of this overture, its repeated second section (m. 14 to the end), and the absence of a final, slow section in contrast to Ex. 6-A. (These musical examples are based on Edward J. Dent's edition of *Dido and Aeneas* with occasional alterations of continuo.)

7-A

B. Accompanied Recitative and Chorus, Act I, scene i

Purcell's accompanied recitative clearly reveals its relationship to the Italian chamber cantata, particularly where florid passages (mm. 1-15) replace the tedious dominant-tonic cadences that characterize most Baroque operas. Purcell not only allowed for lyrical declamation within a precise rhythmic framework, but also offered us a richly varied harmonic palette in the keys selected for the dialogue between Dido and Belinda (Ex. 7-B, mm. 11-15). The change of key to C major for the following chorus (mm. 26-41) reflects the assurance of Aeneas's love, which Belinda and the Second Woman offer to Dido. Also be sure to notice the frequency of melodic chromaticism throughout this example.

7- B

soft___ in peace, and yet how fierce,___ how fierce in___ arms! A tale so

strong___ and full of woe___ might melt___ the___ rocks as well as___ you. What

stub-born heart un-mov'd could see Such dis-tress,___ such pi - e-ty? Mine with

storms___ of___ care___op-prest, Is taught to pi - ty the dis-

trest, Mean wretch-es' grief can touch, So soft,___ so sen-si-ble my

Purcell's *Dido and Aeneas*, edited and arranged by Edward J. Dent. Copyright 1925 by the Oxford University Press, London. Renewed in U.S.A., 1953. Used by permission.

C. The Witches' Cave, Act I, scene ii

The instrumental music that introduces this scene and the accompaniment to the recitative immediately following (mm. 17-36) are noteworthy for their originality. The contrast of keys, f minor to prepare for the impending sinister projects of the witches (mm. 1-30) and Bb major as the witches rejoice in their plans (m. 37 ff.), discloses Purcell's careful planning, not only of this scene but of the entire opera. The witches decide to raise a storm; they sing a duet in d minor (not reprinted here), which is followed by the Echo Chorus in F major (Ex. 7-D).

SORCERESS

Way-ward sis-ters, you that fright The lone - ly tra-vel-ler by

night, Who like dis - mal ra - vens cry - ing Beat the win-dows of _____ the

dy - ing, Ap - pear, ap-pear at my call, and share __ in the fame Of a

D. Echo Chorus, Act I, scene ii

This chorus displays the typically Baroque fondness for sharp contrasts, echo by means of terraced dynamics. Purcell alternated between the homophonic, homorhythmic choruses of which the audience can understand the words, and polyphonic choruses that project a mood without necessarily communicating every bit of the text. His employment of both styles adds variety to the texture. In the material that connects our two examples (Exx. 7-C and 7-D), the composer inserted still another witches' chorus (Baroque audiences loved them) with imitative entries and a homophonic close, all set to the nonsense syllables, "Ho, ho." This "Ho, ho" chorus represents one of the earliest of a long line of similar choruses in English operas and oratorios.

Purcell's mastery of English text setting also deserves our attention. Observe, for example, how the second syllable of "prepare" (m. 6) and the first syllable of "dreadful" and "practice" (mm. 7-9) receive the proper accentuation.

7-D

this o - pen air.   soft - ed cell.

this o - pen air.   - ed cell.

this o - pen air.   - ed cell.

this o - pen air.   - ed cell.

loud   loud
In our deep vault - ed cell   the

In our deep vault - ed cell   the

In our deep vault - ed cell   the

In our deep vault - ed cell   the

Purcell's *Dido and Aeneas*, edited and arranged by Edward J. Dent. Copyright 1925 by the Oxford University Press, London. Renewed in U.S.A., 1953. Used by permission.

E. Aria Over a Ground Bass, Act I, scene i

In the next two examples, we can see how Purcell contrasted two different arias, both written over a ground bass. Each act of *Dido and Aeneas* contains a long aria of this type as part of the overall plan of the opera. Both of our examples are sung by Dido, one in the first act where she expresses her premonitions of tragedy, and the other at the conclusion of the opera, her lament. "Ah, Belinda" has a four-bar ground that repeats eleven times in c minor (mm. 1-44), twice in g minor (mm. 45-52), and concludes eight times in c minor. Observe how Purcell increases the agitation in the accompaniment (mm. 54-64) as the emotion intensifies; notice also the anguish in the word-painting on "torment" (m. 15), the listlessness on "languish" (mm. 49-53), and the perpetually overlapping phrase-structure that Purcell employs for variety. For example, only at measures 9 and 25 does the beginning of the vocal melody correspond to the start of the four-bar ground. Elsewhere, the vocalist's phrase commences above the second, third, or fourth measure of the ground.

7-E

ah,____ ah, Be - lin - da, I am____ prest____ with____ tor - ment,

Ah, ah, ah,__ Be - lin - da,__ I____ am prest____ with__

tor - ment not to be con - fest; Peace____ and

I are stran - gers____ grown, Peace____ and I are

stran - gers,____ stran - gers grown, I lan - guish

F. Dido's Lament, Act III, final scene

Purcell uses an eight-bar recitative to introduce Dido's Lament, the aria over a ground in the last act of the opera. Although Exx. 7-E and 7-F are both in the same form, the aria over a ground, their styles differ considerably. The repeated melody in the Lament has an irregular length, five bars instead of the usual four, and a pattern that descends chromatically from G to D and then settles into a cadential formula resolving to the tonic. This ground begins on an upbeat, a customary opening that "Ah, Belinda" lacks, and it appears eleven times in the same key of g minor. No transposition to the dominant occurs here and therefore no subsequent return to the tonic. A shorter piece, yet more pathetic in its reiteration of the one melodic phrase, this Lament also demonstrates traditional word-painting in the flurry of notes that accompanies the word "darkness" at measure 2, the minor 2nd on "death" at measure 7, the tritone descent on "laid in earth" (mm. 16-17) and "trouble" (mm. 20 and 30). Again the various lengths of the vocal phrases act as a foil to the repetitive bass.

We have included only a few bars of the mournful chorus that follows the Lament. The downward plunge of the melody (mm. 64-65) and its repetition in the statement of each of the four imitative voices emphasize the tragic affection of this concluding scene. Notice also how the melody of the introductory recitative makes a chromatic descent of an octave (mm. 1-9).

7-F

Purcell's *Dido and Aeneas,* edited and arranged by Edward J. Dent. Copyright 1925 by the Oxford University Press, London. Renewed in U.S.A., 1953. Used by permission.

III

Late Baroque Opera

Rome, Naples, London
Dresden, Hamburg, Paris, Vienna
(c. 1680-1750)

In the late Baroque, four composers made major contributions to the development of opera: Scarlatti in Italy, Keiser in Germany, Handel in England, and Rameau in France. Alessandro Scarlatti (c. 1660-1725), an exceedingly prolific composer, is relatively unknown to today's audiences because of the lack of modern editions of his works. Although his operas were performed in Rome, Florence, and Venice, his name is generally associated with the city of Naples, an early center of comic opera (see Chapter V). Scarlatti incorporated folk elements in comic scenes in several of his operas; he also was among the first to conclude an act with an ensemble. He assimilated many of the new features that appeared in the violin music of this period and was thus able to include idiomatic accompanimental figures in his writing for four-part string sections. Two of his operas, *La Griselda* of 1721 (HAM 259; see also MA, plate 17) and *La caduta de' Decemviri* of 1697 (TEM, 44), open with fine examples of the *sinfonia avanti l'opera* (see p. 1), the Italian overture, which, with its three-part form, fast-slow-fast sequence of tempos, and extensive use of homophonic texture, was a predecessor of the classical symphony. A da capo aria (Ex. 8) from one of Scarlatti's earlier operas already reveals the traditional Italian emphasis on melody and bel canto line. Notice also the continued preference for the tripartite vocal form as it appears firmly established in Scarlatti's capable hands (compare Ex. 5-C).

In 1678, the first public opera house outside of Italy opened in Hamburg. Initially, Italian composers and Italian operas (often with German recitatives) dominated the scene. (See *Boris Goudenow*, 1710, by Mattheson, a German composer, who utilized both languages in this opera!) Later, German composers, Keiser among the most outstanding, began to write complete operas in German. Keiser achieved notable advances in the orchestral accompaniments to his recitatives (see Ex. 9); and in his arias, he usually avoided the stereotyped da capo form.

The Doctrine of Affections, a set of musical clichés or melodic conventions that could be classified and taught by composers to their apprentices, became the established technique for the composition of vocal works. Its basis was an attempted analogy between music and speech. By means of the *Affektenlehre* (as it was called in German), the composer could communicate with his listeners much as a speaker talks to his audience. Related to this doctrine was the restriction to one mood (or affect) in each aria: joy, sadness, jealousy, anger. Because of this limitation, much Baroque music is monothematic.

Handel (1685-1759), the German-born composer who studied in Italy and produced most of his works in England, resembles Purcell in his fusion of international styles. His operas are usually to Italian texts; his oratorios are in English. Both his oratorios and his operas generally begin with a French overture (see Ex. 6-A). Handel's excellent facility with English texts, noticeable in his famous oratorio, *Messiah*, appears to advantage also in *Acis and Galatea,* a *serenata* to texts by several prominent English poets. Inasmuch as *Acis and Galatea* is not always classified as an opera, we have selected an excerpt from one of the recently revived operas by Handel, *Giulio Cesare* (1724). Our example displays Handel's imaginative instrumentation. A horn obbligato appears in the aria "Va tacito e nascosto" (Ex. 10) and underlines the meaning of the words.

Rameau (1683-1764), a theorist and a composer of keyboard works, wrote his first opera at the age of fifty. He continued along the path begun by Lully and used mythological subjects, extensive choral sections, ballets, and outdoor scenes. He tended to prefer the enlarged scene-complex, a feature that also appealed to Gluck. Rameau's principal contribution lies in the instrumental music of his operas, several of which (*Zoroastre,* for example) begin with overtures that move without pause into their first act. The attached overture of *Zoroastre* (1749) summarizes the plot through the music and contains one of the earliest uses of clarinets in the orchestra. Otherwise, Rameau's treatment of the orchestra is not remarkable. His reduction of string parts from five to four only brought the French opera orchestra in line with contemporary practice. Example 11, the two minuets and the storm scene from *Hippolyte et Aricie* (1733), Rameau's first opera, provides us with an excellent sample of operatic nature painting.

To summarize, by the late Baroque, Italian opera seria reigned supreme in all countries except France. However, national differences were beginning to emerge and later figured prominently in the various styles of comic opera (see Chapter V).

8. THE DA CAPO ARIA

Pompeo (1683)

Minato   Alessandro Scarlatti (c. 1660-1725)

In this strophic da capo aria from one of his early opere serie, Scarlatti favored a stepwise melody consisting of major and minor seconds that emphasize the bitterness of the text. The downward leap of a minor sixth on "lasciate" (m. 7) heightens the expression of that word. The accompaniment does not actually double the vocal line; rather, it offers the soloist harmonic and rhythmic support while allowing the singer a degree of independence. The B section (m. 11 ff.) in the dominant effectively balances the two A sections that surround it.

Translation

[5]O cease wounding me, or let me die, merciless lights, more cold and deaf to my suffering than ice and marble. O cease wounding me. . .

More cruel and deaf to my suffering than a serpent, than an adder, cruel proud eyes, you can cure me and still enjoy my yearning. O cease wounding me. . .

8

A. Scarlatti's "O Cessate di piagarmi" from *Pompeo*, arranged and edited by Knud Jeppesen in *La Flora*, vol. 1 (copyright Wilhelm Hansen, Copenhagen, 1959). Used by kind permission.

9. RECITATIVE AND ARIA IN GERMAN OPERA

Die römische Unruhe, oder Die edelmüthige Octavia (1705)

Act III, scene viii

Feind

Reinhard Keiser (1674-1739)

In this fine example of German Baroque opera, we can examine Keiser's control of the longer scene with its extensive alternation of accompanied and secco recitative (mm. 1-55) that precedes the aria. Strings and continuo provide the fairly sophisticated accompaniment to this highly expressive recitative and aria. Notice how carefully Keiser has considered text underlay and accentuation, a slightly more difficult task in German than in the euphonious Italian language. Also observe the unorthodox voice leading in the accompaniment, further proof of the composer's originality. (I am indebted to my colleague, Joel Lazar of the University of Virginia, for his realization of the continuo from the full score as it appeared in the Handel-Gesellschaft edition, Leipzig, 1902.)

Translation

Ah! Nero is no longer Nero! Poor prince! No, no, poor slave! Where are dignity and honor? [11]Vanished. Vanished, alas, through unjust wounds. O woe! What self-reproach do I feel? Ha, Agrippina shows herself. Antonia back, Antonia! Ah, Burrhus, Crispin, Aulus, Tuscus, mother Agrippina—[23]What? Are not the hangmen here to seize thee, forsaken Nero? Ah, yes! What have I committed, what have I done! Done heedlessly! [30]Who's there? What do I hear? Ah, Nero is no longer Nero.

[35]Afflicted soul, are you ashamed? Do your dry lips wither? My voice becomes hoarse, my tongue cracks. Oh! A drink! I am thirsty. Is there no goblet of wine here? I am thirsty; will no one quench my thirst? [44]Draw water, unlucky prince! See, see, how he drinks from a pool; he whom once the best wine could not satisfy. [49]Will no one offer a towel to dry a king's hands, that my son's soft hair must serve instead? Is it thus that bliss ends?

[57]Marvel, safe orbit of the world; marvel, ye rulers, and see how here a mighty emperor falls, how Nero perishes in blood.

[83]Something stirs; ears, listen, what is it? A leaf from a tree; the branch of an ash tree sways indifferently; I feel as if in a dream.

[91]My eye glazes, my lips pale, my heart pounds and my veins throb! What executioners are these? Who am I? Ah! Nero is no longer Nero!

A dilapidated, thatched hut on a bare field; a village in the distance. Nero disguised and in flight.

9

Ne - ro, dich zu fan-gen? Ach ja! ach ja! Was hab'ich doch be - gang-en! was hab' ich doch voll-

bracht! voll-bracht und nie be - dacht! [Accomp.] [Secco] Wer kommt? was

[Accomp.] ist es, das ich hör'? Ach, Ne - ro ist nicht Ne - ro mehr! ach, Ne - ro ist nicht Ne - ro mehr!

[Secco] Be - trüb - te See - le, schmach-te - stu? ihr trock-ne Leff-zen, dür - ret ihr? Die

Stim - me wird mir rauch, die Zun - ge spal-tet sich, ach, ein - en Trunk! mich

wie Ne - ro blu - tig, wie Ne - ro blu - tig un - ter - ge - het.

Adagio
(Secco)

Es regt sich was

ihr Oh - ren, horcht, was ists? Ein Blatt von ei - nem Baum, ein

Es - chen-Laub rührt sich, von ohn-ge - fehr; ich bin nur noch als wie in ei - nen

Traum

(Accomp.)

Mein Au - ge starrt, der Mund wird blass,

legato

84

das Hert-ze pocht, die A-dern be-ben mir! Was zei-gen sich vor Hen-ker hier? Wer bin ich, wer bin ich, wer bin ich? Ne-ro,—ach, ach Ne-ro, du bist nicht Ne-ro mehr, ach Ne-ro, du— bist nicht Ne-ro mehr.

10. ITALIAN OPERA IN ENGLAND

Giulio Cesare (1724)

Act I, scene iv

Haym
George Frideric Handel (1685-1759)

Caesar's aria with horn obbligato appeared in one of Handel's most successful operas, *Giulio Cesare,* written about nine years before his earliest oratorio. In this excerpt we can observe another da capo aria (cf. Ex. 8); the B section begins in measure 42. This aria, written for one of the leading male altos of the day, the castrato Senesino (c. 1680-c. 1750), was originally set an octave higher than indicated in our example. Today, with the era of the castrati long passed, the part is sung by a baritone as scored here. In addition to the castrato role (typical of the Italian school of opera, which dominated Europe during this period), other Baroque characteristics include the imitative counterpoint of the instrumental introduction to the aria; the terraced dynamics effected by the alternation of tutti and solo (implied in the texture at mm. 6-7 and 16-17); the use of the horn, an established convention in arias whose subject was hunting (because the French horn was originally a hunting horn); the flurry of notes that regularly underlines the word "nascosto" ("concealed"); and the traditional dotted rhythm of the horn melody itself.

Translation

Caesar: The astute hunter, when he is avid for prey, moves silently, unseen [concealed]. And he who is disposed to evil wants nobody to see the deceit within his heart. The astute hunter. . . unseen.

spo-sto,   non bra-ma che si   ve-da   l'in-gan-no_del suo_   cor,   l'in-gan-no_   del   suo cor.

D.C.

Handel's *Julius Caesar*, ed. Walter Gieseler (Bärenreiter-Verlag, Kassel, Basel, London, Paris).
Used by kind permission of Bärenreiter.

11. INSTRUMENTAL AND VOCAL MUSIC IN FRENCH OPERA

Hippolyte et Aricie (1733)

Pellegrin   Jean-Philippe Rameau (1683-1764)

Rameau contrasted both tonality and texture in this pair of minuets that preceded
the storm scene of Act IV. In the full score we notice that the composer omitted the
customary basso continuo, which usually provided the harmonic support, and that
instead he allotted the chordal underpinning to the strings and featured oboes of this
piece. In his use of woodwinds in the second minuet (B), he anticipated a later practice;
minuet/trio movements of the classical period often employed woodwinds in the trio, or
second minuet. Our excerpt, a typical French *minuet doublé* with the second minuet *en
rondeau*, should be played in the following sequence: A:| |:A':| |:B:| |A A' C A A'
(capital letters in the score have been added by the editor).

In the storm scene that concludes the act (m. 57 ff.), Rameau anticipated Weber's
coloristic use of the orchestra (see Ex. 30-A). The chorus, commenting on nature's
powers and also on the events of the drama, alternates with the three soloists,
Hippolyte, Aricie, and Phèdre. Notice that the solo melody has the arioso quality
peculiar to French opera (see Ex. 6-B). Rameau (as Lully did before) also used frequent
changes of meter in order to conform to the rhythm and accents of the French language
(see m. 94 ff). Observe the various accompanying figures (mm. 76-87), the use of the
chorus at climactic moments, and the more continuous music, for example, between
scenes iii and iv. All of these features influenced Gluck in his later reform operas.

Translation

Chorus: What noise, what winds, O heaven, what a mountainous sea! What a monster the sea has
    brought before us. O Diane, hurry to help us! Fly down from the sky.

Hippolyte: Come, in her absence, I'll be your guide.

Aricie: Stop, Hippolyte, where are you hurrying? What will become of him! I tremble, I am
    shaking. [82] Is this the way the gods protect virtue? Even Diane abandons him.

Chorus: O Gods, what flames envelop him!

Aricie: What thick clouds! All is clearing. . . Hippolyte does not appear. I am dying. . .

Chorus: O cruel fate, Hippolyte is no more. . .

Scene iv

Phèdre: What plaints summon me here?

Chorus: Hippolyte is no more.

89

11

94

Scène IV - Phèdre, band of hunters and huntresses

IV
Opera in the Early Classical Period
Berlin, Vienna, Paris
(c. 1750-1775)

Before the end of the third decade of the eighteenth century, we notice two distinct kinds of opera: serious and comic. Opera seria, a continuation of late Baroque aristocratic opera, had entrenched itself in most of the Italian centers and in German cities where Italian composers like Steffani (1654-1728) and Italian-oriented German composers like Hasse (1699-1783) wrote in the older style (see AAA 3). Opera buffa (see Chapter V), characterized by music in the new, lighter, homophonic texture of the classical period, differed considerably from the seria. One type of buffa seems to have originated in Naples as *intermezzi* (interludes) between acts of the seria. These intermezzi expanded and in time broke loose from the seria to become separate, self-contained works. Another category of buffa probably developed independently of the seria, and in time the two types of buffa united.

Conceivably, one of the reasons for the rapid growth of the buffa was the reform of opera seria undertaken by two Italians, Apostolo Zeno (1668-1750) and Pietro Metastasio (1698-1782), his successor as court poet in Vienna. Zeno and particularly Metastasio, whose dramas provided the book for hundreds of eighteenth-century operas, sought to eliminate all extraneous material, such as comic episodes, from the libretti of the seria. A typical Metastasian libretto consisted of three acts with several scenes in each. Every scene started with a recitative, during which several characters appeared on stage and engaged in dialogue, and ended with an aria sung to the audience (*not* to his fellow actors) by the principal character of that scene (see SHO, p. 186 ff.). At the conclusion of his aria, the singer left the stage and the action of the drama came to a temporary halt. Metastasian operas resembled a chain of recitatives on which were strung a variety of different arias. This tendency to stress the aria increased the importance of singers, who soon began to indulge in excessive ornamentation of the given vocal line. Other objectionable conventions followed, among them the persistent use of the da capo aria, the irrational, but everpresent "happy ending" to each opera, and the precise indication of the amount, the style, and the sequence of successive arias (see SHO, p. 189). These features together tended to create a highly stylized opera whose arias could be interchanged from one opera to another, providing that the new aria sustained the same mood as the one it replaced. Therefore, borrowing from oneself or from others was prevalent and certainly accepted.

The refashioned opera libretto gave rise to various abuses (see above) that in time required reforms in the music. Much of the credit for musical reforms belongs to Christoph Willibald Gluck (1714-1787), a Bohemian composer who studied in Italy and produced operas in Vienna and Paris. In his renowned preface to *Alceste* (1767), probably written with the aid of his gifted librettist Calzabigi (1714-1795), Gluck expressed his desire "to restrict music to its true office of serving poetry," essentially to make music subservient to the drama (see SR, p. 673 ff.). Like Monteverdi and Wagner, however, both of whom professed a primary concern for the drama, Gluck's principal innovations related to the music. In his reform operas, beginning with *Orfeo* (1762), he removed excessive ornamentation from the arias, reduced the amount of secco recitative and instead wrote more orchestral accompaniments for his recitatives. Gluck's frequent use of large choruses (absent from operas based on Metastasio's works) and his penchant for classical mythology and its concomitant tomb scenes show the influence of Rameau and French opera. His long lyrical melodies derive from Italian opera; his instrumental pieces indicate his understanding of the new symphonic style of early classicism as seen in the symphonies and quartets of his teacher, Sammartini (c. 1700-1775).

Gluck's treatment of the orchestra reflects his view of the function of music in opera. In his preface to *Alceste,* he stated that

... instruments ought to be introduced in proportion to the degree of interest and passion in the words; instruments are to be employed not according to the dexterity of the players, but according to the dramatic propriety of their tone.[1]

Besides parts for flutes, oboes, and bassoons, Gluck provided two parts for clarinets and occasional parts for piccolo. He added three trombones to pairs of horns and trumpets, occasionally included bass drums, cymbals, a side drum, and triangle in his percussion, and reintroduced the harp in *Orfeo.* In his last scores, we find practically no trace of *basso continuo;* in other words, by this time, one group of instruments of the orchestra is providing the accompaniment for another group of instruments, thereby eliminating the need for the supportive harmonies of the continuo. As evidence of Gluck's dramatic use of the orchestra, we might note that Berlioz, in his instrumentation treatise of 1844, cited seventeen examples from Gluck's last five operas.[2]

12. RECITATIVE, ARIA, AND CHORUS IN REFORM OPERA

Orfeo ed Euridice (1762)

A. Choral Lament, Act I

Calzabigi   Christoph Willibald Gluck (1714-1787)

After an overture that has no particular relevance to the opera that follows, *Orfeo* opens with a *tombeau* or mourning scene. The chorus laments an offstage action (Euridice's death) and thus informs the audience of events that occurred before the start of the drama. (Compare messenger scene in Exx. 1 and 3-A.) Orfeo's cries, heard above the chorus, reach a climax at measure 62 ff., when he pleads to be left alone with his sorrow. A short *ballo* or dance (a part of which is reprinted here) is followed by the return of the choral lament, whose concluding instrumental section balances the instrumental introduction (mm. 1-14). Thus, the first 151 measures of the opera form a large ABA design. In the last half of this first scene, Orfeo sings his strophic song (Ex. 12-B) with interpolations of recitative that become increasingly agitated with each successive strophe. (Compare Orfeo's song in Ex. 3-A.) The dance piece (mm. 75-88) and the extended scene-complex reveal Gluck's indebtedness to Rameau. The *cornetti* (m. 1) are obsolete wind instruments (see p. 18); Bach and Gluck are among the last composers to write for them. Trombones were traditional in infernal scenes from the time of Monteverdi.

As the curtain is raised to the sounds of a mournful introduction, one sees the stage occupied by groups of shepherds and nymphs, followers of Orfeo. Some of them carry wreaths of flowers and garlands of myrtle, and while others burn incense, they bedeck the marble and strew flowers around the grave. Others sing the following chorus, interrupted by the mournful cries of Orfeo, who lies outstretched on a rock in the foreground, and from time to time passionately cries out the name of Euridice.

[1] Adam Carse, *The History of Orchestration* (New York: Dover Reprint, 1964), p. 155.
[2] *Ibid.,* p. 157.

12 - A

101

Gluck's *Orfeo ed Euridice* piano-vocal score by Heinz Moehn (Bärenreiter: Kassel, Basel, London, Paris, New York, 1962).

Translation

Chorus: Ah! if around this funeral urn, Euridice, fair shade, thou wanderest; hear the plaints, the laments, the sighs, that sound in mourning for thee.

Orfeo: [25]Euridice, Euridice!

Chorus: And hearken to thy unhappy spouse, who, weeping, calls thee and still laments as on that day he lost his sweet companion, his loving turtle-dove.

Orfeo: Enough my friends, your lament only increases my anguish. Strew the crimson flowers, garland her tomb and take leave of me. [69]I want to remain here alone with this somber, funereal shade, impious companion to my misfortune.

B. Orfeo's Strophic Song, Act I, scene i

For the three strophes of Orfeo's song and the changing accompanied recitative that succeeds each strophe, Gluck required two orchestras. An echo orchestra (Orch. II) onstage consists of strings and *chalumeaux* (early clarinets); horns replace flutes for the second stanza (mm. 50-81); English horn and bassoons combine with strings and *cembalo* (harpsichord) for the third stanza (not printed here). Compare Monteverdi's "Possente spirto" of Ex. 3-B. The string tremolos that accompany the last recitative of this song (not included in our excerpt) proceed in the slow harmonic rhythm characteristic of the new classical style.

Translation

Orfeo: I call to my love from daybreak to sunset, but vain sorrow, the idol of my heart does not answer me.
[35]Euridice, Euridice, dearly beloved, where are you hiding? Breathlessly, your faithful husband calls you, in vain. I implore the gods, but my tears are scattered by the winds and my lament is in vain.
[51]I seek my love on these sad shores where she died, but Echo alone replies to my sorrow.

Gluck's *Orfeo ed Euridice,* piano-vocal score by Heinz Moehn (Bärenreiter: Kassel, Basel, London, Paris, New York, 1962).

C. Accompanied Recitative

The melody of the following excerpt appeared first as an aria in two earlier operas, *Ezio* (1750) and *Antigono* (1756). In our example, where this same melody functions in an accompanied recitative, Gluck supported it with flowing accompanimental figures whose extensive continuity anticipate the symphonic texture of recitative of the mid-nineteenth century. That Gluck was experimenting in this first of the reform operas appears obvious when we notice that in each of the three acts he employed a different style of recitative. (Compare Exx. 12-B and 12-C.) Gluck never returned to the style of recitative in Ex. 12-C. However, with this piece he provided a model for later composers, who, like him, began to alter the texture and the design of their recitatives in order to obtain greater variety. Notice the assortment of instruments and their precise assignments.

Translation

Orfeo: How pure the sky! How clear the sun! What a bright, serene light. What sweet, alluring
    sounds blend together in the song of the birds, in the murmuring of the brooks, in the
    whispering of the breezes! This is the home of fortunate heroes. All goes peacefully to rest
    here, but this tranquillity gives me no happiness. [38]If I do not find the idol of my heart, I
    lose all hope. Your sweet voice, your loving glances, your lovely smile is my only delight.
    [56] Where might you be? I shall ask the happy group that is approaching.

Chorus: Here comes Euridice!

il cor - rer de' ru - scel - li, dell'
au - re il sus - sur - rar!
Que - sto è il sog - gior - no de for - tu - na - ti E - ro - i!
Qui tut - to spi - ra un tran - quil - lo con -

Vln. I   Ob.
Fl.   Ob.
Strings, Horn
Bassoon, Cemb.

110

ten - to,   ma non per me.

Se l'i - dol mi - o non tro - ve,   spe - rar non pos - so!

Strings, Bassoon, Horn, Cemb.

I   suo - i so - a - vi ac -

Vln. II

Fl.

Ob.

Ob.

Ob.

Ma in qual par - te ei sa - rà?

Chie - da - si a que - sto che mi vie-ne a in - con - trar stuo - lo fe - li - ce.

Ob.

Gluck's *Orfeo ed Euridice,* piano-vocal score by Heinz Moehn (Bärenreiter: Kassel, Basel, London, Paris, New York, 1962).

D. Aria and Duet

Unlike the two versions of *Alceste* which differed considerably from one another, the *Orfeo* (1762) of Vienna and the *Orfée et Euridice* (1774) of Paris were relatively similar. A cursory comparison of the two scores reveals that Gluck added the *Don Juan* (1761) ballet music for Paris; Moline rewrote the text of the recitatives, which, because of the different rhythm, accent, and inflection of the French language, often necessitated a change of key for the succeeding arias; and the composer refashioned the role of Orfeo for tenor. We must remember that the original Orfeo was sung by the castrato Gaetano Guadagno. The French had never been enthusiastic about castrati, and Gluck decided to rewrite the part. Today's best productions draw on both versions of the opera. The following example is from the Paris *Orfée.* Notice that Euridice's aria frames the duet, again forming a ternary design. Also observe the use of parallel 3rds and 6ths in the duet (mm. 49-63), a feature that probably derived from Italian opera and continued to appear later in the works of Rossini, Bellini, and Donizetti. (Duet begins at *.)

Translation

Euridice: Fortune, my enemy, how cruel to restore me to a life of torment! *I tasted the delights of the tranquil life and today, in my unhappiness, my tears are flowing. [47] I tasted . . . I shake, I tremble. Fortune, my enemy . . .

Orfée: [49] Her unjust suspicions increase my torment. What can I say? What can I do? She is driving me to despair. Will I be able to calm her, allay her fears? [66] What can I say? What can I do? It is my fate to complain. I cannot restrain myself.

114

E. pour___ les tour - ments, ne me rends-tu la vi - e que pour_____

E. ___ les tour - ments, que pour_____ les tour - ments?

Duet *Andante*

E. Je goû - tais les char - mes d'un re - pos sans a -

ORPHÉE

O. Ses in - ju - stes soup - çons

E. lar - mes, d'un re - pos_____ sans_ a - lar - mes, le

O. re - dou - blent mes tour - ments! Que

E. trou - ble, les lar - mes rem - plis-sent au - jour - d'hui mes mal-heu -

O. di - re? que fai - re?

E. reux__ mo - ments. Je goû - tais les char - mes d'un re -

O. El - le me dés-es - pè - re, ne pour-rai - je cal -

E. pos sans a - lar - mes, d'un re - pos__ sans a - lar - mes, le

O. mer le trou-ble de ses sens? Que

E. trou - ble, les lar - mes rem - plis-sent au - jour - d'hui mes mal-heu -

O. di - re? que fai - re?

Gluck's *Orfée et Euridice* (G. Schirmer, 1957, 1959).

13. INSTRUMENTAL MUSIC IN REFORM OPERA

Alceste (1767)

Calzabigi   Gluck

The overture to *Alceste,* the first of many tragic overtures in d minor (compare Mozart's overture to *Don Giovanni* and Brahms' *Tragic Overture*), is neither a sinfonia nor a French overture (see Ex. 6-A). Instead, we find here a binary form of the type that Domenico Scarlatti used in many of his piano sonatas, where, after the double bar (m. 60), the first section is simply repeated in the dominant key. Gluck did not write a synoptic overture as Rameau had already done in *Zoroastre* (1749), nor can we associate specific themes from the overture with characters in the drama (see Ex. 30). In this overture we have a mood-piece that creates the proper atmosphere for the opening of the opera. (See Gluck's ideas on the function of the overture in SR, p. 674.) The open-ended conclusion on the dominant moves directly into a five-measure choral statement before resolving in the trumpet call with which the action of the opera begins.

121

Scene i follows without pause.

V

Eighteenth-Century Comic Opera
Naples, London, Paris, Leipzig, Madrid
(c. 1715-1775)

The spread of comic opera throughout eighteenth-century Europe reflected the social mores of the rising middle class. These people enjoyed the newer, lighter style of opera that was written in the vernacular, included more contemporary plots, and contained fewer characters and no chorus. In all but the Italian comic operas, spoken dialogue replaced recitative. Syllabic text settings in numerous arias as well as in recitatives enabled audiences to understand the words more readily. Arias were shorter with fewer embellishments; melodies were generally in the major mode with precise, easily remembered tunes, sharp rhythmic accents, and occasional syncopations. The texture of the instrumental music and the accompaniments was generally homophonic with very few contrapuntal insertions. The element of the spectacular, common to serious opera, was missing from comic opera, thus making this kind of opera less expensive to stage. With costs down, more operas appeared; more people heard them; and eventually more composers began to write them. Known by various names in different countries, Italian *buffa,* French *vaudeville* and *opéra-comique,* English *ballad opera,* German *Singspiel,* and Spanish *zarzuela* and *tonadilla* flourished in the first half of the century and soon rivalled the popularity of serious opera. Comic characters had appeared in early opera libretti of the seventeenth century; comic episodes sometimes closed an act of the seria; and, often, *intermezzi* (short comic plays with music) alternated with acts of the seria. In addition to these *intermezzi* and comic episodes, independent, self-contained comic operas in dialect were produced in Naples and in Venice. In these operas, stock characters, some from the commedia dell'arte, engaged in routine plots already known to the audiences, who enjoyed them all the more because of their familiarity. Finally, the reforms of Zeno and Metastasio (see Chapter IV) aided the growth of comic opera, as serious opera became cleansed of the impurities of the *intermezzi.*

One of the most significant musical forms to emerge from the comic opera was the ensemble finale, unexcelled as a musico-dramatic feature. With recitative excluded and everything sung, the plot and the music progress simultaneously to a logical conclusion. Ex. 14 is a second-act closing ensemble from one of the few extant comic operas by Scarlatti, whom Dent called the "first composer to unite voices in a formal movement at a moment of high dramatic tension." Composed almost seventy years before the finales of *The Marriage of Figaro* (1786), it represents an early attempt at this difficult genre.

The English, because of their extensive heritage of spoken drama, did not succumb to foreign opera. They did, however, enjoy the political and social satire suggested by the libretti of ballad operas, such as *The Beggar's Opera* (1728), which included among its cast pickpockets, prostitutes, and jailbirds of various sorts. We have reprinted two excerpts from this opera, a short solo and a bouncy duet (Exx. 15-A and 15-B), both in the infectious comic style that eventually found its way into Gilbert and Sullivan operettas.

In the 1660s, the comédie-ballets of Lully and Molière became the first examples of comic opera in France. In the later seventeenth century, at the Italian Theater in Paris,

Italian comedies appeared with intermittent French scenes. With the increased use of the French language, presumably brought about by audience preference, the Italians, for the moment, were forced to leave. Their influence, however, remained in evidence for more than seventy-five years, during which time three successive groups of musicians rallied round the Italian banner to challenge French music (see SR, Chapter XIV).

In the early eighteenth century, several Parisian theaters that staged performances during the two annual fairs in the French capital merged to form the Théâtre de l'Opéra-Comique. The management presented spoken comedies with interspersed *vaudevilles,* popular tunes to which new words had been added. The comedies themselves were soon called *vaudevilles,* after the name of the parodied song. Further impetus to the growth of French comic opera resulted from the visit to Paris of a troupe of Italian buffa players in the 1750s. In 1752, the *second* performance of Pergolesi's *La Serva Padrona* (Ex. 16) achieved such a resounding success that it provoked the War of the Buffoons, a quarrel between the supporters of French serious opera (including the king and his followers) and those (among them the queen and Rousseau) who favored the Italian buffa. Rousseau, calling for a return to nature, away from the myths and historical tragedies that provided the subject matter for serious opera, and at the same time scorning the vaudevilles, wrote *Le Devin du village* (Ex. 17). He called his piece an *intermède* and believed he had written it in the Italian style, even using recitatives instead of the customary spoken dialogue of French comic opera. However, Rousseau's short-range melodies (spanning less than an octave) and uninspired harmonizations display too strong a kinship to French folktunes to sound Italian, although one of his airs, "J'ai perdu tout mon bonheur," reveals a suspicious similarity to Pergolesi's "Sempre contrasti" (Ex. 16-A) from *La Serva Padrona! Le Devin du village* has a degree of historical importance in that Mozart, after viewing a French parody of *Le Devin* by Favart (1710-1792), one of the most important figures in the growth of opéra-comique, wrote his own Singspiel, *Bastien und Bastienne* (1768), based on the same story.

Several years after Rousseau's innocuous attempts, genuine French comic opera appeared in the works of Duni (1709-1775), Philidor (1726-1795) and Monsigny (1729-1817). Their *comédies mêlée d'ariettes,* comedies with *ariettes* (newly composed songs) instead of the *vaudevilles* (parodied songs), prepared the way for the unique blend of romantic rescue opera that Grétry (1741-1813) shaped in the mold of opéra-comique. These operas used spoken dialogue instead of recitative and retained the vaudeville finale, a strophic song with refrain, in which each of the principals in succession sang a verse to conclude the opera. Both Mozart's *Die Entführung aus dem Serail* (1782) and *Der Schauspieldirektor* (1786) and Rossini's *Il Barbiere di Siviglia* (1816) end in this manner.

German Singspiel received its start from a travelling English company that appeared in Berlin in 1743 with a German translation of an English play set to English music. Revised and rewritten to German music, *Der Teufel ist los* appeared again in Leipzig in 1752 and began the trend to popular opera in the vernacular. Among the most successful composers of Singspiel before Mozart were Hiller (1728-1804), an example of whose work may be found in Ex. 18, and Dittersdorf (1739-1799), whose *Doktor und Apotheker* (1786) is still presented on the German stage today (see AAA 7).

Zarzuelas, named after the palace near Madrid where they were performed, were very popular in seventeenth-century Spain. These plays with music lost their popularity to the *tonadilla* in the eighteenth century. The tonadilla began life as the final song of the Spanish intermezzo or *entremes;* it expanded and gained its independence as a short comic opera of perhaps twenty minutes' duration. None has been recorded and we have therefore omitted any example from our anthology. The best source for printed examples of the tonadilla is the three-volume work *La Tonadilla escénica* (Madrid, 1930) by Jose Subirá. Current zarzuela recordings offer music of the nineteenth century, when a new type of zarzuela emerged.

14. EARLY ENSEMBLE IN OPERA BUFFA

Il Trionfo dell'onore (1718)

Tullio   Alessandro Scarlatti (c. 1660-1725)

A conversation among four characters prefaces the quartet they are about to sing. The composer uses simple continuo accompaniment to support the secco recitative. Chordal movement proceeds from the tonic towards the dominant or subdominant and then back again to the tonic. Although Scarlatti made modulations to neighboring keys, the music remains basically within the orbit of b minor/D major. Notice the diminished-7th chord at measure 11, perhaps underscoring Riccardo's dismay. The recitative concludes in D, and the quartet begins in b minor (m. 24). This quartet is not an aria *a 4* where each singer takes his turn in succession. In Ex. 14 all four performers engage in song, sometimes by twos, and at the conclusion as an ensemble. Notice the dovetailing of parts at measures 33-37, the textual pairing of alternate voices at measures 60-62, and again the singing in 3rds and 6ths. Whereas this piece is not in the rapid tempo we have come to associate with a finale, it does include the patter, parlando style of short motives, repeated figures, and fragments of melodic declamation that, when woven together, provide the fabric of the quartet.

Translation

Erminio: My whole being is struggling for revenge.

Leonora: O, what is this? Riccardo is here?

Erminio: So, here is the scoundrel!

Doralice: Alas, my Riccardo!

Leonora: My brother is waiting in ambush.

Erminio: The traitor shall die by betrayal.

Doralice: No, stop!

Riccardo: Who dares attack me?

Leonora: Hold back!

Erminio: Unworthy sister to defend the one who dishonors us!

Riccardo: Leonora here? Bad luck!

Erminio (challenging Riccardo): Rascal!

Riccardo (drawing his sword): In spite of you, my sword.

Leonora: Stop, what are you doing?

Doralice (to Erminio): For the sake of the love you had for me, calm your fury.

Erminio: Cruel woman, I am forced to obey you in spite of myself. (Then to Riccardo) But you shall know the anger of a man wounded in his honor, and I shall have my revenge.

Riccardo: A heart like mine does not fear your fury.

Erminio: [32] Beautiful.

Doralice (to Erminio): Silence! What hope have you? What? I do not hear you. My heart is now another's. Silence!

Erminio: Ah, but think of the anguish that my heart suffers.

Leonora: [51] My love! Ah, but see the torment that besieges my heart. My love, etc.

Riccardo (to Leonora): Be silent. What do you ask? What? I do not hear you. My heart is now another's, etc.

14

(In brac-cio al-la ven-det - ta   son tut-ti i sen - si miei.)   (Ah, che veg-

15. AIR AND DUET IN ENGLISH BALLAD OPERA

The Beggar's Opera (1728)

Gay   John Christopher Pepusch (1667-1752)

The Beggar's Opera is a *pasticcio*, an opera whose close to seventy airs (arias) are derived from more than twenty different sources, some identifiable as the work of specific composers, and others that originated as anonymous Scotch, Irish, and English folk or popular songs (see Dent, GBO). John Gay was the librettist, or in any event the creator, of this opera, for it was he who selected the various pieces to be included in it. Gay then requested Pepusch to supply an overture and accompaniment to the songs. Gay himself produced the finished work, a political satire and parody of opera seria whose plot still delights audiences today. Witness the revival of Brecht's *Three Penny Opera* to new music by Kurt Weill.

Our examples, Macheath's solo and the duet by Polly and Lucy, are consecutive numbers in the opera, separated only by the intervening spoken dialogue. Notice the syllabic text setting in each excerpt, the rhythm derived completely from the rhythm of the text (a good reminder of the difficulties that beset the translator, whose new text must fit the rhythm and pitch inflection of another language and also have the same meaning as the original), the simple accompaniments, the very short phrases and the extreme brevity of each piece. Sources for most of the pieces have been identified by W.H. Grattan Flood. Dent, in his edition (1954), reprints a list of the sources with corrections by Mr. Handley Taylor. From this list we notice that Ex. 15-A was originally an Old Irish tune published as "The Rant" in *Apollo's Banquet*, 1690; Ex. 15-B was an Irish Trot printed by Playford in 1651. Although we have not reprinted the overture, we might describe it as another example of the Baroque French overture. It provides a vivid contrast with the light tuneful airs of the opera, whose style is most emphatically representative of early classicism. We might note that Benjamin Britten prepared a modern version of this opera in 1948.

15-A

16. AIR AND DUET IN INTERMEZZO

La Serva Padrona (1733)

A. Aria

Federico   Giovanni Batista Pergolesi (1710-1736)

On 1 August 1752, *La Serva Padrona,* with an overture by Telemann (1681-1767), was presented in Paris on the same bill with Lully's last opera, *Acis et Galatée* (1686). This performance of the Pergolesi piece provoked the aforementioned War of the Buffoons (see p. 126). If we compare Ex. 16-A with its imitation by Rousseau (Ex. 17), we can appreciate the vastly superior music of the Italian original. As with most of the eighteenth-century comic operas, the texture is homophonic, the short, catchy phrases of the text are easily remembered, and the music is instantly accessible. In both the solo and duet (Ex. 16-B) we find slow harmonic rhythm (infrequent chord changes), a tendency toward syllabic text setting, and a lack of vocal embellishments. This straightforward, simple vocal style was essential, because singers in comic operas were often hired more for their thespian abilities than for their musical talents. Observe also that both pieces are in da capo form.

Translation

Uberto: Always dissension because of you, now this, now that, now here, now there. It's yes or no, but enough of that. Let's finish it now, [19] what do you say, must I explode? No sir, no sir. Always dissension . . . [56] You ought to weep for your disgrace, you know I'm right. Do you agree? Say yes or no. It is just so. Always dissension . . .

16-A

pa-re? Ah! Ma che ti pa-re? Ah! Ho io a cre-pa-re. Si-gnor mio, no, Ho io a cre-

pa-re? Si-gnor mio, no, _____ si-gnor mio, no, _____ si-gnor mio, no.

Fine

Pe-rò ____ do-vrai pur ____ sem-pre ____ pian ____

____ ge-re la tua dis-gra-zia, e al-lor di-rai che ____ ben ti

Dal Segno al Fine

B. Duet

Translation

Serpina: In my heart a little bell is ringing, it strikes me constantly.

Uberto: I too feel something throbbing, a drum beats repeatedly.

Serpina: I hear it go tippiti, tippiti, tippiti.

Uberto: I hear it too. Mine goes tappata, tappata, tappata.

Serpina: I do hear it. What can it be, what can it be? I don't know. O love, I think it's that.

Uberto: What can it be, what can it be? I don't know. O love, I think it's that.

Serpina: It strikes me constantly, this little bell that's ringing.

Uberto: What? What can it be? (***)

Serpina: I don't know.

Uberto: What can it be?

Serpina: I don't know. I hear a tippiti, tippiti, tippiti.

Uberto: I hear a tappata, tappata, tappata. . .(***to the close is repeated).

140

143

Pergolesi's *La Serva Padrona*, arranged by Albert Stoessel (Kalmus, 1934).

17. AIR IN FRENCH INTERMÈDE

Le Devin du village (1752)

Rousseau   Jean-Jacques Rousseau (1712-1778)

In this first number from the opera, Colette's air in the Italian style, we notice the paucity of Rousseau's melodic inspiration. The sharp, precise profile so attractive in the Pergolesi aria (Ex. 16-A) is totally absent here. Instead, excessive repetition, unimaginative rhythmic patterns, and dull harmonizations characterize the piece. The dynamics are Rousseau's own. Already in Lully's works (see Ex. 6) we find frequent indications of *doux*, *f* and *p*. We have included the recitative that follows immediately after the da capo air in order to demonstrate further Rousseau's need to imitate the Italians. Remember that except for the opera buffa, comic operas used spoken dialogue instead of recitative. Rousseau's recitative is therefore an exception. A chorus from this *intermède* has been reprinted in HAM, 291.

Translation

Colette: I have lost my delight, I have lost my mate. Colin has forsaken me. Alas. He has changed. I don't even want to think about it. Alas, alas, I dream about it constantly. I have lost my delight. . .

[Recit.] [1] He used to love me, that's my misfortune. Whom does he prefer to me? She's probably quite charming, [6] an indiscreet shepherdess. Don't you believe me when I say how I've been wronged? Colin has changed. Your turn will come. . .

On one side of the stage is the soothsayer's house; on the other, some trees and fountains, and at the back, a hamlet. Colette, crying and wiping her eyes with her apron.

mais quelle est donc cel - le qu'il me pré - fè - re? elle est donc bien char-

man - te! Im-pru - den - te ber - gè - re, ne crains tu point les maux que j'é-prouve en ce

jour? Co - lin a pu chan - ger; tu peux a - voir ton tour...

Rousseau's *Le Devin du village*, arranged by Charles Chaix (Editions Henn 1924).

18. LIED IN GERMAN SINGSPIEL

Lisuart und Dariolette (1766)

Schiebeler
(partly founded on Favart's *La Fée urgèle,* 1765)   Johann Adam Hiller (1728-1804)

One of the significant composers of Singspiel was Hiller, the first conductor of the Leipzig Gewandhaus Concerts (begun in 1781), an editor of an important musical periodical, the *Wöchentliche Nachrichten.* . .(4 vols., 1766-1770), and a man who anticipated Weber in his understanding of the specifically German type of folksong. The peppery melody of Ex. 18 bears a strong resemblance to popular song. It contains frequent repetitions of short phrases of text, each supported by a light accompaniment. New formal patterns emerged in comic opera, and our example displays an alternative to the established da capo form. (The subject matter resembles that found in Leporello's Catalogue Aria from Mozart's *Don Giovanni.*) The song is sung by Derwin, Lisuart's servant.

149

Translation

Now the blonde, now the brunette,
Now the lean one, now the stout one,
Oh, the capricious whims,
Oh, that beautiful butterfly!
To give one's soul and body
[37]To the soft glance of only one,
That I consider fair. But the Devil take it!
To be constantly changing, that is asking too much.

18

VI
Synthesis of Buffa and Seria
Vienna and Prague
(c. 1786-1791)

Mozart wrote twenty-one operas of which four (see Exx. 19, 20, 21, 22) rank with the greatest masterpieces of dramatic music ever written, and two others, *Idomeneo* (1781) and *Die Entführung aus dem Serail* (1782), deserve honorable mention. Mozart excelled both in musical characterization and in musico-dramatic organization. Although we know that he wrote fluently and easily and that his instinct served him well at most times, his letters to his father reveal some of the numerous problems that beset him before the completion of an opera. Occasionally, the dramatic situation within the plot concerned him, or the professional rivalry between prima donnas, or even the meddlesome local authorities who could become a nuisance before a performance. Despite the difficulties, however, Mozart's last works indicate his complete mastery of the balance between words and music. His ensembles, both the finales and the shorter ones that appear in the course of an act, are plays within a play. Rarely does the action come to a halt for the singers to display their talents. Both story and music proceed simultaneously. Mozart extended his finales in such a way that their music, particularly the finales of the second act of *Figaro* and of the last act of *Don Giovanni*, accounts for more than half of the entire act.

In his last three operas in the Italian language, *Le Nozze di Figaro* (1786), *Don Giovanni* (1787), and *Così fan tutte* (1790), Mozart combined elements of buffa and seria. He uses secco recitative[1] as well as accompanied recitative; he includes elaborate coloratura arias as well as simple ariettas; his plots deal with real people in understandable situations, those with which his audience can identify. He does not make extensive use of the chorus, but he certainly includes numerous instances of ensemble singing from duets and trios to quartets, quintets, and sextets (see Ex. 21). A comparison of his style in the sextet in Example 21 with Beethoven's style in the quartet of Example 23-A shows the difference between their orientation: Beethoven's approach is essentially instrumental, symphonic in outlook, while Mozart's concern is for a heightened expression of the drama. Except in rare instances, Beethoven achieves dramatic presentation of the text through instrumentation, texture, dynamics, rhythm, harmony, and form, but not through the action of the drama itself. Mozart's gifts as a genuine dramatic composer show to best advantage in his ensembles, where the plot never stands still while the music pushes forward. Most of his ensembles proceed so effortlessly that the audience is unaware of the consummate skill required of composer and librettist to accomplish this feat. In contrast, during the canon of our Beethoven example, the action has literally come to a standstill.

On his first visit to Vienna, in 1768, Mozart had met Gluck, and the two certainly saw one another during Mozart's second stay in that city for the production of *Die Entführung* in 1782. Relations, however, were not exactly cordial inasmuch as Gluck championed Salieri, Mozart's rival at court. In Chapter IV, we remarked on the extent of Gluck's reforms and observed that along with Monteverdi and Wagner he should be cited as a pioneer in the historical development of opera. Now we should like to indicate some

---

[1] See E. Downes, "Secco Recitative in Early Classical Opera Seria," *JAMS* XIV (Spring, 1961), 50 ff.

differences between the later works of Gluck and the last three or four of Mozart's operas, written barely a dozen years afterwards. Despite occasional sections in the new, early classical style, the music and plot of Gluck's operas belong to the Baroque period, the era of the aristocratic, stately, even static opera seria. The music, plots, textures, and dynamic action of Mozart's operas reflect the full force of the high classical style. Gluck's characters are ideal types; Mozart, on the other hand, depicts individual human beings. Gluck still thought in terms of classical mythology, while Mozart was attracted to Beaumarchais! Therefore, we should not be too surprised that Mozart's operas are still fresh today, while most of Gluck's works have been relegated to history.

19. CAVATINA, RECITATIVE, ARIETTA
Le Nozze di Figaro (1786)

Act II

Da Ponte   Wolfgang Amadeus Mozart (1756-1791)

Figaro, who has just told the Countess how he intends to teach the Count a lesson, leaves her presence singing the final flourish (mm. 1-12) of his *cavatina* from Act I. (A cavatina is generally a short solo song, shorter than an aria and with fewer instances of textual repetition. See p. 254.) Mozart thus uses thematic recurrence to connect the acts and to remind us that Figaro's attitude implies "if the Count wants to dance, he'll dance to my tune." Tempo and meter suggest the aristocratic minuet to which the Count would dance.

The following recitative, a conversation, shows how precisely Mozart adhered to speech rhythms and inflections. Chordal support derives mostly from tonic-dominant movement with modulation first to the relative minor (mm. 17-19), then to the dominant (G major via the progression II-V-I at mm. 21-23), the tonic minor (m. 25), and finally through the subdominant and dominant to the eventual resolution in the new tonic, B♭ major, the key of the next arietta.

This *arietta* (short aria) is Cherubino's specially written love song to the Countess and as such we can expect it will be carefully planned. The introductory instrumental prelude (mm. 42-49) that precedes Cherubino's entry utilizes measures 50-53 and 58-61 of the vocal part. Cherubino's repeat of this material has been extended (mm. 54-57), and it now includes several chromaticisms (mm. 54 and 56) to emphasize his feelings. The middle section in F major starts at measure 62, and only to heighten the meaning of *martir* does Mozart change to f minor (m. 76). From here we proceed to the next middle section in the relative major (A♭) of f minor (m. 78). Rhythm and melody resemble the earlier sections (compare with mm. 1-8), but the distant key of A♭ stresses the textual meaning of *gelo* ("I am chilled") in contrast to the warm feeling of the B♭ opening. At *fuori di me* ("beside myself"), Mozart leaves the key of A♭ and begins the gradual return to the tonic B♭ at measure 103. We shall not always analyze each excerpt harmonically. However, this short piece in ternary form affords an excellent example of the various and frequent modulations that Mozart has included without making the piece seem contrived.

Translation

Figaro: Should my dear master want some diversion, I'll play the music on my guitar.

Countess [Recit.]: How pained I am, Susanna, to think that Cherubino heard all the nonsense my husband told you. Ah, you don't know yet. . .but for what earthly reason didn't he see me in person? Where did you put his love song?

Susanna: Here it is; as soon as he comes we'll have him sing it. Listen, who is it? Our hero! Come in, most worthy major general.

Cherubino: Please do not call me by such a fatal name. It reminds me that soon I must leave her, my dearest, kindest lady.

Susanna: Who is so pretty!

Cherubino: So sweet, so lovely.

Susanna: So sweet, so lovely! [30] You little hypocrite, now quickly sing that love song you gave me this morning so that the Countess may hear it.

Countess: Who wrote the song?

Susanna: Who wrote it? Look at his face and see him blush like a schoolgirl.

Countess: Take my guitar, Susanna, and accompany him.

Cherubino: Today I'm not in good voice, but if Madame desires. . .

Susanna: She certainly does, let's have the words.

Cherubino [Arietta]:
[50] You know the answer, you hold the key,
Love's tender secret, share it with me, Ladies I beg you,
Share it with me.

[62] This new sensation I undergo, It is so different from all I know.
Filled with excitement, walking on air,
First I am happy, soon I despair.

[78] Now I am chilly, next time aflame,
Not for a moment am I the same.
I am pursuing some sunny ray, but it alludes me, try as I may.
I can't stop sighing, hard as I try, and then I tremble, not knowing why,

[97] From this dilemma I find no peace, and yet I want it never to cease.
You know the answer. . .

19

155

Quan - to duol-mi, Su - san-na, che que-sto gio-vi - net-to ab-bia del Con-te le stra-va-gan-ze u-

di - to! ah! tu non sa - i ma per qual cau-sa ma - i da me stes-sa ei non

ven-ne? Dov' è la can-zo - net-ta? Ec - co-la, ap-pun-to fac-ciam che ce la can-ti.

Zit - to, vien gen-te, è des-so: a-van-ti, a-van-ti, si-gnor uf-fi-zi -

a - le! Ah, non chia-mar-mi con no-me sì fa-ta-le! ei mi ram-men-ta, che ab-ban-do-nar degg'

i - o co-ma-re tan-to buo-na! E tan-to bel - la. Ah sì, cer-to! Ah

156

sì, cer - to! i - po - cri - to - ne! via pre - sto la can - zo - ne, che sta - ma - ne a me de - ste,

COUNTESS   SUSANNA (pointing to Cherubino)

a ma - da - ma can - ta - te. Chi n'è l'au - tor? Guar - da - te, e - gli ha due bra - ci di ros - sor sul - la

COUNTESS   CHERUBINO

fac - cia. Pren - di la mia chi - tar - ra, e l'ac - com - pa - gna. Io so - no sì tre - man - te,

SUSANNA

ma se ma - da - ma vuo - le Lo vuo - le, sì, lo vuol, man - co pa - ro - le.

Arietta

Andante con moto   (Susanna plays the ritornello on the guitar.)

W.W.,
Horns,
Strings

157

Sen - to un af - fet - to pien di de - sir,____ Ch'o - ra è di - let - to, ch'o - ra è mar - tir. Ge - lo,e poi sen - to l'al - ma av-vam - par, E in____ un mo - men - to____ tor - no a ge - lar. Ri - cer-co un be - ne fuo - ri di me, Non so chi il tie - ne, non so cos' è. So-spi-ro e ge - mo sen - za vo -

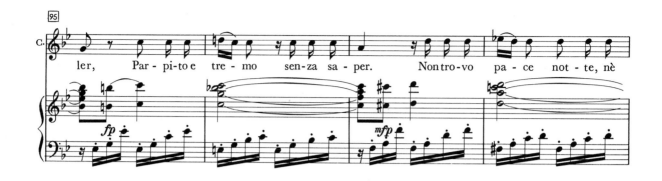

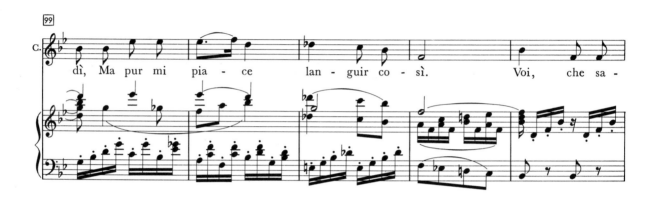

Mozart's *Le Nozze di Figaro* (G. Schirmer, 1947, 1948, 1951).

20. ACCOMPANIED RECITATIVE AND ARIA
Don Giovanni (1787)

Act II

Da Ponte   Mozart

Mozart wrote the following *scena* (dramatic aria) at the request of Madame Cavalieri, the first Donna Elvira. For the accompanied recitative (mm. 1-36), the composer uses a short, vigorous orchestral motive that expresses the lady's agitation. This motive appears alternately in the keys of c minor and d minor before concluding in c minor with a poignant anticipation of the recurrent sigh of the aria (mm. 30-36). The following E♭ aria, *"Mi tradì,"* with its insistent rhythmic figure in the accompaniment, further emphasizes Elvira's unhappy state. The binary form of this aria might easily be overlooked owing to the frequent insertions of the introductory figure in flowing eighth notes (m. 37 ff.) in both orchestral and solo parts. The A section begins on the upbeat to measure 37; B starts with *"Ma tradita"* ("but betrayed," a variant of *"Mi tradì,"* "he betrayed me") at measure 54; A returns at measure 75; A′ in the tonic minor (e♭ minor) starts at measure 91; A (m. 117) and B (m. 135) and a six-measure codetta (mm. 160-165) conclude the piece. Notice the word-painting that underlines *palpitando* (mm. 107-112) and also observe Mozart's colorful use of the woodwinds.

Translation

Elvira [Recit.]: What unspeakable sins, o gods, what more terrible crimes will attract his fancy! Ah, no. Heaven will not permit him to continue unpunished. [17]Heaven's vengeance will soon fall on him and endless torments await him in Hell. Miserable Elvira, with my heart so pained, why am I trembling? Why do I sigh?

[Aria] Betrayed by that ungrateful wretch! He's made me so unhappy, Oh God! [54]Betrayed and abandoned, do I still try to protect him, pity him? This ungrateful soul betrayed me. Oh God, he's made me so unhappy. [91]When I am aware of my torment, I think of vengeance, but I restrain myself. [103]My heart palpitates within me. Betrayed by that ungrateful wretch. . .

20

Allegro assai

DONNA ELVIRA

In qua-li ec-ces - si, o Nu-mi, in qua i mi-sfat - ti or-ri-bi-li, tre-men-di è av-

vol-to il scia-gu-ra-to! Ah no! non

puo-te tar-dar l'i-ra del cie-lo, la giu-sti - zia tar-dar.

Sen-tir già par-mi la fa-ta - le sa - et-ta, che gli piomba sul ca-po!

Strings throughout Recit.

162

Mozart's *Don Giovanni* (G. Schirmer, 1961).

168

21. ELABORATE ENSEMBLE

Così fan tutte (1790)

Act I

Da Ponte   Mozart

Mozart's most extended ensemble-finales appear at the close of the second act of *The Marriage of Figaro* and during the second scene of the second (last) act of *Don Giovanni*. Here, composer and librettist gather their characters together for one final fling. Recitative is completely absent, and music and drama move swiftly forward. Tempo, meter, key, musical figuration, and instrumentation change as the music progresses. Unless a fermata (m. 126) or distinctly different figuration pinpoints the start of a new section (mm. 9-10 and 43-44), the audience may not always be aware of the changes. Characters dart on and off stage as the plot thickens (if this finale occurs in an interior act) or as the drama resolves (if the finale concludes the opera).

Like *Figaro* and *Don Giovanni, Così fan tutte* contains an ensemble finale to close each of its two acts (see Da Ponte's description quoted in Dent, MO, p.104). Because of the limitations of space, however, we have decided to include a shorter ensemble, a sextet (instead of the finale) from the first act of *Così.* The six principal characters appear here in the same manner as they do in the finale: singly, in pairs, by threes, by fours, and in a group of six. We can observe both their successive and their simultaneous entries from the score. We might consider the entire musical plan of this excerpt by consulting the schematic diagram that follows.

TEMPO	KEY	METER	MEASURE	DRAMATIC SITUATION
Allegro	C	$\frac{4}{4}$	1-10	Don Alfonso introduces Despina to
Allegro	C	$\frac{4}{4}$	10-22	Ferrando and Guglielmo, who acknowledge her presence through flattery.
Allegro	G	$\frac{4}{4}$	22-38	Despina and Don Alfonso discuss the boys.
Allegro	C	$\frac{4}{4}$	38-54	Singing together the boys believe that Despina is favorably impressed with them. However, she tells Don Alfonso that she has her doubts.
				Dorabella and Fiordiligi are heard from within and Don Alfonso leaves the stage.
Allegro	F	$\frac{3}{4}$	54-62	Girls are exasperated.
Allegro	C	$\frac{3}{4}$	62-82	Girls turn deaf ear to the boys' pleas.
Allegro	a	$\frac{3}{4}$	82-104	Despina and the boys kneel down and plead.
Allegro	modulating	$\frac{3}{4}$	104-125	Successive and simultaneous singing with boys pleading and girls rejecting their advances.
Molto Allegro	C	$\frac{2}{2}$	127-the close.	The girls will not be won. The answer is no.

In order to understand the vast difference in size between this sextet and the second act finale of *Figaro,* for example, we might compare the number of bars in this excerpt (219) with the number of bars in that finale: 939 in all!

Translation

Don Alfonso: To the pretty Despinetta, I present you, my friends. Nobody knows more than she does when it comes to affairs of the heart.

Ferrando and Guglielmo: By this hand that I kiss with pleasure, by those grateful glances, see to it that my beloved turns favorable eyes upon me.

Despina: What looks! What clothes! What a physique! What mustaches! I don't know if they're Poles or Turks!

Don Alfonso: How do they strike you?

Despina: [32] To be frank, their whiskers are out of date, really an antidote to romance. What a mustache! What a physique!

Ferrando, Guglielmo, Don Alfonso: Now things are settled. If she doesn't recognize us, there's nothing more to fear.

Fiordiligi, Dorabella: [48] O Despina!

Despina: The mistresses!

Don Alfonso: Now's the time! Do well. I will hide here.

Fiordiligi, Dorabella: You arrogant hussy! What are you doing with those people? Send them away immediately or you'll be sorry.

Despina, Ferrando, Guglielmo: [82] O Madame, excuse us. Look at us two wretches languishing at your lovely feet, your adoring lovers.

Fiordiligi, Dorabella: Great gods, what do I hear? Who's responsible for this treachery?

Despina, Ferrando, Guglielmo: Calm down, please.

Fiordiligi, Dorabella: [127] I cannot restrain myself! I'm filled with horror and despair!

Despina, Don Alfonso, Ferrando, Guglielmo: I'm slightly suspicious of this rage and fury. Such excitement brings contentment!

Fiordiligi, Dorabella: Ah, forgive me, my love. This heart is innocent.

21

170

171

bian - ze! che ve - sti - ti! che fi - gu - re! che mu -

stac-chi! Io non so, se son Val - lac-chi? o se Tur-chi son co - stor? Val-lac-chi,

Tur-chi, Tur-chi, Val - lac-chi? Che ti par di quell' a - spet-to? Per par -

D. ALF. (softly to Despina)   DESP.

lar - vi schiet - to, schiet - to, han-no un mu - so fuor dell' u - so, ve-ro an-

f

173

Allegro   (He retires, Enter Fiordiligi and Dorabella)

A. stan-te! fa con ar - te: io qui m'a - scon - do.

FIORD. Ra-gaz-zac - cia tra-co-tan-te! che fai

DORAB. Ra-gaz-zac - cia tra-co-tan-te! che fai

FI. lì con si-mil gen - te; ra-gaz-zac-cia tra-co-tan-te, che fai lì con si-mil

DO. lì con si-mil gen - te; ra-gaz-zac-cia tra-co-tan-te, che fai lì con si-mil

FI. gen - te, con si-mil gen - te, con si-mil gen - te: fal-li u-sci - re im-man-ti-

DO. gen - te, con si-mil gen - te, con si-mil gen - te: fal-li u-sci - re im-man-ti-

175

177

178

179

182

181

FI. pie-na ho_ l'al-ma in pet - to di_ di - spet-to e_ di_ ter - ror!

DO. te - gno, tut - ta_ pie-na ho_ l'al - ma in pet - to di - di - spet-to e_ di_ ter -

DE. *cresc.* quel - la rab - bia *f* e quel fu - ror.

FE. *cresc.* pet - to, quel - la rab - bia *f* e quel fu -

A. *cresc.* quel - la rab - bia *f* e quel fu - ror,

G. pet - to, *cresc.* quel - la rab - bia *f* e quel fu -

185

FI. *sotto voce* Ah, per - don mio bel di - let - to,

DO. *sotto voce* ror. Ah, per - don mio bel di - let - to,

DE. *sotto voce* mi da un po - co_ di so - spet - to, mi da un

FE. *sotto voce* qual di -

A. *sotto voce* mi da un po - co di so - spet - to, quel - la rab - bia quel fu - ror,_ mi da un

G. ror, *sotto voce* qual di -

p

185

Mozart's *Così fan tutte* (G. Schirmer, 1951, 1952).

187

22. ARIA IN FOLK STYLE

Die Zauberflöte (1791)

Act I

Schikaneder [and Giesecke?]   Mozart

    Unlike Weber (see Ex. 30), Mozart did not call this aria a *Lied*. There is no doubt, however, that the following example provides us with a fine specimen of the short, strophic song in the popular style, the *volkstümliches Lied*. Notice the immediate accessibility of the tune, its short range, symmetrical phrases, and simple harmonizations. Always with a flair for drama, Mozart directs the orchestra to play the entire tune before Papageno begins to sing, thus providing the birdcatcher (Schikaneder in the first performance) with enough time to pirouette in front of the audience before he begins his song.

Translation

Tamino: What do I hear? Where am I? What a strange place! I see a queer figure approaching.

Papageno:

I am a man of widespread fame, And Papageno is my name.
To tell you all in simple words, I make my living catching birds.
[36]The moment they attract my eye, I spread my net and in they fly.
I whistle on my pipe of Pan. In short I am a happy man.

Although I am a happy man, I also have a future plan.
I dearly love my feathered friends, but that's not where my interest ends.
To tell the truth I'd like to find a pretty girl of my own kind.
In fact I'd like to fill my net with all the pretty girls I met.

Once all the girls were in my net, I'd keep the fairest for my pet.
My sweetheart and my bride-to-be, to love and cherish tenderly.
I'd bring her cake and sugarplums and be content to eat the crumbs.
She'd share my little nest with me. A happier pair could never be!

22

(Papageno, dressed in a suit of feathers, hurries by, carrying a large bird cage on his back and a pan pipe in his hands.)

PAPAGENO

P.

Der__ Vo - gel - fän - ger__ bin ich ja, stets__ lu - stig hei - sa hop - sa - sa! ich
Der__ Vo - gel - fän - ger__ bin ich ja, stets__ lu - stig hei - sa hop - sa - sa! ich
Wenn__ al - le Mäd - chen__ wä - ren mein so__ tausch - te ich brav Zuk - ker ein, die

P.

Vo - gel - fän - ger__ bin be - kannt bei alt und jung im gan - zen Land.
Vo - gel - fän - ger__ bin be - kannt bei alt und jung im gan - zen Land.
wel - che__ mir am__ lieb - sten wär, der gäb' ich gleich den Zuk - ker her.

Mozart's *The Magic Flute [Die Zauberflöte]* (G. Schirmer, 1941, 1951).

190

VII

Nineteenth-Century French Opera Before Wagner

Vienna, Paris

(c. 1790-1860)

While Mozart was active in Prague and Vienna, several new operatic styles began to develop in Paris. Indeed, the French capital slowly emerged as the center of dramatic musical entertainment for all of Europe and retained its dominant position past mid-century. Two kinds of opera attracted Parisian audiences: first, the older serious opera derived from Gluck and characterized by the use of classical and historical subject matter and large-scale tableaux, for example, Cherubini's *Medée* (1797), Méhul's *Joseph* (1807), and Spontini's *La Vestale* (1807); second, the rescue operas, so called because of their suspense-filled plots and heroic episodes. These operas gained popularity during and immediately after the French Revolution. Cherubini (1760-1842) and Méhul (1763-1817), along with Lesueur (1760-1837) and Grétry (see p. 126), turned out numerous operas in this mold. Rescue operas also incorporated crowd scenes (similar to those in serious operas), but replaced recitative with spoken dialogue and were therefore considered *opéra-comique.* Both the Gluck-inspired serious operas as well as the rescue operas anticipated the later massive productions of grand opera in the 1830s. Although no French work in the serious vein remains in the repertory, one rescue opera, a German variant of the genre, still holds the stage today. Technically a Singspiel because of its use of spoken dialogue, Beethoven's *Fidelio* (Ex. 23) is based on a supposedly true rescue story. The composer wrestled a long while with this work, revising it three times between 1805 and 1814. Conceivably, the humanitarian idealism of the libretto justified his continuing interest, for Beethoven would not have applied himself to a frivolous libretto, not even to one by Da Ponte. (Beethoven called *Don Giovanni* "immoral"!)

Besides the rescue opera, another type of *opéra-comique,* with libretto and music more suited to the title, appeared in the second and third decades of the century. Performers in these operas acted in farcical situations, parodied accepted moral standards, and usually sang simple, tuneful airs to light-textured orchestral accompaniments (see SHO, p. 331 ff.). After the Paris performance of Rossini's *Le Comte Ory* (1828), the newer *opéra-comique* assimilated some of the bounce and vigor of Rossini's music, his sparkling orchestration and his Italianate melodies. A link among composers of these operas, in particular Auber (1782-1871), Hérold (1791-1833), and Boieldieu (1775-1834), existed in the person of Scribe (1791-1861), a prolific dramatist who reworked countless numbers of his more than 400 plays into successful libretti.

Auber's *Fra Diavolo* (1830), one result of the collaboration between Scribe and this composer, includes an abundance of strophic songs, couplets, romances (see Ex. 24), duets, and ensembles of a musical, non-dramatic nature. The popularity of operas of this type extended into the 1860s and enraged Wagner, who insisted that this preference only confirmed his opinion of the moral degradation of the French populace under the

Empire. Despite Wagner's pronouncements, however, the new style of *opéra-comique* not only influenced many German opera composers, among them Lortzing (1810-1851) and Flotow (1812-1883), but in Paris led directly to the composition of operetta.

Scribe's name is most often associated with the impresario Louis Veron (1798-1867) and the composer Giacomo Meyerbeer (1791-1864). These three men together created the magnificent spectacle of grand opera. Meyerbeer, who during the twentieth century has been more reviled than revered, was, in his lifetime, perhaps the single most popular composer in Europe. A superb dramatic craftsman, he was also a better musician than he recognized. Unfortunately, he seems to have catered exclusively to the public taste for sensationalism. His principal operas, *Robert le Diable* (1831), *Les Huguenots* (1836), *Le Prophète* (1849), and the posthumously produced *L'Africaine* (1865), a work that obviously influenced Verdi's *Aida* (1871), are all based on glamorous, heroic subjects. Calling for several soloists, large choruses (Ex. 25), and numerous dancers, these operas require unlimited resources to stage. One significant difference between *opéra-comique* and grand opera lies in the use of recitative in the latter to replace spoken dialogue.

The operas of Berlioz (1803-1869) belong to the category of grand opera. Berlioz did not live to see a performance of his masterpiece, *Les Troyens* (1856-1859, with libretto by the composer after Vergil's *Aeneid*); only the second part was performed during his lifetime. The organization of the opera into a series of scenes or tableaux is significant in that it antedates a similar technique of Mussorgsky's in *Boris Godunov* (1874).

French lyric opera represents the middle road selected by those composers, among them Gounod (1818-1893) and Thomas (1811-1896), who rejected the extremes of grand opera and operetta. Of all lyric operas, Gounod's *Faust* (1859) and Thomas's *Mignon* (1866), both based on dramas by Goethe, have been among the most successful.

To summarize, French opera before Wagner catered to the rising middle class in Paris with five different types of opera: serious opera, rescue opera, lighter comic opera, grand opera, and lyric opera. Operetta, an offshoot of the lighter comic opera, also held the boards.

23. ENSEMBLE, ARIA, AND MELODRAMA IN RESCUE OPERA
Fidelio (1814)[1]

A. Quartet, Act I

Sonnleithner and Treitschke
after Bouilly

Ludwig van Beethoven (1770-1827)

By virtue of its plot, the prisoners' chorus that closes the first act, and the dungeon scene that opens the second (last) act, *Fidelio* more than qualifies as a bona fide rescue opera. The following example, a four-voice canon, illustrates some of the many problems Beethoven encountered in operatic writing. The voices enter successively, each stating the original melody (mm. 8, 16, 24, 32). Each person's text is different because he is speaking in character: Marcelline jubilant in her love for Fidelio; Leonora (Fidelio) afraid lest this infatuation foil her plans to rescue her husband; Rocco delighted with his daughter's choice; and Jacquino enraged at the prospect of Marcelline's marriage to Fidelio. Although their respective texts differ, their melodic lines are identical because of the canonic texture. By contrast, Verdi, in his famous quartet from *Rigoletto,* differentiates not only the text but also the melody of each of his characters. Beethoven, always instrumentally oriented, provides a musically perfect form that falls slightly short dramatically. The quartet is beautifully scored for violas and celli divisi (see opening bars). This quartet antedates several static ensembles in later German opera,

---

[1] Our excerpts are from the third version of the opera, which was completed in 1814.
The date "1805," appearing in the Table of Contents, is the date of the first version.

among them the quintet from Wagner's *Meistersinger* and the trio from Strauss's *Rosenkavalier* (1911). [2]

Translation

Marcelline: I'm so astonished, my heart is content,
It's clear he loves me, how happy I shall be.

Leonora: [16] How great is the danger, how faint is my hope,
It's clear she loves me, oh nameless agony.

Rocco: [24] It's clear she loves him, yes, lass, he'll be thine,
A nice young couple who will surely get on fine.

Jaquino: [32] I'm ready to pull out my hair, her father agrees to the match,
I'm so astonished, I know not how my love to snatch.

23 - A

[2] Because of the growing complexity of orchestral scores, only the most unusual features of instrumentation will be indicated in our examples hereafter.

197

B. Aria, Act I

In this dramatic "vengeance aria," Beethoven vividly portrays Pizarro's personality through music. Beginning in the stormy key of d minor, the tonality changes to D major (m. 71) as Pizarro delightedly envisions Florestan's death. Despite the textual repetition of the first stanza (m. 44 ff.), Beethoven alters the music to emphasize Pizarro's increasingly evil intentions. The *sotto voce* chorus of guards that sounds above a string tremolo while Pizarro is singing provides an example of this typically romantic feature, later popular with Bellini and Verdi. The rhythmic drive and orchestral color of this aria anticipate Weber's technique in *Der Freischütz* (Ex. 30). We know that Weber conducted *Fidelio* numerous times and was undoubtedly influenced by Beethoven's music. The Queen of the Night's "vengeance aria" from *Die Zauberflöte* and Dr. Bartolo's "La Vendetta" from *Le Nozze di Figaro* might be compared with this excerpt. (Notice, also, the sudden key change at m. 89 and accented dissonances throughout.)

Translation

Pizarro: Ah, such a moment, my vengeance shall be tasted. Fate calls you, gnaws at your heart. [14]Oh joy, oh fortune. Already in their power, I saw the rabble glower and mock me in my fall. [31]Now nothing more can happen, for I will be the murderer. [75]In his dying hours, I'll shout aloud my triumph, my revenge.

Chorus: He speaks of death and wounds. It's time to make our rounds. How important it really is!

23 - B

PIZARRO

Ha! Ha! Ha! welch' ein Au - genblick! Die Ra - che werd' ich küh - len! dich, dich ru - fet dein Ge - schick! In sei - nem Her - zen wüh - len, o Won - ne, gro - sses Glück! in sei - nem Her - zen wüh - len, o Won - ne, o Won - - - ne, gro - sses Glück!

mor - - den, den Mör - der selbst zu mor - den!

Ha! Ha! welch' ein Au - genblick! Die

Ra - che werd' ich küh - len! dich, dich ru - fet dein Ge -

schick! In sei - nem Her - zen wüh - len, o

Won - ne, o Won - - - ne, gro - sses

202

57 Glück! Schon war ich

60 nah', im Stau - be, dem

63 lau - ten Spott zum Rau - be, da -

66 hin, da - hin ge - streckt zu

69 sein! Nun, nun ist es mir ge -

fp

cresc.

ff

p

wor - den,   den Mör - der____ selbst zu mor - den! In sei - ner

letz - - - ten Stun - de, den Stahl in sei - ner

Wun - de,   ihm noch in's Ohr zu schrei'n:

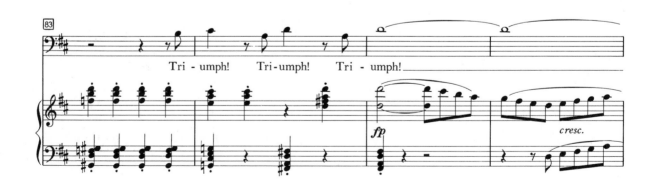

Tri - umph! Tri - umph! Tri - umph!_____

Beethoven's *Fidelio,* arranged by Gustav F. Kogel (G. Schirmer, 1907; renewed 1935).

C. Melodrama, Act II

Beethoven wrote only two recitatives in *Fidelio.* Both are *accompagnato* and both introduce arias: Leonora's first-act "Abscheulicher" and Florestan's opening aria in the second act. For the text of the dungeon scene, however, Beethoven used another musico-dramatic technique: *melodrama,* speech alternating with or sounding above the orchestra. Among the first composers to essay this feature in opera was the French philosopher-musician, Rousseau, who applied it in his play *Pygmalion* (1770).

Translation

Leonora (in an undertone): How cold it is in this underground vault!

Rocco: That is natural, it is so deep.

Leonora (anxiously glancing all about her): I really thought we could not even find the entrance.

Rocco (turning toward Florestan): There he is.

Leonora (her voice breaking as she seeks a glimpse of the prisoner's face): He seems quite motionless.

Rocco: [6]Perhaps he's dead.

Leonora (shuddering): You think so?

Rocco: No, he is sleeping.

Leonora: It's impossible to distinguish his features. God help me, if it is he.

Rocco: [17]Here under this rubbish is the old well of which I've spoken. (Sets his lantern on the heap.) We need not dig far to reach the opening; give me a pickaxe, and come stand here. (Descends into the hollow up to his waist, setting the pitcher down near him. Leonora hands him a pickaxe.) You tremble. Are vou afraid?

Leonora: Oh no! Only it is so cold.

Rocco (quickly): Then get to work; working will make you warm enough.

23-C   *Poco sostenuto*

(Rocco and Leonora, descending the stairway by the light of a lantern, carrying a pitcher and the tools for digging)

LEONORE (in an undertone): Wie kalt ist es in diesem unterirdischen Gewölbe!
ROCCO : Das ist natürlich, es ist ja so tief.

Allegro

LEONORE (anxiously glancing all about her):
Ich glaubte schon, wir würden den Eingang
gar nicht finden.

Poco adagio

ROCCO (turning toward Florestan) :Da ist er.
LEONORE (with a broken voice, while seeking
to catch a glimpse of the prisoner's face) :
Er scheint ganz ohne Bewegung.

ROCCO:Vielleicht ist er todt.   LEONORE: Ihr meint es?   (Florestan makes a movement)

Allegro

ROCCO:Nein, nein, er schläft.   sempre pp

ROCCO:Das müssen wir benutzen,
und gleich an's Werk gehen; wir
haben keine Zeit zu verlieren.

Strings   LEONORE:Es ist unmöglich, seine Züge zu unterscheiden.   Gott, steh' mir bei, wenn er es ist.

Andante con moto

Strings
Horns

ROCCO:Hier unter diesen Trümmern
ist die Cisterne, von der ich dir gesagt
habe. (Sets his lantern on the heap.)

Wir brauchen nicht viel zu graben,
um an die Öffnung zu kommen; gieb
mir eine Haue und du, stelle dich
hieher.
(Descends in the hollow up to his
waist, setting the pitcher down near
him. Leonora hands him a pickaxe.)

Du zitterst,

Beethoven's *Fidelio,* arranged by Gustav F. Kogel (G. Schirmer, 1907; renewed 1935).

LEONORE: O nein, es ist nur so kalt.

ROCCO (quickly): So mache fort, im Arbeiten wird dir schon warm werden.

24. ROMANCE IN FRENCH OPÉRA-COMIQUE

Fra Diavolo (1830)

Scribe

Daniel François Auber (1782-1871)

We can easily anticipate the turn of the melody in this modest little aria. Its tunefulness, simple harmonization, recurrent rhythm, and sprightly pizzicato accompaniment provide the reason for its instant popularity. The design for this *romance* could not be patented, and Auber had many imitators. Notice that measures 4-8 of the introduction present the melody of measures 21-25. Observe also that the repeat of the melody at measure 26 accompanies a different text, after which text and music change ever so slightly.

Translation

Zerlina: See that gallant, proud man on the rocks, his musket is near him. It is his faithful friend. [25]Watch him approach, a red feather in his hat, and wearing a coat of sumptuous velvet. [34]Tremble. In the bosom of the distant tempest, the echo repeats, Diavolo, Diavolo, tremble. In the bosom . . .

24   *Allegretto*

210

Vo-yez sur cet-te ro-che ce brave à l'air fier et__ har-di, son mous-quet__ est pres de lui, C'est son fi-dèle a-mi, Re-gar-dez il s'ap-pro-che, un plu-met rouge à son__ cha-peau, et cou-vert__ de son man-teau

Dia-vo-lo,   Dia-vo-lo.

Auber's *Fra Diavolo* (Novello & Company, Ltd., n.d.).

25. CHORAL MUSIC IN GRAND OPERA
Les Huguenots (1836)

The Benediction of the Daggers, Act IV

Scribe   Giacomo Meyerbeer (1791-1864)

Among the most brilliant features of Meyerbeer's operas are his finales, or *strette* as he called them, using the term to describe the increasingly intensified activities of music and drama as they both surge forward to a climax. Although the following example is not a finale, it serves the same purpose. A self-contained musical unit that superbly illustrates Meyerbeer's thespian gifts, this scene of the benediction of the daggers most certainly merits our close attention.

With the chorus of Catholic leaders on stage, the orchestra begins with a characteristic dotted-note figure, which persists (despite interruptions at m. 26 and at m. 70) until the new section at measure 104. During both interludes (mm. 26 and 70), the forte-piano alternation of Ab-major and E-major chords proved startling to contemporary critics. Beethoven and Schubert had both utilized this relationship between keys a third apart, but Meyerbeer viewed them enharmonically (Ab as G♯) anticipating his later section in E major. Excitement mounts as three monks move about from one group to another repeating the words: *Dieu le veut* ("God desires it," or "Death to all heretics!"). Furiously hammering, fortissimo triplets supply the orchestral underpinning to suit the action. Unison choruses (also fortissimo) gather momentum. Suddenly, at measure 194, texture and dynamics change. Meyerbeer begins (pianissimo) to fragment his choral statements, dropping swiftly to *sotto voce* cadential figures as the monks leave the stage to begin preparations for the morrow. (The events of the next day will go down in history as the Massacre of St. Bartholomew's Day.)

It would be a frightfully difficult task to establish the chronology of all the different musical and dramatic effects that appear in the history of nineteenth-century opera. And should we attempt to do so, we would unquestionably incur the wrath of partisans of one or the other composer. However, none can deny that Gounod, Bizet, Massenet, Verdi, Tchaikovsky, and certainly Wagner were sufficiently impressed by various aspects of Meyerbeer's musical theatricalism to borrow unhesitatingly from his works when the occasion required it. An immediate example that comes to mind is Senta's magnificent ballad from Wagner's *Der fliegende Holländer* (Ex. 31), an ill-concealed plagiarism of Raimbault's ballad in *Robert le Diable,* Meyerbeer's opera of 1831.

Translation

1st Monk: Glory, glory to God, the avenger. Glory to the faithful warrior, whose sword flashes to serve Him.

St. Bris and the Three Monks (together): [35]Sacred blades, holy swords that will soon be drenched in impure blood, you for whom the Heavens smite your enemies, sacred blades, be blessed by us!

Chorus (sopranos, tenors, basses): Glory to God the avenger. . .

St. Bris: [71]Let this white scarf and this spotless cross from Heaven distinguish the chosen.

Three Monks and St. Bris (together): Show no mercy and no pity! Strike down all relentlessly, the enemy who flees and the enemy who hides.

Chorus: [84]Let's strike, strike, strike!

St. Bris: The pleading warrior struck down at your feet.

Chorus: Let's strike, strike, strike!

St. Bris: [89]No mercy, no pity, let the sword and the flame reach old and young; and women, accursed let them be. God takes no cognizance of them.

Chorus: [109]God desires it. He orders it. No mercy for anyone. For this price will He pardon the sinner, the repentant sinner. Let swords flash, blood flow, and immortality awaits you in Heaven. God desires it. . .the repentant sinner. Spare nobody!

1st Monk (alone): [171]Silence, my friends!

St. Bris: Let nothing betray us. Let's withdraw without a sound. For this Holy Cause.

Chorus, St. Bris, Monks: [178]For this Holy Cause will I obey fearlessly. God, my King, rely on my courage. I pledge myself completely to you, for you. At midnight no noise!

25

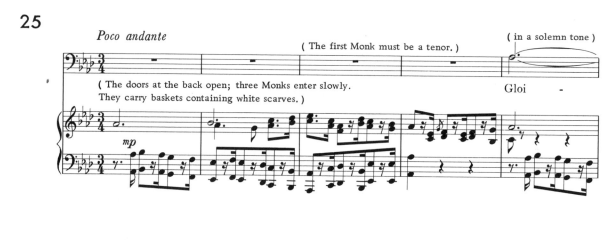

214

215

sang im-pur ser-ez bien tôt trempé-es, vous par qui le Très Haut fra - pe ses en-ne-mis,

glai - ves___ pi - eux par nous soy - ez bé - nis!___ Ven-

SOP.

gloi - - -

TEN.

gloi - - -

BASSES

oui, gloire au Dieu ven-

(St. Bris, the 2nd and 3rd Monks with the basses in the chorus; the first Monk with the tenors.)

S.

- - re, oui, gloire au Dieu ven - geur!_____

T.

re, oui, gloire au Dieu ven - geur!

B.

geur,_____ gloi - re, gloire au Dieu ven - geur!_____

dimin.

220

222

CHŒUR ET CORYPHÉES

223

224

225

* In full score, each part has its own dynamic indications.

227

229

26. SCÈNE, RÉCITATIF, CAVATINE, CHANSON IN FRENCH LYRIC OPERA

Faust (1859)

Barbier and Carré
Based on Part I of Goethe's *Faust*

Charles Gounod (1818-1893)

Less spectacular than grand opera, more concerned with serious subject matter and psychological concepts, the lyric opera, of which *Faust* is an example, flourished in France from about mid-century. After its first performances with spoken dialogue, Gounod substituted recitative, and the new *Faust* in time became the most popular French opera ever written. Unfortunately, lack of familiarity with the contextual position of its separate numbers tends to prejudice our appraisal of the total plan of the opera. We must observe these pieces in their proper context to see that there is an overall plan and that each number leads easily into the next.

Act III opens with a short instrumental introduction containing the barest suggestion of evil to come. Without a real pause, melody, harmony, rhythm, tempo, texture, and dynamics change to usher in Siebel's simple, almost strophic flower song ("Faites-lui mes aveux"), interrupted several times by recitative. In the scene and recitative that follow (again notice their sequence: *not* recitative and scene, because recitative occurs here in the natural course of the drama), Mephistopheles advises Faust that he need not fear his rival, Siebel, because he (Mephistopheles) will give Faust more tantalizing bait with which to seduce Marguerite. Alone now (m. 67), Faust sings his cavatine (modified ABA form), in which we note Gounod's frequent use of the sequence (mm. 86-89; 94-97), a hallmark of his style. Mephistopheles returns to bring Faust a casket of jewels for Marguerite, whose innocence prompts Faust to plead that Mephistopheles leave them alone. Marguerite then enters, sits in her garden, and sings the famous song of the "King of Thule," wherein we notice Gounod's solution to the problem of song placed within the normal recitative-aria fabric of opera. (Compare Cherubino's arietta, Ex. 19.) As Marguerite muses softly to herself, Gounod alternates between recitative and arioso before continuing without pause into the equally well-known jewel song (m. 297). (We might compare Gounod's treatment of recitative with the techniques of Lully, Rameau, and Gluck. We find that similar tendencies exist in their works—for example, the insertion of recitative in the middle of an aria.)

Our longest single excerpt proves that in *Faust* the drama and the music are in fact continuous. Even the opening of this opera is not delayed by an overture. Instead, an instrumental introduction merely sets the mood before the first scene begins.

Translation

[Scene and Recitative]

Faust: Is it here?

Mephistopheles: Follow me!

Faust: Whom are you looking at?

Meph: Siebel, your rival.

Faust: Siebel?

Meph: Hush, he's coming.

Siebel: My bouquet! Isn't it lovely?

Meph: Lovely!

Siebel: Victory! Tomorrow I'll tell her all. If she wants to know my heart's secret, a kiss will tell all.

Meph: Seducer!

[Allegro]

Meph: [49]Wait for me, dear doctor, to keep company with the flowers of our friend. I shall look for a treasure for you, more marvelous, even richer than any of which you might dream!

Faust: Leave me!

Meph: I obey. Deign to wait for me here.

[Cavatine]

Faust: [71]A peculiar uneasiness grips me. I sense that love has taken possession of my soul. O Marguerite, I kneel before thee. All hail, O dwelling pure and holy, where one feels the presence of an innocent, sacred soul! [94]What riches in such poverty! In short what happiness. [105]O nature, it's there you made her beautiful. It's there she grew, beneath your guidance. There, that with your breath infusing her soul, you watched her blooming womanhood, this heavenly angel. There! [123]All hail. . .sacred soul.

[Scene]

Mephistopheles: [145]Careful! Here she comes. If the bouquet prevails over the casket, I shall consent to lose my power.

Faust: Let's go! I never want to see her again.

Meph: What scruples are you displaying now? The casket is right on the threshold. Come! I have hopes.

[Scene and Air]

Marguerite: [188]I'd like to know who that young man was, if he is of noble birth and also his name.

[202]Reigned a King in Thule of old,
Who unto death was true-hearted,
And, for sake of one departed,
Treasured a goblet of gold.
[210]He was gentle of bearing,
His voice was very kind.
This rare cup so tenderly cherished,
Aye at his side the King did keep,
[219]And every time it touched his lips,
He wept, and thought of her long perished.
[228]Over the sea at last came death;
On his couch the old King lying
Called for the cup when he was dying,
Almost with his last breath.
[236]I knew not what to answer, and blushed like any child!
Once more with the old, true devotion,
The King would have his cup of gold,
Then, with hand in death growing cold,
He flung the goblet in the ocean!

[251]Nobles alone can bear them with so bold a mien. Let's be off! Think of him no longer. If God hears my prayer, I'll see you again. Here I am all alone.

[Recit.] [266]A bouquet! Siebel's no doubt! Poor boy. What's this? Where could this casket have come from? I dare not touch it. I think this is the key. If I open it! My hand trembles! Why? I shouldn't be doing anything wrong in opening it. And yet. . . [278]Oh Heaven, what jewels! Is this a dream? A dazzling fantasy? Or if I am awake, I must say I've never seen the likes of these before.

[287]If I dared for a moment to try this lovely pair of earrings. . .
And here, so handy, at the back of the casket is a mirror.
Who wouldn't want to preen before it?
[304]Ah, I laugh to see myself so lovely in this mirror.
Is it you, Marguerite? Is it you?
Reply, reply quickly. No, no. It's not you.
It's not your face; it's the daughter of a King,
Whom one greets in passing. [351]Ah if he were here. . .

If he could see me thus, as a fair lady.
He would certainly adore me.
[378] Let's make the change.
Heavens! It's like a hand resting on my arm. [399] Ah. . .
I laugh. . .whom one greets in passing.

26

234

CAVATINE

où se de-vi-ne La pré-sen-ce d'une âme in no-cen - te et di-

vi - ne!

MEPHISTOPHELES (reëntering)
A - ler - te, la voi - là! Si le bou-

quet l'em-por-te Sur l'é-crin, je con-sens à per-dre mon pou-

FAUST
voir. Fu-yons! je veux ne ja-mais la re-voir. Quel scru-pu-le vous

SCÈNE ET AIR

Je vou-drais bien sa - voir quel é - tait ce jeune hom - me; Si c'est un grand sei-

gneur,___ et com-ment il se nom - me?

CHANSON DU ROI DE THULÉ

Moderato maestoso (♩=72)

MARGARITA *poco ritenuto*

Il é - tait un Roi de Thu-lé,___ Qui, jus-qu'à la tom - be fi-

dè - le, Eut, en sou-ve-nir de sa bel - le, U-ne coupe en or ci - se-

242

228
M. Quand il sen-tit ve - nir la mort,___ É-ten-du sur sa froi-de cou - che,

p

232
M. Pour la por-ter jus-qu'à sa bou-che, Sa main fit un su-prême ef-fort!___

rit. Andante

f *pp* *rit.*

236 (breaking off) Tempo I (resuming the song)
M. Je ne sa-vais que di - re, Et j'ai rou-gi d'a-bord. Et puis,

239
M. en l'hon-neur de sa da - me, Et puis, en l'hon-neur de sa da - me, Il but u-

243 *rit.* *più lento*
M. ne der-niè - re fois.___ La cou-pe trem - bla dans ses doigts,___

rit. *p*

Et dou-ce-ment il ren-dit l'â - - me!

Les grands sei-gneurs ont seuls des airs si ré-so-lus, A-vec cet-te dou-ceur!

pp a piacere Moderato

f

dolce

Al - lons, n'y pen-sons

cresc. *dim.* *p* *cresc.*

Andante

plus!___ Cher Va-len - tin! si Dieu m'é-cou - te, Je te re-ver-

f *dim.*

Andantino

(noticing the flowers)

rai!___ Me voi - là tou-te seu - le!

p

(Puts down the casket, and kneels to adron herself with the jewels)

je ris_____ de me voir Si belle en ce mi - roir!

Ah! je ris_____ de me voir Si belle en ce mi - roir! Est - ce

toi,____ Mar - gue - ri - te, Est- ce toi? Ré-ponds-moi,

ré-ponds-moi, ré-ponds, ré-ponds, ré-ponds vi - te! Ah! s'il é - tait i - ci!

S'il me vo - yait ain-si, Comme u-ne de-moi-sel - le Il me trou-ve-rait

251

Gounod's *Faust* (G. Schirmer, 1902, 1930). Used by kind permission of the publisher.

VIII

Nineteenth-Century Italian
Opera Before Wagner

Rome, Milan, Naples
(c. 1790-1860)

In the later eighteenth century and during the first two decades of the nineteenth century, Italy lost her position of leadership in the production of opera. However, before the third decade of the century, several Italians had already returned to the limelight. Rossini (1792-1868), Bellini (1801-1835), and Donizetti (1797-1848), three leading opera composers before Verdi, studied and produced their early works in Italy, but matured in Paris. Certainly, all achieved some of their greatest successes at the Paris Opera. Of Rossini's thirty-eight operas in as many years—he stopped writing in 1829 after the success of his grand opera, *Guillaume Tell*—his best known is his delightful comic opera, *Il Barbiere di Siviglia,* based on the first play of Beaumarchais's trilogy. (Mozart had already set the story of the second play, *Le Nozze di Figaro.*) Rossini's inexhaustible supply of melodies, his vigorous rhythms, his entertaining buffa arias, his ensembles, his scintillating orchestration, and even his occasionally overdone crescendi, combine to make the *Barber* (Ex. 27) one of the perennial favorites. We might note that, to his credit, Rossini wrote out his cadenzas and fioriture to avoid excesses by singers.

Bellini and Donizetti, despite many differences between them, are usually mentioned together. Bellini wrote nine operas, seven to libretti by Felice Romano; he wrote no comic operas. Donizetti wrote more than seventy operas, of which his comic operas, notably *L'elisir d'amore* (1832) and *Don Pasquale* (1843), represent the last examples of the genre in the nineteenth century. Our anthology, however, contains the famous "mad scene," a coloratura aria (Ex. 29) from one of Donizetti's best known romantic operas, *Lucia di Lammermoor.* The presence of superb singers, a *sine qua non* for the vocal acrobatics expected in such scenes, led to the use of the words *bel canto* ("beautiful song") to describe those operas that include an abundance of this kind of virtuosity. (Bukofzer notes the "emergence of the bel canto style between 1630 and 1640." See MBE, p. 118. His use of the term to describe the earlier style, however, should not be confused with the florid vocalism of the nineteenth century.) Our example is but one of many "mad scenes" that dot the libretti of nineteenth-century Italian opera.

Norma, one of Bellini's operas that combine elements of grand opera (chorus and spectacle) and romanticism (long-line melodies and extended lyricism), elicited much praise from Wagner. Because he had earned his livelihood making piano arrangements of the works of Donizetti and Bellini, among others, Wagner was familiar with many of their scores. He preferred Bellini's, probably because they showed marked superiority in the treatment of the orchestra. Bellini's melodies, with their broken-chord accompaniments, resemble figurations in numerous piano pieces by Chopin, particularly the nocturnes. However, despite many authors' comments to the contrary, we have no proof that Chopin knowingly imitated the older composer's style.

The cavatina from *Norma,* "Casta Diva" (Ex. 28), suggests that Bellini agreed with the textbook definition of the term: a slow piece, in one section and one tempo, shorter than an aria, with few melismas and little textual repetition; a sentence in song, extracted (*cavato*) from a few notes. This description, however, applies only to the first section of the aria (included in Ex. 28). Numerous other cavatinas, for example Mozart's "Se vuol ballare" from *Figaro,* the comic aria from Rossini's *Barber* (Ex. 27) along with two additional cavatinas from the same opera, and Faust's cavatine included in Example 26, all reveal varying characteristics. Unfortunately, there is no single definition that covers the period during which the term was extensively used, the second half of the eighteenth century and the first half of the nineteenth century.

27. CAVATINA IN COMIC OPERA
Il Barbiere di Siviglia (1816)

Sterbini   Gioacchino Rossini (1792-1868)

The following cavatina provides an illustration of yet another feature of Rossini's style: the comic *patter* aria. The word patter supposedly derives from the whispered "Pater Noster" rapidly recited in church, although here it describes the style of singing wherein each syllable of each word is closely wed to its own note, an effect particularly appropriate to the euphonious Italian language. (Gilbert and Sullivan's "Modern Major-General" from *Pinafore* is a patter aria in the English language.) Our cavatina is longer than most, and it also includes much textual repetition not generally found in this form.

The vigorous opening instrumental figure paints Figaro's portrait in music. Most of the melodic and rhythmic material of the aria is contained in the orchestral introduction and the vocal refrain that precede the appearance of Figaro onstage (m. 44). Simple, almost routine harmonizations (see m. 253 ff. and the entire introduction, mm. 1-43), short-range, tuneful melodies with leaps that occasionally emphasize the volatile nature of the character who is singing, numerous sequences, and a kind of perpetual movement in persistent $\frac{6}{8}$ rhythm are featured in this excerpt, which owes much of its popularity to its rapid delivery.

Rossini uses rests very effectively. Following one at measure 80, he wraps up the first section of the piece with textual repetition, a vocal refrain, and a snappy instrumental flourish (mm. 81-100). The cavatina continues with the orchestra sounding a motive that has been anticipated earlier (mm. 17-18). The piece seems to be eternally unwinding, moving gradually, but assertively, to its whirlwind finish. Rossini unifies the work through recurrent short, recognizable, rhythmic and melodic motives. Then, too, he reuses blocks of material. Compare, for example, measure 150 ff. and its earlier appearance in measures 59-70. Observe that Rossini still uses secco recitative (m. 275 ff.). He is one of the last nineteenth-century composers to do so. Rossini's orchestration, besides supporting the singers in their arias, also displays a markedly individual instrumentation that unfortunately does not appear to advantage in a piano reduction of the score.

Translation

Figaro: Make way for the factotum of the town! [52] I must get to my shop. It's already dawn. Ah, what a merry life, what pleasure awaits a barber of quality! Ah, bravo Figaro, you are truly most fortunate. [112] Ready for everything night and day, always in perpetual motion. What a godsend! What nobler life for a barber than mine! [127] Razors, combs, lances, and scissors! At my command everything's there. Then there are the perquisites of this business with gay ladies and cavaliers. [153] Ah, what a merry life. . .for a barber of quality. All of them call me. All of them want me. Women and girls, old and young! What's with my wig? Quickly, my beard! Here bleed me! [179] Carry this message! All of them call me. . .message. Figaro, Figaro, etc. Oh me! Oh my! What fury! What a crowd! [198]One at a time, for mercy sake! Figaro! I'm here! Eh, Figaro! I'm here! Figaro here! Figaro there! Figaro what? Figaro where? Quick, even quicker! I'm fast as lightning. I'm the factotum of the town! Ah bravo Figaro, Oh but I'm fortunate! [245]There's nothing I need! I'm the factotum of the town!

[Recit.] [275]Ah what a happy life! A little fatigue, but a lot of amusement! And in my pocket always several doubloons, [278]the noble fruit of my reputation. It's like this: without Figaro, not a girl in Seville could get married!

tis - si - mo per ve - ri - tà, for - tu - na - tis - si - mo per ve - ri-

tà! La le ran la la le ran la la re la re la la la ran la la ran la.

Pron-to a far tut - to, la not-te il gior - no sem-pre d'in-

tor-no in gi - ro sta. Mi-glior cuc - ca-gna per un bar - bie - re, vi-ta più no-bi-le, no, non si

259

le rà, col ca-va-lie-re, la le ran la,   la,   la.

Ah che_bel vi-ve-re,   che bel_pia-ce-re,   che bel_pia-ce-re   per un bar-

bie — re di qua-li-tà!   di qua-li-tà!

Tut-ti mi chie-do-no,   tut-ti mi vo-glio-no,   don-ne, ra-

gaz-ze,   vec-chi e fan-ciul-le: Qua la par-ruc-ca,

per ca - ri - tà, per ca - ri - tà, per ca - ri - tà! u-no al-la

vol - ta, u-no al-la vol - ta, u-no al-la vol - ta per ca - ri - tà!

Fi - ga-ro! Son qua. Ehi, Fi - ga-ro!

Son qua. Fi-ga-ro qua, Fi-ga-ro là, Fi-ga-ro qua, Fi-ga-ro

là, Fi-ga-ro su, Fi-ga-ro giù, Fi-ga-ro su, Fi-ga-ro giù! Pron-to pron-

tu - na non man-che - rà, so - no il fac-to - tum del - la cit - tà,____

so - no il fac-to - tum del - la____cit - tà,____del - la____cit tà,____del -

la____cit - tà, del - la cit - tà!

Recit.

Ah, ah! che bel-la vi - ta! Fa-ti-car po-co, di-ver-tir-si as-

sa - i, e in tas-ca sem-pre a - ver qual-che do-blo - ne. Gran frut - to del-la mia ri-pu-ta-

265

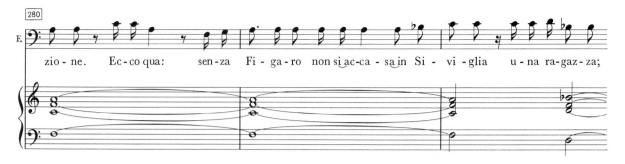

zio - ne.   Ec - co qua: sen - za Fi - ga - ro non si ac-ca - sa in Si - vi -glia   u - na ra-gaz - za;

Rossini's *Barber of Seville* (G. Schirmer, 1962).

28. CAVATINA IN BEL CANTO OPERA
Norma (1831)

Scene and Cavatina, Act I, Scene iv

Romano   Vincenzo Bellini (1801-1835)

Composers often wrote specific arias or even entire roles with certain soloists in mind. In such instances, responsibility for the projection of a mood or the excitement of the plot rested almost completely with the singer. Many of the operas in which the composers focus on the abilities of the vocalists are called *bel canto* operas. Our excerpt illustrates one facet of the bel canto tradition in Italian Romantic opera. Similar to their counterparts in France and Germany, these operas usually included a libretto based on a story set in the Middle Ages or derived from legendary sources; they contained numerous outdoor scenes, nocturnal happenings, and elements of the supernatural.

As Norma addresses the Druids, observe how Bellini's music matches the intensity of the text in his accompanied recitative (mm. 1-55). In the cavatina that follows, we have a model of the form that prevailed through much of the nineteenth century. An instrumental introduction states the melody in its entirety (mm. 56-69), holding momentarily on a fermata before the vocalist's introductory bar (m. 70). Notice that the entire section is essentially monothematic. One melody appears in the introduction (mm. 56-70), recurs in the vocal line slightly ornamented (mm. 71-85), offers its decorative turn for sequential treatment (compare the original at m. 59 with its treatment in mm. 87-88), and returns intact at measure 96. At impassioned fortissimo portions of the text, the orchestra, in addition to providing a Chopinesque broken-chord accompaniment, doubles the vocal line (mm. 82-84). Occasionally, the soloist has fragments of the melody that continues in an unbroken line in the orchestra and chorus (m. 85 ff.). This sotto voce, homorhythmic chorus in the background alternates with or accompanies the soloist. Such choruses became a feature of Italian Romantic opera. (For an earlier instance, see chorus in *Fidelio*, Ex. 23-B, m. 89 ff.). We have not printed the second section of this cavatina. It is in a lively tempo and is often described as a *cabaletta* (cf. Ex. 36).

Translation

Norma [Recit.] : Seditious voices! Does anyone dare to raise the voices of war at the altar of our deity? Does anyone presume to dictate answers to the all-seeing Norma and hasten the mysterious fate of Rome? It does not depend on human power.

Oroveso: And how long must we be oppressed? Are not our native groves and ancient temples sufficiently contaminated by the Latin eagles? Now the sword of Brenno can no longer remain idle.

Chorus: [22] Let it be brandished at once!

Norma: And it will fall, broken. Yes broken, if any of you should dare to draw it before the time. [29] The days are not yet ripe for our vengeance. The Roman spears are still stronger than the axes of the Sicambre.

Oro. and Chorus: [34] And what does Heaven tell you? Speak! What will happen?

Norma: I read in the hidden volumes of Heaven; in pages of death the name of proud Rome is written; she will die one day, but not through you. She will die by her vices; consumed she will die. [47] Await the hour, the fatal hour that fulfills the great decree. I summon you for peace, and the sacred mistletoe I gather.

Norma [Cavatina]: [71] Chaste Goddess, who dost bathe in silver light these ancient, sacred trees, [78] Turn thy fair countenance upon us unclouded and unveiled.* [96] Do temper the burning hearts, and also the excessive zeal of thy people.** [103] Spread on earth the peace, which, through you, reigns in heaven.

Oro. and Chorus: * Chaste Goddess. . .

Oro. and Chorus: ** Oh, God, spread on earth. . .

28

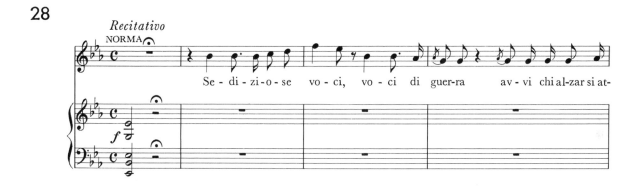

267

NORMA

Allegro moderato

Io ne' vo-lu-mi ar - ca-ni leg-go del cie-lo: in pa-gi-ne di mor-te del-la su-per-ba Ro-ma è scrit-to il no-me el-la un gior-no mor-rà; ma non per vo - i. Mor-rà pei vi-zi suo-i; qual con-sun - ta mor-rà. L'o-ra a-spet-ta-te, l'o-ra fa-tal che com-pia il gran de-cre-to. Pa - ce v'in-ti-mo. e il sa-cro vis-chio io mie-to.

pp sempre

(Cuts the mistletoe; the Priestesses gather it in wicker baskets. Norma advances and raises
her hand to heaven. The moon shines with its full light. All kneel.)

*56 *Andante sostenuto assai*

*) The original key of this aria is G major. Because of its difficulty, it is usually transposed down to F major, as here.

271

gen - ti que - - ste sa - cre, que - ste

sa - cre, que - ste sa - cre an - ti - che pian - te, a noi vol - gi il bel sem-

bian - te, a noi vol - gi, a noi vol-gi il bel sem - bian

sempre cresc. sino al.........

sempre cresc. sino al..........

- - - te, il bel sem - bian - te sen - za nu - be e sen - za

273

Bellini's *Norma* (G. Schirmer, n.d.).

29. THE COLORATURA ARIA IN BEL CANTO OPERA

Lucia di Lammermoor (1835)

Cammarano   Gaetano Donizetti (1797-1848)

From *Lucia di Lammermoor,* another singer's opera, derived this time from Sir Walter Scott's novel *The Bride of Lammermoor,* we have included the mad scene to illustrate the virtuoso coloratura style. Here, too, a *sotto voce* chorus introduces the solo aria and reappears once (m. 141) before its conclusion. The breathless quality of the vocal line reflects Lucia's agitation. The asterisks at measures 41, 88, and 136 indicate those places where singers usually provide further ornamentation of the given vocal line, in addition to the numerous delicate traceries already notated (mm. 87 and 111). The enormous technical facility and vocal agility required for the execution of this aria are always recognized by audiences, whose applause invariably drowns out the following chorus. Most singers today offer an extended and brilliant cadenza at measure 162 in which the flute and soloist echo one another as they sing the same devilishly difficult passages, the motives of which derive from measures 89-90 and 99-102.

Notice the full accompaniment of the recitative (mm. 11-41) and observe also that in the succeeding aria, it is the orchestra and not the soloist who presents the complete melody (mm. 42-51). Donizetti has employed the voice here as an obbligato instrument darting in and out of the texture. The numerous tempo changes and the interruptive recitative suggest a scena rather than an aria.

Translation

Raimondo: Here she comes!

Chorus: Great Heavens! She looks as if she's come from the grave!

Lucia: The sweet sound of his voice struck me, that voice has pierced my heart. [17] Edgardo, I am yours once more. I have fled from your enemies.

[Recit.]: [29] A chill creeps into my breast, every fibre of my body trembles, my foot falters. Sit beside me near the fountain for a little while. Yes, sit near the fountain with me.

[Aria] [52] Oh my! The dreadful phantom arises and separates us! Oh Edgardo, the phantom is separating us!

[Recit.]: [85] Let us take refuge here, Edgardo, at the foot of the altar. It's strewn with roses! Celestial music, don't you hear it? Ah!

[Aria] [100] Ah! They are playing the wedding hymn! Soon time for our marriage! How happy I am! [114] Oh joy that I feel and cannot express. [121] The incense burns, the holy candles shine, shine all over! Here is the minister! [129] Give me your right hand. Oh happy day! Oh happy! At last I am yours! You are mine! God gives you to me.

Norman, Raimondo and Chorus: Oh, what a sad state you are in!

Lucia: Every pleasure sweeter, yes, every pleasure shared with you.

Norman, Raimondo and Chorus: Oh Lord, have mercy upon her!

Lucia: From a kind heaven, life will be a smile for us.

29

voce m'è qui nel cor di - sce - sa! Ed - gar - do! io ti son

re - sa, Ed - gar - do! ah! Ed - gar - do mi - o! sì, ti son

re - sa; fug - gi - ta io son da' tuoi ne - mi - ci, da' _____ tuoi _____ ne - mi -

ci. Un

ge - lo mi ser - peg - gia nel sen! tre - ma o - gni

285

Donizetti's *Lucia di Lammermoor* (G. Schirmer, 1898; copyright renewed 1926).

IX

Nineteenth-Century German Opera Before Wagner

Berlin, Prague
(c. 1800-1840)

While the Parisians concerned themselves with rescue opera, opéra-comique, and the early stages of grand opera, and while the Italians concentrated on singers and the bel canto tradition, one German composer, whose advanced compositional techniques cleared the way for Wagner's "music of the future," achieved success in Berlin. Although he composed significant works in other genre besides opera, Carl Maria von Weber would be assured of his place in musical history had he left us only *Der Freischütz*.

Like most romantic operas, *Freischütz* offers outdoor scenes, nocturnal scenes, and elements of the supernatural, but in addition it includes a folk tale already known to its audiences. Weber, long interested in German folksongs, so successfully shaped his melodies in folk style that shortly after their initial performances, the tunes from *Freischütz* were whistled in the streets of Berlin! Historically speaking, the earliest examples of German romantic opera are *Undine* (Berlin, 1816) by E. T. A. Hoffmann (1776-1822) and *Faust* by Ludwig Spohr (1784-1859), presented the same year in Prague. Both composers anticipated Weber's techniques in *Freischütz,* Hoffmann in his use of supernatural elements and his preference for folklike melodies, and Spohr in his employment of recurrent motives. However, *Undine* and *Faust* are today mere historical novelties, whereas *Freischütz* can still thrill contemporary audiences.

Before the appearance of Wagner, Weber is clearly the single most important composer of German romantic opera and all it connotes. Like Wagner, Weber was born and raised in a theatrical family and was therefore thoroughly familiar with sets, staging, lighting, and the erratic behavior of actors. Weber's first cousin, Constanze, had married Mozart, and Weber's father (brother to Mozart's deceased father-in-law) sought to make of his son an equally successful prodigy. Young Weber had other ideas and in time earned his living almost entirely as a conductor, first in Breslau and Prague and then, for the last ten years of his life, in Dresden. His legacy is extensive. He emerges as one of the few innovators in the history of dramatic music. Before Berlioz, Liszt, Wagner, Strauss, and Debussy, Weber experimented with orchestral color. We can observe his techniques in the remarkable Wolf's Glen Scene (Ex. 30-A), where he has combined elements of melodrama, scena, recitative, and aria, all tightly meshed within an orchestral fabric. He was among the first composers to associate a particular tone color with a specific character: the clarinet for Max, the brave hunter, and the diminished seventh chord played tremolando by the strings to identify Samiel, the evil spirit. Weber included folklike choruses of hunters and bridesmaids (Ex. 30-B), invented nonsense syllables and magical incantations to heighten the suspenseful atmosphere of the drama, and fashioned *Der Freischütz* as the supreme example of German romantic opera. A synoptic overture, an outline of which appears on page 291, presents all the significant themes of the opera. Skillfully, Weber molds this material into sonata form.

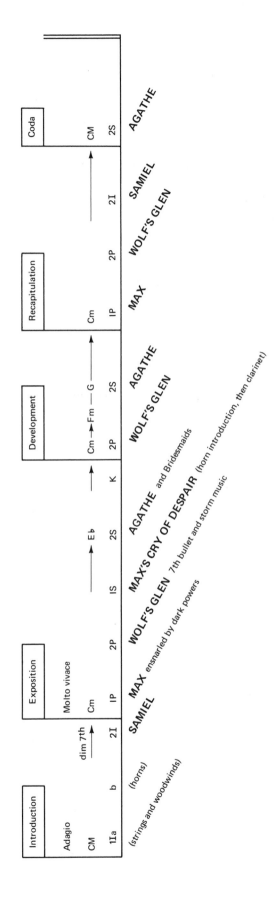

Weber's
Der Freischütz: OVERTURE (1820)
performed a year before the opera's premiere

KEY: All the themes used in the overture, with the exception of the first introductory elements (1Ia, 1Ib) and a short cadential section (K), are taken from music in the opera. The derivation is indicated below the symbol and the key scheme appears above the symbol.

I   Introductory themes

P   Primary themes

S   Secondary themes

K   Closing themes

M   Major

m   Minor

→   Modulating

Notice that here, as in the concert overture (cf. Mendelssohn's *Midsummer Night's Dream*), we do not find the repeated exposition so typical of the classical period. However, the sonata form is clear.

The early form of this type of analysis first appeared in print in Professor Jan LaRue's article "A System of Symbols for Formal Analysis," in JAMS, x (Spring, 1957). Fuller details appear in his forthcoming book *Guidelines for Style Analysis*, New York: W. W. Norton & Company, Inc. 1970.

30. VOCAL AND INSTRUMENTAL MUSIC IN GERMAN ROMANTIC OPERA

Der Freischütz (1821)

A. Finale, Act II

Kind   Carl Maria von Weber (1786-1826)

The Wolf's Glen Scene illustrates a finale whose primary emphasis on the drama differentiates it from both the Italian ensemble of perplexity and ensemble finale as well as from the French vaudeville finale. (For a typical ensemble of perplexity, see the Sextet from Donizetti's *Lucia di Lammermoor;* for an ensemble finale, see the second-act finale of Mozart's *Figaro;* and for a typical French vaudeville finale, see the last number of Rossini's *Barber.*) Because we are so very much involved with the story at this point in the opera, we are apt to lose count of the variety of musical techniques—melodrama, accompanied recitative, spoken dialogue, aria, arioso, chorus of invisible spirits, echoes—and the blood-curdling theatrical tricks that Weber employs to increase the tension in the drama. Numerous sophisticated stage directions are the composer's own. (A facsimile of the manuscript exists for comparison with the printed edition.) Additional instructions have been taken from Friedrich Kind's libretto. Samiel, exclusively a speaking role, seems to have been a novelty for the time. Notice also the musical continuity through the various scene changes (in mm. 39 and 110) and the unusual instrumentation with which Weber achieves his desired dramatic ends. Thus the entire scene is a landmark in the history of opera.

Translation

Chorus of Invisible Spirits:
Milk of moon fell on the sod, Uhui!
Spider webs are stained with blood, Uhui!
[31] Ere another eve is sped, Uhui!
A sweet gentle bride is dead, Uhui!
Ere the next descent of night, will the sacrifice be done? Uhui!

Kaspar:
Samiel, Samiel, appear!
By the wizard's skull,
Samiel, Samiel, appear!

Samiel: Why do you call?

Kaspar: You know that my term has almost run out.

Samiel: Tomorrow!

Kaspar: [61] Once more prolong this life to me!

Samiel: No!

Kasper: Another victim I'll give thee!

Samiel: Whom?

Kaspar: My comrade, he nears. He who never yet dared here appear!

Samiel: What does he seek?

Kaspar: [74] It is magic bullets on which he builds his hopes!

Samiel: Six will obey. The seventh betray!

Kaspar: The seventh shall be yours! Speed it from his barrel to his bride. Despair will make him yours, him and the father.

Samiel: I have no stake in her yet!

Kaspar: But you will set a term. And for another three years I'll bring him to you as your prey!

Samiel: [104] So be it! By the gates of Hell! Tomorrow, he or you!

Kaspar: Excellent service! Blessings on you Samiel! He has made me warm! But where is Max? Could he break his word? Samiel, help!

Max: [157] Ha! Fearful yawns the gloomy chasm. What horror! My eyes fancy themselves gazing into a slough of Hell! Look how the stormclouds cluster there! The moon gives up its beams. [169] Ghostly, misty shapes waver. The rock is alive! And here! Hush, hush! Nightbirds fly up in the bushes! [178] Branches, ruddy grey and scarred, stretch out gigantic arms at me! No! Though my heart may be horrified, I must! I defy all terrors!

Kaspar: Thanks, Samiel. My term is achieved. Have you come at last comrade? Was it right to leave me all alone? Can't you see how distasteful it is for me?

Max: [198] I shot the eagle out of the lofty air! I cannot turn back. My destiny calls! Woe is me!

Kaspar: Come on, time is flying!

Max: I can't get down!

Kaspar: You usually climb like any rabbit!

Max: [215] Look over there, look what's coming in view! It is my mother's ghost. As she lay in her coffin, she rests in her grave now. She looks and weeps and warns me. She is waving me back!

Kaspar: Help, Samiel! Ridiculous fancies. Ha! Look again and you'll see what comes of your cowardly stupidity!

Max: Agatha! She's jumping into the water! Down! I must follow!

Kaspar: [258] I think so too!

Max: Here I am. What do I have to do?

Kaspar: First have a drink! The night air is cold and damp. Will you do the casting yourself?

Max: No, that goes against our agreement! What do I have to do?

Kaspar: Nothing. Whatever you may say or hear, keep quiet. If someone unknown to you should come and help us, what matter to you? But if you see me tremble, then come and help me, and call out what I call out, otherwise we're both lost!

Max: Kaspar!

Kaspar: Hush! Every moment is precious! Watch me so that you learn the art. [261] First the lead. Some ground glass from broken church windows; you can find that! Some quicksilver! Three bullets that have hit their mark. The right eye of a lapwing! The left eye of a lynx. *Probatum est!* And now the blessing of the bullets.

Protect us, you who watch in darkness! Samiel, Samiel, give ear! Stand by me in this night! Till the spell is complete. Bless them by seven, nine and three, that the bullet be obedient. Samiel, Samiel, to me!

Kaspar: One!

Echo: One!

Kaspar: [290] Two!

Echo: Two!

Kaspar: Three!

Echo: Three!

Kaspar: Four!

Echo: Four!

Kaspar: [327] Five!

Echo: Five!

Kaspar: Alas, the savage pack!

Chorus (invisible):
[340] Over hill, over dale! Through abyss and pit. Over dew and clouds,
tempest and night, over chasm, bog, abyss, through fire, earth, sea, air, Yahoo! way away! Ho, ho!

Kasper: Six!

Echo: Six!

Kaspar: Samiel! Samiel! Samiel! Help! Seven!

Max: Samiel!

Samiel: Here I am!

(Kaspar, without hat or cloak, but with hunting bag and knife, busies himself with large rocks, laying out a circle in the middle of which a skull lies; a few steps away are the excised eagle's wings, a casting-ladle, and a bullet mold.)

FOURTH SCENE

30-A

CHORUS OF INVISIBLE SPIRITS

FIFTH SCENE

(Kaspar: Shortly afterwards, Samiel. The clock strikes twelve in the distance. The circle of stones is complete.)

(Rips his hunting knife out, plunges it into the skull, raises the knife with the skull, turns round three times and calls out.)

SIXTH SCENE

(Kaspar raises himself up, slowly and exhausted, and wipes the sweat from his brow. The skull with the hunting knife has disappeared; in its place a little fire with glowing coals comes up from below, and some bundles of rushes.)

301

Vivace

191 (He climbs down a few paces.)

194

KASPAR (standing up and looking at him):
Dank, Samiel! die Frist ist gewonnen!

KASPAR (to Max): Kommst du endlich, Kamerad?
Ist das auch recht, mich so allein zu lassen?
Siehst du denn nicht, wie mir's sauer wird?

(He has been fanning the fire with the eagle's wing
and points it at Max as he speaks.)

198   MAX (staring at the eagle's wing)

Ich schoß   den Ad - ler aus ho - her Luft;   ich kann   nicht

204   *Rezit.*   *Vivace* (He climbs down a few paces, then

rück - wärts,   mein Schick-sal   ruft!

207   stops again and gazes fixedly at the rocks on the other side.)

the moon begins to darken.)

KASPAR (aside, mocking) MAX (impetuously to Kaspar):
Ich denke wohl auch.   Hier bin ich! Was hab ich zu tun?

KASPAR: (Throwing him the hunting flask, which Max sets down.) Zuerst trink einmal! Die Nachtluft ist kühl und feucht.   Willst du selbst giessen?

MAX: Nein, das ist wider die Abrede.

KASPAR: Nicht? So bleib ausser dem Kreise,   sonst kostet's dein Leben!

MAX: Was hab ich zu tun, Hexenmeister?

KASPAR: Fasse Mut!   Was du auch hören und sehen magst, verhalte dich ruhig.   (Disguising his own horror.) Käme vielleicht ein Unbekannter, uns zu helfen, was kümmert es dich?   Kommt was anders, was tut's? So etwas sieht ein Gescheiter gar nicht!

MAX: O, wie wird das enden!

KASPAR: Umsonst ist der Tod! Nicht ohne Widerstand schenken verborgene Naturen den Sterblichen ihre Schätze. Nur wenn du mich selbst zittern siehst, dann komm mir zu Hilfe und rufe, was ich rufen werden, sonst wir beide verloren. (Max, with a gesture as if to object.) Still! Die Augenblicke sind kostbar! (The moonlight has dwindled to a tiny beam. Kaspar takes the casting ladle.) Merk, was ich hineinwerfen werde, damit du die Kunst lernst! (He takes the ingredients out of his hunting bag and throws them in one after another.)

NB. Both repeat signs were put into the manuscript with pencil, and the repeat is used only if Max should not have enough time.)

KASPAR: Hier erst das Blei. Etwas gestossenes Glas von zerbrochenen Kirchenfenstern; das findet sich. Etwas Quecksilber. Drei Kugeln, die schon einmal getroffen.

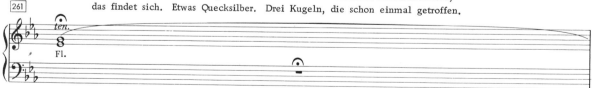

262 Das rechte Auge eines Wiedehopfs, das linke eines Luchses! *Probatum est!* Und nun den Kugelsegen!

Andante (Bowing to the earth in each of three pauses) Schütze, der im Dunkeln wacht,

264 Samiel! Samiel! hab

pp Vl. Vla.   Timp. D.B.

268 acht! Steh mir bei in dieser Nacht, bis der Zauber ist voll - bracht! Salbe mir so Kraut als

Blei, segn es sieben, neun und drei, dass die Kugel tüchtig sei, Samiel! Samiel! herbei!

271

Cl.,Hrn.,Str.

Timp.

(The mixture in the mortar begins to ferment and bubble and gives out a greenish-white glow. A cloud passes over the moon, so that the whole surroundings are lit only by the fire, the owl's eyes, and the rotten stump of the tree.)

Allegro moderato

276 VI. I   KASPAR (Pours, lets

pp Str.

the bullets fall out of their mold, and

282 calls): Eins!   ECHO (repeats): Eins!

Str.

KASPAR (counting anxiously) : Vier!
ECHO : Vier!

W. W. Str. (A rustling is heard.   Crack of whips and trample of horse's hooves; four fiery wheels run past, throwing

off sparks,   though at their speed, one cannot trace their real form or the shape of any wagon.)

KASPAR (counting, still more anxiously) :   (Barking of dogs and neighing in the
Fünf! ECHO: Fünf!

air; misty images of hunters on foot and horseback, stags and dogs fly past overhead.)

Bsn., Tbn.

CHORUS (invisible)

TENOR *ff*

BASS

Durch Berg und Tal,___ durch

D.B.

Schlund und Schacht,___ durch Tau und Wol- ken, Sturm und Nacht,durch Tau und Wol- ken,

Sturm und Nacht!___ Durch Höh - le, Sumpf___ und

Hrn.

ff Str.

Bsn., Tbn., D.B.,

Er - den - kluft,___ durch Feu - er, Er - de, See und Luft, jo ho, wau wau, jo

Bsn., Tbn.

ho, wau wau, ho   ho   ho   ho   ho   ho   ho

KASPAR : Wehe, das wilde Heer! Sechs! Wehe!
ECHO : Sechs! Wehe! *Presto* (The whole sky turns black as night.   Stormclouds clash; thunder

ho!

sounds and lightning flashes; torrential rain pours down; the earth spouts dark blue flames; will-o-the-wisps appear

on the mountains; trees crack as they are torn out by the roots; the waterfall roars and looms up; the rocks

avalanche; tempestuous sounds come from all sides; the earth quakes.)

KASPAR (shuddering and calling out): Samiel!

Samiel!
(thrown to the ground)

MAX (Buffeted hither and thither by the storm, Max jumps out of the circle, seizes a branch of the rotten tree and calls out.)

hilf!

Sieben!

(At this very moment the storm begins to calm down, and in the place of the rotten tree there stands the black huntsman, reaching out for Max's hand.)

Samiel!

SAMIEL (in a dreadful voice):
Hier bin ich!

(Max makes a sign of the cross and falls to the ground)

(The clock strikes one. Sudden silence. Samiel has disappeared.

Kaspar is still lying with his face to the ground. Max gets to his feet convulsively.)

(curtain falls)

End of Act II.

Weber's *Der Freischütz*, ed. by Kurt Soldan (C. F. Peters, 1926; renewed 1954).

B. Volkslied

This delightful strophic song with refrain (mm. 19-28) demonstrates how closely Weber's own creation resembles the genuine article in its short range, simple harmonizations, symmetrical phrasing, and syllabic text setting. The composer himself titled this piece. We might compare it with Example 22, a composition. that Mozart chose to call an *aria*.

Translation

Chorus of Bridesmaids:

We wind a bridal wreath for you with silken thread of azure,
We're leading you through play and dance to luck and love and pleasure.

[19]Bridal garland, beautiful green wreath,
Silken thread of azure, may your life have pleasure.

[11-2]Lavender, myrtle, and thyme grow in my garden. How long must we await the suitor?

Bridal garland . . . pleasure.

[11-3]They spun the flax for seven years. The little shirt is oh so sheer, and even the wreath is ready.

Bridal garland. . .pleasure.

[11-4]Before her suitor came around, seven years had elapsed. And when he came and took her hand, with bridal wreath he crowned her.

Bridal garland. . .pleasure.

füh - ren dich zu Spiel und Tanz, zu Glück und Lie - bes - freu - de!
lang bleibt doch der Frei - ers - mann, ich kann es kaum er - war - ten!
Hemd - lein ist wie Spinn - web klar, und grün der Kranz der Lo - cken.
weil er die Herz - lieb - ste nahm, hat sie den Kranz ge - won - nen. (⊕)

ALL (dancing in a circle around Agatha)

Schö - ner, grü - ner, schö - ner, grü - ner Jung - fern - kranz, veil - chen - blau - e

Sei - de, veil - chen - blau - e Sei - de!

Weber's *Der Freischütz*, ed. by Kurt Soldan (C. F. Peters, 1926; renewed 1954).

X

Wagner's Operas
Dresden, Weimar, Munich, Bayreuth
(c. 1843-1876)

Wagner's operas seem to emerge as the keystone of nineteenth-century music; we often describe operas as being before or after the production of his principal works. Writer, musician, dramatist, philosopher, statesman, Wagner was, with Darwin and Marx, one of the three most significant figures of the nineteenth century. His influence has extended even into the twentieth century. All but three of his thirteen operas are staples of the repertory on both sides of the Atlantic. Like Monteverdi and Gluck, Wagner placed the drama before the music in importance. He hired singers for his operas and trained them first as actors, insisting that they recite their roles before singing them. This procedure may strike us as particularly amusing in view of the relative inactivity on stage during extended portions of the operas. Wagner's plots unfold very slowly; his dramatic situations might be summarized briefly as the redemption of man through the love of a good woman. (See, for example, the plots of *Der fliegende Holländer, Tannhäuser, Lohengrin,* and the *Ring* operas.)

Wagner attempted what he called the *Gesamtkunstwerk,* the total work of art, a synthesis, in which one man would be responsible for the prose poem of the libretto, its versification, its music, the hiring of the singers, musicians, and even the stage designers in order to realize his own ideas for stage settings. Wagner wrote his own libretti; he derived his material from numerous mythological and legendary sources and often combined two or more different tales, never hesitating to change events in order to achieve his dramatic ends. He used a new type of recitative, *Sprechgesang,* in an effort to combine both melodic and declamatory functions of the voice. He abolished purely musical set forms in favor of continuous music that suited the dramatic requirements. Wagner made frequent use of *Leitmotiven* (leading motives), although he did not employ the term himself or designate individual motives by name. These musical tags for people, objects, places, and ideas were transformed in the course of the opera. Because Wagner entrusted these motives to the orchestra, it became one of the principal protagonists of the drama.

Wagner was among the first to call for a darkened hall and a covered pit for the players. He expanded the woodwind and brass choirs so that full chords could be presented with uniform timbre and even stimulated the invention of the so-called Wagner tuba (whose origin has remained frustratingly obscure). He subdivided strings further than any previous composer had. From all members of his orchestra Wagner demanded virtuoso techniques. Conductors, too, were treated to his ideas in special pamphlets prepared for the execution of specific operas. Wagner's experimental harmony paved the way for Strauss and Schoenberg after him. His dissonances with long-delayed resolutions extended the realm of tonality.

Whereas the earlier operas (*Rienzi* through *Tannhäuser*) belong to the genre of German romantic opera, his music dramas, for whose successful presentation Wagner had to build his own theater at Bayreuth, represent the apotheosis of the play in music. Wagner

315

eliminated the division into aria and recitative, the separate numbers of opera. His music is continuous, sounding through every scene change, narrative, monologue, and action on stage, ceasing only at the conclusion of an act.

31. BALLAD IN ROMANTIC OPERA

Der Fliegende Holländer (1843)

Wagner

Richard Wagner (1813-1883)

Wagner tells us that the entire *Dutchman* grew out of Senta's Ballad, which he composed before any of the other sections of the opera. Although it is a self-contained, removable number of a type we do not find in his later operas, in many ways this excerpt points to the future. (In German literature, a ballad is usually a narrative poem with emphasis on the supernatural.) Senta, the first of Wagner's psychopathic women, sits in a chair and sings of the tale of the mystery ship and its captain, the Dutchman, who is doomed to sail the seven seas until redeemed by a faithful woman's love.

Each of the three stanzas of our excerpt (beginning at mm. 15, 59, and 103) is followed by a two-part refrain, the first part (with the chromatic bass line at mm. 24-38) describing the elements that batter the Dutchman as he roams the seas, and the second part (in a melody akin to the principal theme of Schumann's piano concerto, m. 39 ff.) announcing his means of redemption. Notice the overlap at measures 53-54, where the end of the refrain and the beginning of the Dutchman's horn call that opens the stanza follow on one another's heels. After the third stanza of the Ballad, the maidens (a unisexual chorus, also typical of romantic opera) softly sing the redemption motive that rounds out the strophic form of the song. A diminished version of this motive is then proclaimed anew, even more vigorously this time, by Senta. Notice the text repetition at measure 150 ff., a feature rarely found in later Wagner operas. Instead of a genuine break or cessation of sound, Wagner continues the music through Erik's arrival (m. 162), thus offering us a foretaste of the endless melody, the musical continuity of the later operas.

The overture to *Der fliegende Holländer,* in quasi-sonata form, includes the horn call that opens Senta's Ballad and the three motives of the ballad as well. After Wagner had completed *Tristan und Isolde,* he returned to this overture and changed the conclusion, adding the final ten bars in G major, in which woodwinds and harp present the redemption motive in its regular state before resolving to D major, pianissimo instead of the original fortissimo.

Translation

Senta: Yohoho! Have you seen the ship with blood-red sail and black mast? On board, a pale man, the ship's master, keeps watch unceasingly. [24]Hui, how the wind roars. Yohoho! Like an arrow he flies, without aim, without rest. [39]But the pale man can be freed of his curse if he finds a woman who'll pledge him her love eternal. Ah, when will you, pale seaman, find her? Pray God that you'll find a true woman soon.

[59]Against the wrath of wind and storm he once would sail around a cape. He cursed and swore a foolish oath, "Come what may, I'll never give up!" [68]Hui, and Satan heard it. Yohoho! Took him at his word and condemned him to sail on the sea without aim, without rest. [83]In order that the poor man may find salvation, an angel of God showed him how he may be redeemed. Ah, could you, pale man but find her? Pray God you'll find a true woman soon.

[103]He anchors every seven years. He lands to seek a woman. He hasn't yet found her. Hui, unfurl the sails! Yohoho, weigh the anchor, Yohoho. Faithless love, faithless troth. To the sea, without aim, without rest.

Chorus of Maidens: [126]Ah, where is she, to whom the angel might guide you? Where are you lingering, you who will be true unto death?

Senta: [134]I am she, who by her love will redeem you! May God's angel guide you to me!
Through me should you achieve salvation!

Mary and the Maidens: Heaven help us! Senta!

Erik: Senta! Do you want to destroy me?

31

(Towards the end of the verse, Senta turns toward the picture. The maidens listen with interest. Mary has left off spinning.)

finden? Be - tet zum Him - mel, dass bald ein

Weib Treu - e ihm halt'!

Bei bö - sem Wind und Stur - mes-wuth um -

se - geln wollt' er einst ein Cap; er flucht' und schwur mit

tol - lem Muth: „in E - wig-keit lass' ich nicht ab!"

CHORUS OF MAIDENS

SENTA (carried away by a sudden inspiration, and springing up from the chair.)

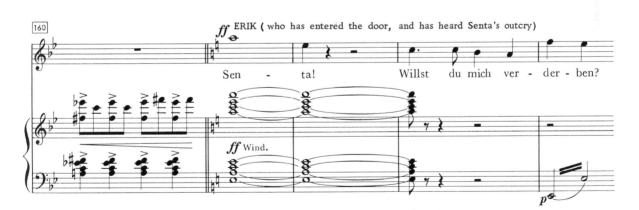

Wagner's *The Flying Dutchman [Der fliegende Holländer]* (G. Schirmer, 1897; renewed 1925).
Used by kind permission.

32. NARRATIVE
Lohengrin (1850)

Wagner   Richard Wagner

As one of his principal operatic reforms, Wagner favored narrative instead of recitative or dialogue to carry on the action of the drama and thus inform the audience of events of the plot. The character himself relates the story, occasionally, where necessary, reporting on events or incidents that have occurred even before the curtain rises. *Lohengrin,* a choral opera with 67 entries for the chorus,[1] is the last of Wagner's romantic operas. Picturesque, with castles, knights, and much chivalry, *Lohengrin* is staged as grand opera at Bayreuth today! "In fernem Land," the Grail Narrative, is the key scene of the opera. By Wagnerian standards, it is a very short narrative. (Compare, for example, Isolde's Narrative from Act I of *Tristan und Isolde!*) In this narrative, Lohengrin reveals himself to Elsa as the son of Parzival. (Notice that the spelling differs from that used in the later opera, *Parsifal.* Similar inconsistencies often appear within the Wagnerian operas because of the vast amount of time—almost thirty years for the *Ring*—that separates the initial conception of a plot from its final realization.)

Observe the lack of textual repetition, the early use of *Stabreim* (a kind of alliteration) in *höchste Heiligthum,* and the speechlike melody of the entire excerpt. Notice Wagner's typical harmonic devices in the hymn style of the opening chords, the extended pedal point (miniscule by comparison with the sustained E♭ in the Prelude to *Rheingold*), almost 11 measures of an A-major tonic chord held through the commencement of Lohengrin's narration, the chromatic bass (mm. 18-19), and the typical Wagnerian sliding motion (mm. 30-36) after already establishing the F♯ major at measure 27. Finally, note the manner in which the entire excerpt has been embedded in the musical canvas, with music sounding before the start and after the conclusion of the narrative. (The Prelude to Act I of *Lohengrin* opens with mm. 1-4 followed by mm. 12-20 of our excerpt.)

Translation

In distant land, by ways remote and hidden, there stands a mountain called Monsalvat. [9] A shrine is there, more precious than any known on earth. It holds an immortal cup enthroned in light. Whoever sees it is cleansed of earthly sins. It was carried here by angels. [20]Once a year, a dove descends from Heaven, to strengthen it again for works of grace. It's called the Grail; the power of Heaven attends the faithful knights who guard that sacred place. [27]He who chooses to be its servant is made invincible. All evil is powerless against him. Before him, the spirit of night pales. [36]Although he may be called to distant land as defender of the cause of virtue, while he is unknown, he still commands its spell. [43]The holy Grail is graced by a lofty manner; no profane eye may see its light. Its knight should be guarded from doubts. If known to man, he must immediately flee. [52]Now hearken, this is how I deal with forbidden questions! I was sent here from the Grail. My father, Parzival, wears a crown. I am his knight and Lohengrin is my name.

32

[1]*See* Jack Stein, *Richard Wagner and the Synthesis of the Arts* (Detroit: Wayne State University Press, 1960).

liegt ei - ne Burg, die Mon-sal - vat ge-nannt; ein lich - ter Tem - pel ste-het

dort in-mit - ten, so kost - bar, als auf Er - den nichts be-kannt; drin ein Ge-

fäss von wun-der thät' - gem Se - gen wird dort als höch - stes Hei - lig-thum be-wacht; es

ward, dass sein der Men - schen rein - ste pfle - gen, Her - ab von ei - ner En - gel -

schaar ___ ge-bracht; all - jähr - lich naht vom Him - mel ei - ne Tau - be, um

neu zu stär- ken sei- ne Wun- der- kraft: es heisst der Gral,— und se- lig rein- ster

Glau- be er- theilt durch ihn sich sei- ner Rit- ter- schaft. Wer nun dem

Vla., 'Cello, Trombs. & Tb.

Gral zu die- nen ist er- ko- ren, den rü- stet er mit ü- ber- ir- di- scher

Macht; an dem— ist je- des Bö- sen Trug— ver- lo- ren, wenn

ihn— er- sieht,— weicht dem des To- des Nacht, Selbst wer von ihm in fer- ne

Wagner's *Lohengrin* (G. Schirmer, n.d., plate no. 12946).

33. SPRECHGESANG IN MUSIC DRAMA[2]
Siegfried (1865-1871)

Wagner   Richard Wagner

We have taken the following excerpt from the vast musico-dramatic canvas of the
Ring; this passage must have been of particular significance to the composer, for it was
here (m. 13) that he first stopped work on the *Ring* to begin *Tristan*. Unquestionably,
Wagner's treatment of the orchestra in *Tristan,* his remarkable and continual thematic
transformation within the orchestral tissue, influenced his technique on his return to the
score in 1867.

Siegfried, furious with Mime and convinced that the dwarf is not his father, sends
him away. He then lies down beneath a lime tree and begins to reflect on who his
parents might be. Wagner uses a slow harmonic rhythm (infrequent chord changes) and

[2]Although the term *music drama* is commonly applied to these operas, Wagner did
not approve of its use in connection with his works.

exploits the low register of the horn (one of the first composers to do so) in an extended pedal point D (beginning at m. 1). The trills in the strings, the sound of which provides an association with nature that we have begun to take for granted, had their counterpart in earlier forest scenes: Weber's Wolf's Glen Scene (see Ex. 30-A) and Beethoven's "Pastoral" Symphony. This feature will reappear later in Debussy's *Pelléas et Mélisande.* Just as in each of the *Ring* operas we find musical references to its companion operas, so here in the "Forest Murmurs" from *Siegfried* we notice that the entire orchestral fabric is composed of repetition or transformation of motives already heard in *Rheingold* and *Walküre.* Each mention of a character, place, object, or event in the text will find the orchestra stating the motive related to it. For example, as Siegfried muses that if he were Mime's son, surely he would resemble him, the orchestra plays the motive (mm. 39-48) of the dwarfs in *Rheingold,* the smithy motive. When Siegfried wonders about his mother, the orchestra plays the Wälsung's motive (mm. 58-64 and 74-78) from the first act of *Walküre.* Later we hear the motive (mm. 90-100) associated with love in the first act of *Siegfried,* where the hero speaks of the mating of the beasts of the forest. Our excerpt closes with a reminder of Freia, the goddess of youth and love, in her motive (mm. 110-111) from *Rheingold.*

Notice the excellent example of alliteration in measures 33-48, and the passage (mm. 60-74) that Melchior rated among the finest examples of the Wagnerian style of singing, a combination of recitative and bel canto. Of this glorious synthesis of music and drama, the critic Lawrence Gilman once said, "The whole is somehow greater than the sum of its parts." In just this fragment, we can observe how Wagner has captured not only the sound, but the scent of the forest as well.

Translation

How happy am I that he is not my father! How refreshing seems the forest! How glorious the day! Since that wretch has left me and I no longer have to look at him.! [33] How did my father look? Certainly like me, because if Mime had a son, wouldn't he resemble Mime? [42] Just as grizzled, gruesome and grey, cramped and crooked, halting and hunchbacked, with hanging ears and bleary eyes. Away with that nightmare! I don't want to see it again! [60] But what did my mother look like? That I cannot even imagine! Her clear, shining eyes glistening like a soft doe's, only more lovely! [78] When she bore me in travail, why had she to die? Do all mortal mothers die when they give birth to their sons? [89] How sad that would be! Ah, might the son but see his mother, a lovely mortal's mate.

33

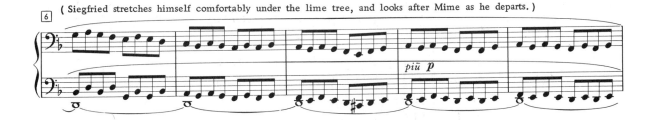

Ha! ge-wiss, wie ich selbst! Denn wär'wo von Mi-me ein Sohn, müsst' er nicht ganz

Mi - me glei - chen? Gra-de so gars - tig, gries - sig und grau,

klein und krumm, höck - rig und hink - end, mit hän - gen-den Oh - ren,

trie - fi-gen Au-gen? Fort mit dem Alp! Ich mag ihn nicht mehr seh'n!

(He leans farther back and looks up through the branches.
Deep silence. Forest murmurs.)

Mässig (wie zuvor)

bang sie mich ge-bo-ren, wa-rum a-ber starb sie da?

Ster-ben die Men-schen-müt-ter an ih-ren Söh-nen al-le da-hin?

Trau-rig wä-re das, traun! Ach,

möcht' ich Sohn___ mei-ne Mut - - - - - ter se-hen!

Mei-ne Mut-ter ein Men - schen-

(He sighs softly and leans still farther back.....Deep silence.....)

weib!

legato

Zart
Vl.

p

più p

pp

Wagner's *Siegfried*, ed. by R. Kleinmichel (G. Schirmer, n.d.).

34. MOTIVIC PROCESS

Tristan und Isolde (1865)

A. Prelude[3]

Wagner   Richard Wagner

Every example in our anthology has been a complete one, not just a few bars to illustrate a particular musical feature or compositional technique. With *Tristan,* however, we have made an exception. Although our example offers only the opening measures of the famous Prelude to *Tristan*, we can notice immediately the enigmatic Tristan-chord (*), the first statements of several of the main motives of the opera, and the way in which Wagner overlaps them. We may also observe the composer's blending and juxtaposition of orchestral colors in what appears (in the piano reduction) to be one melody, but which is, in fact, two distinct motives:

> a solo cello opens with the Grief Motive (a leap of a minor 6th, A to F), which then descends chromatically to D♯, at which point (see * in Example 34-A) the Desire Motive (played by Ob., Cl., Eng. Hn., Bsn.) begins on G♯ and moves to B. Notice the final recurrence of this motive in the concluding bars of the opera (Ex. 34-F).

Indeed, because of the presence of these leading motives (Tristan, m. 16; the Look, m. 18; Love and Death entwined, m. 25), we can state that the Prelude contains the essence of the drama in a highly concentrated form.

In order to show more precisely how these motives intrude upon and pierce the musical texture as the opera unfolds, we have selected several brief passages that include the Grief and Desire motives in combination with other material. (See Exx. 34B-34F

[3] In the score, Wagner referred to this music as the *Einleitung* (Introduction). Writing about it, he often called it the *Vorspiel*, or Prelude, by which name it is best known today. Curiously, the composer described this music as the *Liebestod;* he used the term *Verklärung* (transfiguration) when discussing the conclusion of the opera, which we today know as the *Liebestod.* Liszt, in his piano transcription, apparently switched terms, and it is the "Mild und leise" that now has affixed to it the tag of *Liebestod,* while the opening music is called the *Prelude.*

below.) Among other characteristics of Wagner's later style, we should like to call attention to the sequences (mm. 1-11), extensive chromaticism, continuous melody, and dissonance with delayed resolution, all of which appear in Example 34-A. With the completion of *Tristan und Isolde,* Wagner's compositional techniques reached maturity. The end of *Siegfried,* the entire *Götterdämmerung,* and *Parsifal* exhibit his late style.

Translations:

B. Destined to me, lost to me. Bright and brave! Knight and knave!

C. Know you not well your mother's skill? Do you think that she, who foresees all, had sent me unprepared to seek strange lands with you? I know my mother's counsel full well, and gladly do I prize her art. Vengeance. . .

D. Oh King, that I cannot tell you; and what you ask, that you can never learn.

E. Oh rapture!

34 - B

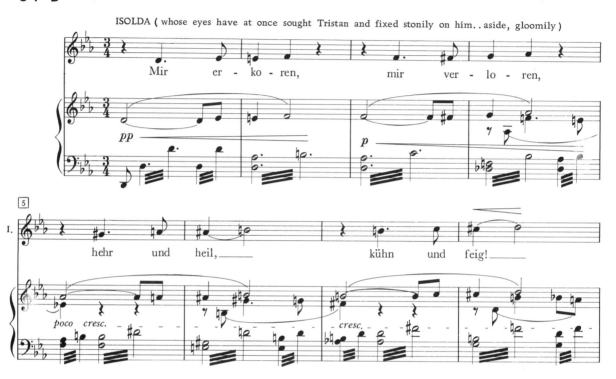

ISOLDA (whose eyes have at once sought Tristan and fixed stonily on him.. aside, gloomily)

Mir er - ko - ren, mir ver - lo - ren,

hehr und heil,_____ kühn und feig!_____

34 - C

BRANGÄNE (Coming close to Isolda with a mien of mysterious familiarity)

Kennst du der

Mut - ter Kün - ste nicht? Wähnst du, die Al - les klug er - wägt,_____

34-D

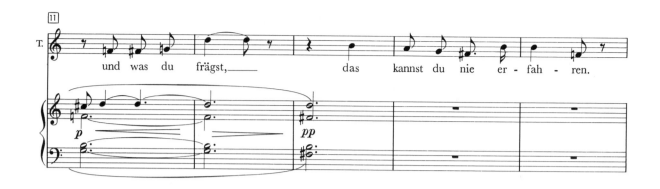

und was du frägst,_____ das kannst du nie er - fah - ren.

34-E

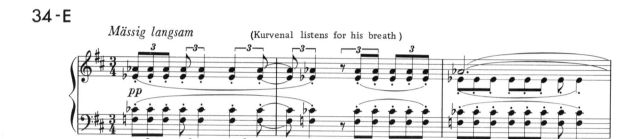

Mässig langsam (Kurvenal listens for his breath)

KURVENAL

sehr zart   *rall.*

leise

O Won - ne!

34-F

(Mark blesses the dead.)

rallentando

morendo   *pp* (The Curtain falls during the final pause.)

Wagner's *Tristan und Isolde*, arranged by Richard Kleinmichel (G. Schirmer, 1906; renewed 1934). Used by kind permission.

35. INSTRUMENTAL MUSIC

Die Meistersinger (1867)

Prelude to Act III

Wagner

Richard Wagner

Beginning with *Tannhäuser,* every Wagner opera with the exception of *Götter-dämmerung* contains an important third-act prelude. These pieces are not entr'acte music, but real second overtures, usually with music derived from what came before and what will come afterwards. Two of the best known of these preludes, both of which we hear often as concert pieces, are the prelude to the third act of *Lohengrin* and the prelude to the third act of *Die Walküre,* the latter known as the "Ride of the Valkyries." Both of these are sizable pieces of about five minutes' duration. Our excerpt, seemingly shorter, actually requires as much time for performance as either of the other two. It is not self-contained, but leads directly into the first scene of the succeeding act. Nevertheless, these few bars of music provide us with an excellent illustration of Wagner's knack for interlacing various themes to prepare a highly concentrated dose of musico-dramatic material. Wagner left us a description of the significance of this music in a letter of 1869 written to his benefactor, King Ludwig II of Bavaria. From its contents we understand the following: the cellos (mm. 1-3) introduce the melody of Sachs's monologue, "Wahn, wahn," whose words we first hear *after* the curtain rises on this third act, but whose melody we have already heard as a countertheme to the last stanza of the cobbler's song in Act II. The melody is taken up by one instrument after another. A new section begins (mm. 16-25) with a foretaste of the chorale melody ("Wach auf!") that the populace will sing in the final scene of the opera. "Wach auf" is a paean to Luther by the original Hans Sachs, who was both cobbler and Meistersinger in sixteenth-century Nüremberg. He wrote this hymn on July 8th, 1523. Next we hear snatches (mm. 25-28) of the cobbler's song from the second act, then the hymn melody again (mm. 43-50), and finally a return to "Wahn, wahn" (m. 51).

344

Wagner's *Die Meistersinger*, ed. by Karl Klindworth (G. Schirmer, 1904).

XI

Late Nineteenth-Century
Italian Opera

Venice, Milan
(c. 1850-1890)

In less than a dozen years after the death of Donizetti, Verdi emerged as the leading opera composer of Italy. And even before the spectacular Cairo premiere of *Aida* in 1871, Verdi had become the only composer in Europe whose dramatic works rivalled the music dramas of Wagner. Although born in the same year, and thus historical contemporaries, Verdi and Wagner were as different from one another as Italian and German musicians have always been.

Verdi composed operas based on libretti that he acquired from various sources and various writers; Wagner composed operas and music dramas based on his own prose poems. Verdi created real people in real situations of genuine, if somewhat exaggerated, dramatic excitement; Wagner modeled supermen engaged in powerful activities in supernatural regions ruled over by legendary gods and goddesses. Verdi, far less given to rhetoric and philosophy, said little, worked furiously on the shape and design of his arias and assorted musical numbers, but concentrated much less on his orchestra. Wagner, protesting that his first interest was the drama, nevertheless showed singular concern with the music of the orchestra. Curiously enough, although Wagner was convinced he had achieved a *Gesamtkunstwerk,* a synthesis of music and drama, entire sections of the orchestral music of these dramas can be successfully detached for concert performance. (And where difficulties arose in their employment in an unaltered state in the concert hall, Wagner provided new endings, as he did later with the third-act prelude of *Die Meistersinger,* our Ex. 35.) By contrast, very little of Verdi's orchestral music can be presented in this fashion. On the other hand, arias from Verdi's operas may be heard in concert, whereas it is well nigh impossible to extract a vocal segment from the continuous musical fabric of Wagnerian operas after *Lohengrin* (1850).

Verdi did not study other composers' scores; Wagner not only studied them, but learned them well enough to assimilate certain features and reuse them in his own works. A unique example of Wagner's borrowing—for he usually did not appropriate melodies—appears in the Prelude to *Tristan und Isolde* (see Ex. 34), which was written in 1859 and presents as its opening motive a theme from Berlioz's *Roméo et Juliette* of 1839! Verdi did not contribute substantially to the development of the orchestra. He sought orchestral effects that would enhance the vocal line. His independent orchestral pieces—overtures, ballets, preludes—are few. Indeed, one of the most unusual examples of his instrumental writing occurs in the short orchestral prelude to Act III of *La Traviata,* where strings divisi sound the mournful notes of the dramatic action that follows. (Unlike Wagner, Verdi rarely employed a second overture.) Verdi's operas contain numerous examples of recurrent motives (see Ex. 37), but little motivic transformation. Of twenty-six operas, all but the last two are number operas with arias, duets, choruses, and ensembles, complete and self-contained. Perhaps because of the intensity of his interest in melody, many of these numbers became and have remained operatic favorites for more than a hundred years! Not only the separate numbers, but also the entire operas, among them *Rigoletto* (1851), *Il Trovatore* (1853), *La Traviata* (1853), *Simon Boccanegra* (1857; rev. 1881), *Un Ballo in Maschera* (1859), *La Forza del Destino* (1862), *Don Carlo* (1867), *Aida* (1871), as well as several earlier operas, have become the mainstay of the operatic repertory. Of his singers, Verdi demanded far less musically and dramatically than Wagner did. (It would be inconceivable for one Verdi opera to have three different male singers in a single role in one night, as *Tristan* has required on occasion!) Verdi's demands on orchestral players are easier to meet, and these, combined with the relatively few difficulties in staging have resulted in more performances for his operas than for those by Wagner.

Although Verdi continued to use traditional accompanied recitative, with the composition of *Rigoletto* and *Traviata* he had already refined his style so that recitative seems to grow naturally out of the drama and to proceed just as effortlessly into aria (see the following example). In his last two operas, *Otello* and *Falstaff* (1893), written after Wagner's death and at a time when there was some speculation with regard to his own health and productivity, Verdi surpassed his finest achievements. Here the separation between aria and recitative is no longer carefully drawn. Instead, Verdi has inched his way into the domain of music drama, Italian style. Although the two operas differ considerably (*Otello* is a tragedy and *Falstaff* a comedy) both have continuous music, and *Falstaff,* particularly, has become the caviar of operatic audiences around the world. *Falstaff* concludes with a fugue to the words "Tutto el mundo è burla" ("All the world's a joke"), as if the eighty-year-old composer needed once and for all to thumb his nose at the world and to announce himself the equal of the Germans even in the complexities of fugal composition.

36. ARIA WITH CABALETTA
La Traviata (1853)

Piave   Giuseppe Verdi (1813-1901)
after the younger Dumas

In Violetta's first solo of Act I, we notice the agitation in her voice as she wonders (first in recitative and then in aria) if she, the ultra-sophisticated Parisian courtesan, is falling in love. Although half of the 22 bars of recitative have absolutely no accompaniment, the orchestral figurations, when they do appear, cement and support the vocal part so that it never sounds dry. A short introduction (m. 23 ff.) connects this recitative to the first stanza of the aria in which Violetta continues to reflect on her situation. In a new key (m. 51), Violetta restates one of the most significant themes of the opera as she sings Alfredo's love motive from the duet they have sung a few moments earlier. (This theme recurs in the melodrama in the last act of the opera, where the dying Violetta reads Germont's letter aloud while the orchestra plays Alfredo's theme in the background.) Verdi repeats this entire section (although it is generally cut in performances of the opera), and concludes with a delicate fioritura (m. 113).

Tempo and texture change as Violetta interrupts her aria with a quasi-recitative (m. 117) that finishes with two coloratura passages to underline the words *vortici* ("vortex") and *gioir* ("to rejoice") in measures 132 and 135. A further change of key, meter, melody, mood, and texture brings us to the introduction to "Sempre libera," the *cabaletta* (m. 137). Once in each stanza we hear the melody of the recurrent love motive as Alfredo sings beneath Violetta's balcony. Verdi showed excellent judgment in his choice of the aria-cabaletta combination to conclude this act. It reflects superbly Violetta's changing moods, from wistfulness and wonderment ("Ah, fors' è lui") to the hysteria and urgency with which she expresses her need for freedom to pursue the life to which she has grown accustomed ("Sempre libera"). Like the term *cavatina, cabaletta* had various meanings during the nineteenth century. Here, however, Verdi has used *cabaletta* in the generally accepted sense of the word: the final section of an aria in several parts, usually faster and more brilliant than the opening sections.

Translation

Violetta: How odd! Those accents are graven upon my heart! Will it bring misfortune, a serious love? What shall you do, my troubled spirit? No man has yet kindled your desire. [13]Oh joy, that I knew not, to be loved and loving. Can I disdain it for the arid follies of my life? [27]Ah, perhaps it is he, my lonely soul amid scenes of pleasure loved to paint in hidden colors! [43]He, modest and vigilant, who came to my door, kindled new flames, directing my heart to love. [51]To that love that makes the world go round, mysterious, proud torment and rapture of the heart. [71]To me, as a young lady, with my honest, fluttery desires, this man of my dreams seemed magnificent, when radiant from heaven he stood before me. Oh if the dream be madness, life has no longer worth. [95]I felt that love makes the world go round, mysterious, proud torment and rapture of the heart. [117]What folly, what vain madness is this! Poor woman, alone, abandoned in this populous desert called Paris. What hope now! [128]What must I do? Surrender to pleasure? Perish in a maddening whirl of delights? Rejoice! [Mm. 71-117 are usually omitted in performance.]

[144]Always free, I must be free to live madly and foolishly from pleasure to pleasure. I will drain a brimming measure from the cup of pleasure. [152]When day breaks, happily I welcome new delights, to which my thoughts are flying, flying. Ah! love. . .

Alfredo: [172]Love, love that makes the world go round, mysterious, proud torment and rapture of the heart.

Violetta: [186]What folly, folly! Joy! Joy!

[194]Always free, I must be. . .flying.

36

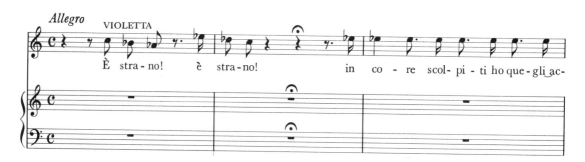

l'uo - mo an-co - ra l'ac-cen - - de-va.   Oh gio - - - ja ch'io non co -

nob-bi,   es-ser a-ma - ta a-a - man-do!   E sde-gnar - la pos-s'i - o   per

l'a-ri-de fol-li - e   del vi-ver mi - - - o?

Andantino (♩=96)

Ah, for - sè   lui   che

l'a - ni - ma   so-lin-ga ne' tu - mul - ti,   so-lin-ga ne' tu - mul - ti,

355

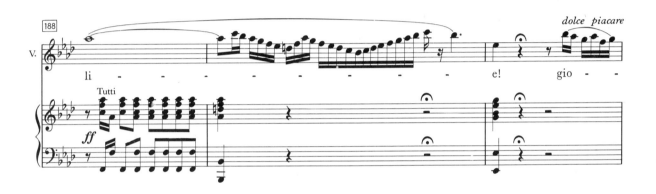

358

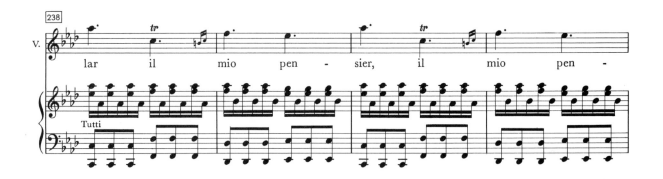

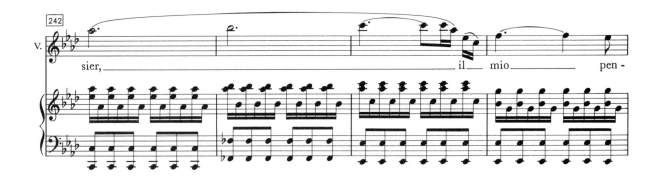

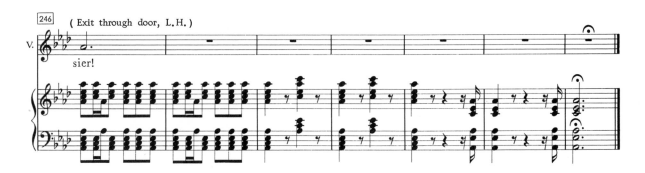

Verdi's *La Traviata,* edited and revised by Berthold Tours (G. Schirmer, 1899; renewed 1926).

360

37. ARIA AND CANZONETTA

Otello (1887)

A. Credo

Boïto   Giuseppe Verdi
after Shakespeare

Iago's "Credo," a unique creation of Arrigo Boïto (1842-1918), a composer in his own right who became Verdi's librettist for *Otello* and *Falstaff,* has no counterpart in Shakespeare. In Example 37-A we have a fine instance of musical illustration that surpasses verbal description. The horrifying sound of Verdi's introductory motive in the brass prepares the audience for Iago's conduct during the balance of the opera. This motive recurs at measure 23 in unison and again at measures 58 and 64 (harmonized) before Iago finishes his aria. The short, choppy, repeated notes in the vocal part (mm. 5-8 and 15-16), as Iago methodically selects the words to describe his personality, sound a sinister tone of impending evil.

Both the "Credo" and the "Willow Song" (Ex. 37-B) are set pieces, exceptional for this opera, but included because they display Verdi's art of musical characterization at the height of his powers. Notice that after the conclusion of the "Credo" (m. 78) the orchestra continues, although the entire musical idiom has changed as Iago scurries about the stage setting his plan in motion. Verdi's increased use of continuous music in *Otello* tends to blur the outlines of many numbers that might otherwise be considered set pieces.

Translation

I believe in a cruel God, who has created me in his likeness and whom, in hate, I name. From the vileness of some germ or base atom was I born. [19]I am wicked because I am a man and I feel the primeval vice in me. Yes, that is my faith. [30]I believe with a firm heart, just as does the widow in church, that the evil that I conceive and which proceeds from me I will fulfill by my destiny. [39]I believe that a just man is a jester, a bad actor, that in face and in heart everything about him is a lie: tears, kisses, glances, sacrifices and honor. [46]And I believe man to be the sport of iniquitous fortune from the germ of the cradle to the worm of the grave. [62]After so much mockery comes death. And then? Death is extinction; Heaven is an old wives' tale.

[81]Here she is! Cassio to her! This is the moment. Bestir yourself! Desdemona comes. (He approaches, greets her and moves closer towards her.) [99]Now I must fetch Otello. Satan help me in my plan! Already they're talking together. Smiling, she leans her face towards him. [111]Only a glimpse of this smile suffices to lead Otello to ruin. Let's get started. In this instance, I'll give my all! [121]Here he comes! In position. . .for work!

37- A

Sì! que - st'è la mia fè!

Cre - do con fer - mo cuor, _____ sic - co - me

cre-de la ve-do-vel-la al tem - pio, che il mal ch'io pen - so e che da me pro-

ce - de per mio de - sti-no a dem - pio.

Cre - - do che il giu-sto è un i-stri-on bef-

363

far-do e nel vi - so e nel cuor, che tut-to è in lui bu - giar-do, la-gri-ma, ba-cio, sguardo,

sa-cri - fi - cio ed o - nor.

E cre - do

l'uom gio - co d'i - ni - qua sor - te dal

ger - me del - la cul - la.

al ver - me del - l'a -

365

(Desdemona and Emilia are seen to enter garden.
Iago goes toward the terrace beyond which Cassio
has taken his position.)

(Cassio goes to Desdemona, bows to her and joins her.)

367

(Verdi's *Otello*, arranged by Michele Saladino (International Music Co., n.d.).

B. Willow Song

The short but exquisitely etched fourth and final act of *Otello* begins with a brief orchestral prelude that includes four significant themes to be heard later. One of these themes, Desdemona's *canzonetta*, the Willow Song, is played on a solo English horn at the start of the prelude. Desdemona had asked Emilia to place her wedding sheets on her bed and to bury her in them should she be the first of the two to die. In this melancholy mood she recalls her mother's maid, Barbara, who had died of love and who used to sing this song. Outstanding characteristics of the song include the pathetically simple accompaniment, the repeated "Salce" ("willow") that acts as a refrain after each stanza, the emptiness between the F's at measures 22 and 26-27, the frequent intrusion of open fifths, and the loneliness of the unaccompanied voice at strategic points in the text. The use of these special devices indicates the care with which Verdi has differentiated the texture of this song from the musical tissue of the opera.

After the close of our excerpt, when Desdemona has already wished Emilia "Buona notte," she cries out fitfully again, like a child suddenly frightened. Once more we are touched by her innocence, but we are immediately distracted, engulfed by the music as the strings begin a swift chromatic descent to prepare for the forthcoming change of scene.

Translation

Desdemona: My mother used to have a poor maid, beautiful and in love. Her name was Barbara. She loved a man who later abandoned her. [7]She sang a song, the willow song. Untie my hair, this evening I have a complete recollection of it.

[23]The poor soul sat pining, alone and lonely
There on the lonely strand. Oh, Willow!
Upon her bosom, her head inclining, Oh, Willow!
[49]Let's sing! The funereal willow shall be my garland.

Hurry, Otello will arrive soon.

[66]The fresh stream ran by her
Where the rushes grow,
And murmured all her moaning;
And from her eyes the sad tears did flow
Which in her heart were rising. Oh, Willow!
[84]Let's sing. The funereal willow will be my garland.

[97]Down from the branches all the birds come flying,
Towards her sweet song.
And her weeping eyes moved the stones to pity.

[110]Put away this ring. Poor Barbara. That was her story, very simple. And it ends:

[125]He was born to live in glory, and I. . .to love him.
Listen, I hear a sigh.
Quiet. Who knocks at the door? [Emilia: the wind]
And I to love him and to die.
Emilia, farewell. How my eyes burn me! Do you think it forebodes weeping?
Good night.

 37-B

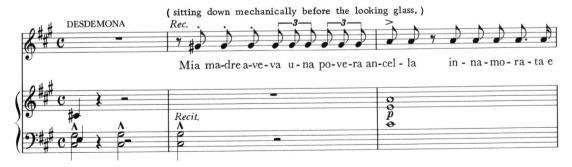

369

370

vol dai ra - mi cu - pi ver - so quel dol - ce can - to.

con espress.   marcato

E gli oc - chi suoi pian - ge - an tan - to, tan - to,_____ da im - pie - to -

(to Emilia, taking a ring from her finger)
parlando

sir le ru - pi." Ri - po - ni quest' a - nel - lo.

mf (rising)

Po - ve - ra Bar - ba - ra!

ppp (parlante)

So - lea la sto - ria con que - sto sem - pli - ce suo - no fi - nir:

Verdi's *Otello*, arranged by Michele Saladino (International Music Co., n.d.).

C. The Kiss Motive

In order to compress the five-act Shakespeare play into a four-act opera, composer and librettist eliminated the first act of the play. They start the opera with a scene on Cyprus as the people await the return of Otello from his victory over the Turks. After

Otello's safe arrival, he and Desdemona (who are already married when the opera begins) recall their courtship in an exquisite duet (end of Act I) that concludes with the Kiss Motive. It is in this duet that Verdi uses a fragment of Otello's famous speech to the Senate. However, nothing in the play approximates the passion of the Kiss Motive, whose recurrence at the very end of the opera reminds us (as well as Otello) of the love he has destroyed through jealousy. Unlike Wagner, who would probably have transformed the motive here, Verdi employs it in the same state as it appeared earlier.

Translation

A kiss, yet one more kiss, another kiss.

37- C

Verdi's *Otello*, arranged by Michele Saladino (International Music Co., n.d.).

XII
Nationalism in Opera
St. Petersburg, Prague
(c. 1836-1900)

Because of the Western orientation of their court in the eighteenth century, native Russian mores and traditions had, for a time, been discouraged. For example, at royal invitation beginning in the 1730s, Italian buffa and afterwards French opéra-comique and German Singspiel were staged in St. Petersburg, the principal Russian operatic center. Later, in the mid-nineteenth century, some Russian composers, among them Tchaikovsky (1840-1893) and Anton Rubinstein (1829-1894), still preferred to emulate French and German musicians rather than to develop their own nationalistic styles. However, changes began to occur in the nineteenth century not only in Russia, but in all countries whose musical life had previously been dominated by French, Italian, and German composers or by native musicians writing under foreign influences. Although Spain and England had not been subjected to foreign musical domination to the same degree as Russia, a parallel situation existed in these countries also, where a kind of musical apathy resulted in little productivity over several centuries.

For our purposes we shall concern ourselves with the new Slavic music coming from eastern Europe, where, perhaps because of their proximity to the exotic music of the mid-East and Asia, or as a result of a sudden self-awareness among composers, a different musical style developed. For the first time in centuries, we notice a reversal of the direction of musical influences, which originated in the East and gradually spread into the West. We probably associate the phrase "nationalism in music" with Russian music because of the intentional exportation of their music and its weighty impact on Western audiences and composers alike.

First Glinka (1804-1857) and then Dargomizhsky (1813-1869) began the revitalization of Russian art music. Their work was carried further by Mussorgsky (1839-1881), Borodin (1833-1887), and Rimsky-Korsakov (1844-1908), three members of The Five (Cui and Balakirev comprised the balance of the group), who often obtained their subjects from the poems and dramas of Pushkin (1799-1837) and Gogol (1809-1852). The music of Mussorgsky, one of the most gifted Russian composers, has been the subject of much controversy among scholars, who believe his opera, *Boris Godunov*, should be performed in the original version[1], and musicians who prefer it with the fuller orchestration supplied by Rimsky-Korsakov. For Example 38 we have

---

[1] This opera exists in five different versions:
  a) the original seven-scene *Boris Godunov* of 1868-69;
  b) the enlarged and reconstructed *Boris Godunov* of 1871-72;
  c) the version of b) cut on the advice of friends, performed and published in vocal score, in 1874;
  d) Rimsky-Korsakov's version of 1896;
  e) Rimsky-Korsakov's revision of 1908.

The Oxford University Press edition that we have used includes (a), (b), and (c); J. and W. Chester's edition of 1926 presents (c); Bessel and Kalmus both present (e). Oxford has recently published a new English edition with the same piano reduction (by Paul Lamm) that we have used in our anthology, but with a new English translation.

elected to use the authorized edition prepared in 1928 by Paul Lamm. Here we can observe Mussorgsky's skillful use of huge choral forces (compare with Ex. 25) in an opera based on historical subject matter. We also notice that the composer has cast the Russian people (the chorus) in the role of the principal protagonist. Only with a knowledge of the Russian language can we appreciate Mussorgsky's particular technique of text setting: melodic declamation derived absolutely and completely from speech inflection. Hopefully, ignorance of the original language of the work will not prevent our recognition of the musical novelties contained in *Boris Godunov.*

Folk opera affords a composer another means for expressing nationalism. Among the most delightful specimens of this genre is *The Bartered Bride* (1866) by the Bohemian composer Smetana. From this opera we have selected an instrumental excerpt, which, because of its obviously national flavor (folklike tune and rhythm, dancers dressed in national costumes), has been omitted from contemporary performances under the Soviet regime.

38. CHORUS IN NATIONALISTIC OPERA

Boris Godunov (1868; rev. 1872)

Coronation Scene

Mussorgsky after Pushkin   Modeste Mussorgsky (1839-1881)

As a musical unit, this coronation scene (ii of the Prologue) provides us with innumerable examples of elements of Mussorgsky's musical style: first, his use of *ostinato* (the persistent reiteration of a melodic and/or rhythmic pattern), here at measures 3-38 further emphasized by the recurrent alternation of the pivotal chords $A\flat^7$ and D^7 (on the common tones C and $G\flat$/F♯) and the treble figure derived from them; second, a feature closely related to the ostinato, the pedal point extending from measures 50-82; third, the wide range that separates the treble from the bass; fourth, the rhythmic permutations of the treble figure in measures 7-38 by which Mussorgsky imitates pealing church bells of various sizes. In addition, irregular phrasing, frequent meter changes (m. 85 ff.) unisons, octave doublings, and the interval of the falling minor third as Boris begins his solo (m. 116 ff.) project the decidedly personal style of this composer. We also notice the hymnlike chords (m. 135) with which he occasionally harmonizes modal melodies. Finally, as Mussorgsky intended, his vocal declamation closely approximates speech inflection.

We find few florid melodies in this opera, and none in our excerpt; even the naive, simple folk melody that the chorus sings first (mm. 52-63) and that the orchestra repeats (in a sequence beginning at m. 64) serves as a refreshing change from the prevailing declamatory idiom. Because of its Slavic flavor, Beethoven used this song in the trio of the third movement of his Razumovsky Quartet, Op. 59, No. 2. Mussorgsky employed recurrent motives in *Boris Godunov*—one of these is Boris's theme at measure 116—possibly as a result of hearing some of Wagner's music during the latter's visit to Russia in 1863. However, we cannot be sure of this source for his inspiration. Another novelty in the opera concerns the manner in which Mussorgsky tried to portray psychological problems, such as Boris's growing anguish, through music. Towards this end, the composer's use of the chiming clock—happily introduced into Russia in time for the second version of the opera—in Boris's great monologue in the second act adds to the suspense.

We might speculate that the works of Berlioz and Mussorgsky illustrate the fortunate results that accrue from the untutored, unrestrained musical imagination. Berlioz, because he could not perform or experiment at the keyboard, used the various instruments of the orchestra as his musical palette from which he drew unique, bizarre sounds. Mussorgsky appears to have done the same with his unfettered approach to harmonic intervals, chord progressions, and modal scales. Both Berlioz (in *Les Troyens*) and Mussorgsky conceived of opera as a series of separate scenes, a chronicle from which the audience themselves shaped and assimilated the complete story.

Relatively few English-speaking people are familiar with the Russian language. For this reason, we have used an English versification of the text.

A square in the Moscow Kremlin. Facing the audience, upstage, the Red Stairway of the Imperial Palace. Right, downstage, the people are kneeling in the space between the Cathedral of the Assumption (right) and the Cathedral of the Archangels (left). Only the stairways of both Cathedrals are visible. Loud peals of bells.

38

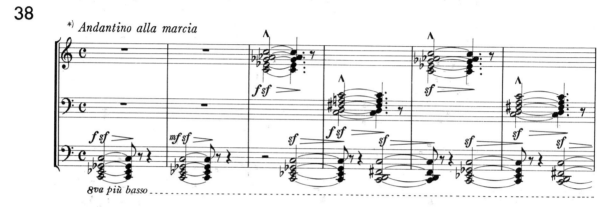

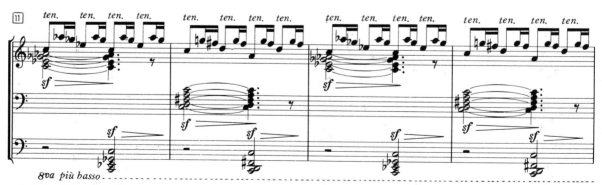

* In the full score: Alla marcia non troppo allegro.

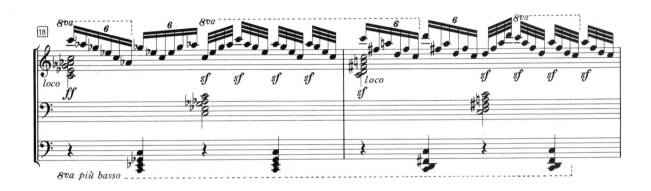

Loud chimes on the stage. From the Red Stairway boyars in solemn pageant start towards the

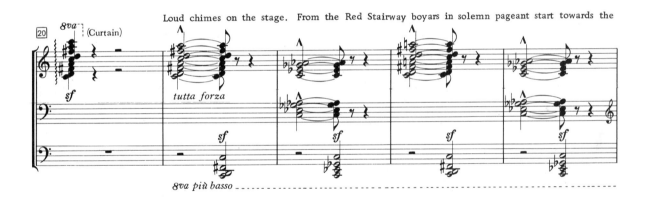

Cathedral of the Assumption; in front are guards, Strelstsy, and young boyars; then comes Shufsky, carrying the crown of

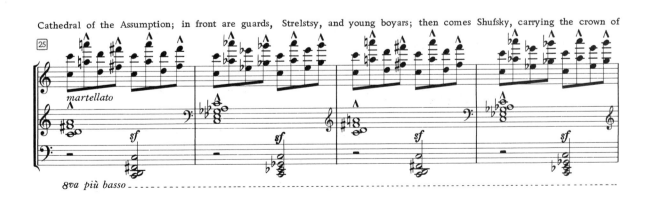

the Monomach on a cushion. Behind them boyars, Shchelkalof carrying the imperial sceptre; then more Strelstsy, the

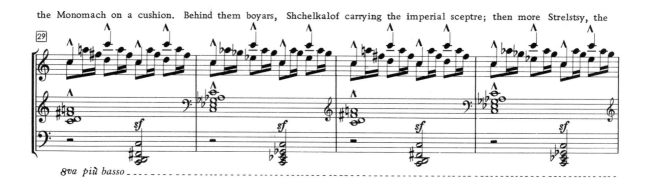

chief boyars, the secretaries, etc. The pageant passes among the crowd and enters the Cathedral. The Strelstsy stand

in files on both sides of the steps.

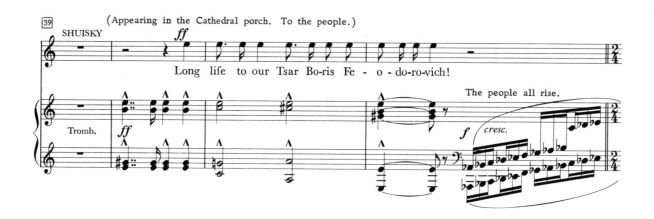

The chimes on the
stage continue.

(Appearing in the Cathedral porch. To the people.)

SHUISKY

Long life to our Tsar Bo-ris Fe - o - do-ro-vich!

The people all rise.

Tromb.

382

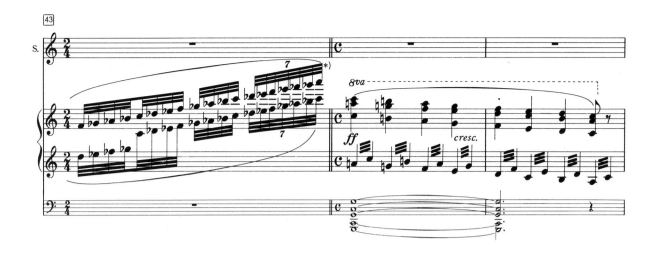

*) In the full score, this run ends with a sextuplet whose last note is B♭.

**) The bar-rest is lacking in the MS. vocal score.

***) Here, in the full score, is a chord given out by the horns: which was struck out, apparently by Mussorgsky himself.

*) In the full score, Moderato cantabile. **) Bar lacking in the 1874 vocal score.

384

glo - ry   glo - ry

The solemn imperial pageant comes out of the Cathedral. The police officers

glo - ry   glo - ry

Long   life   and

marshal the people into rows.

Long   life   and   pow - er!

pow - er!

*) In the full score, the bass remains:

*) In the full score:

Trumpeters take place facing the audience, in front of the people.

387

*) BOYARS. From the Cathedral porch, to the people:

They come down the steps.

Long life to thee, Tsar Bo - ris Fe - o - do - ro - vich!

*) The vocal score of the initial version says: "4 Boyars."

388

life to thee! O - ver Rus - sia Tsar Bo - ris _____ now

life to thee! O - ver Rus - sia Tsar Bo - ris _____ now

the Archangels to the Cathedral of the Assumption.

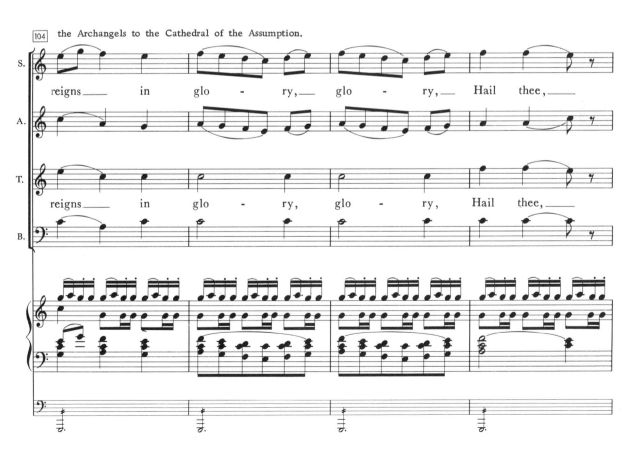

reigns _____ in glo - ry, _____ glo - ry, _____ Hail thee, _____

reigns _____ in glo - ry, glo - ry, Hail thee, _____

Boris appears in the Cathedral porch. Shuisky, behind the Tsar's back, signals to the people to keep silence, and

with Vorotynsky takes his place behind Boris.

The chimes cease.

*) BORIS at the porch. His children, Feodor and Xenia, are behind him.

Meno mosso

My soul is sad! A se-cret ter-ror

*) The key signature is the editor's.

**) The full score says: Poco meno mosso.

390

*) The run is lacking in the 1874 vocal score.

The pageant proceeds towards the Cathedral of the Archangels. The people rush towards the cathedral.

Long life and glo - ry, Tsar our kind fa - ther, Long life and

Long life and glo - ry, Tsar our kind fa - ther, Long life and

Chimes only.

The police maintain order.

**Tempo I Poco allargando*

pow - er to you our fa - ther! As the

pow - er to you our fa - ther! As the

*) The three bars up to Tempo I are lacking in the 1874 vocal score.

**) In the full score: Meno mosso.

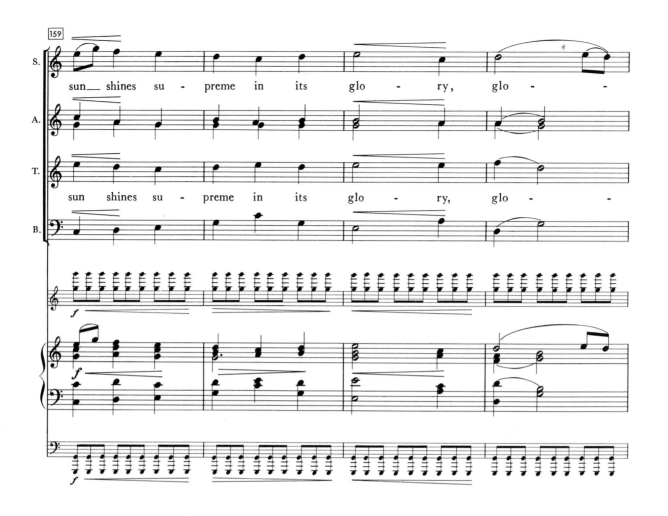

Boris comes out of the Cathedral of the Archangels and proceeds towards his palace.

Mussorgsky's *Boris Godunov*, ed. by Paul Lamm (Copyright 1928 by the Oxford University Press).

39. INSTRUMENTAL MUSIC IN FOLK OPERA

The Bartered Bride (1866)

Sabina

Bedřich Smetana (1824-184)

This vivacious polka is so closely associated with *The Bartered Bride* that few people know the composer added it along with the Furiant in 1869 in his second of three revisions of the opera. The precise rhythmic profile, heavy accents, simple harmonizations, and melodic inevitability hammer home the folksiness of this excerpt. After a slightly varied repeat (m. 25 ff.) of the first section (A), new material (B) appears at measure 90. The transition (m. 118 ff.), whose rhythm stems from B, proceeds through a variant of A (m. 136 ff.) into the finale of the first act, where the chorus enters supported by orchestral material derived from A.

39   (People assemble before the inn; the older ones sit down at the tables, the younger ones get ready to dance.)

399

Ah, with you I do love dancing Now re-treat-ing,
now ad-vanc-ing, Laugh-ing, meet-ing, chaf-fing, greet-ing, Heart to heart with plea-sure beat-ing!

Smetana's *Bartered Bride* (G. Schirmer, 1956).

XIII
Realism in French Opera
Paris
(c. 1875-1900)

Among the first of the Frenchmen to free himself from Wagnerian influences, Bizet, in his last opera *Carmen* (Ex. 40), created what may be the most exciting French opera of all time. A number opera with distinctly separate arias, duets, choruses, and ensembles, *Carmen,* because of its spoken dialogue, was presented at the Opéra-Comique. After Bizet's death, Ernest Guiraud (1837-1892) undaunted and certainly with the best of intentions, wrote recitatives to replace Bizet's dialogue. Unfortunately, it is with these recitatives that we hear the opera today in the United States. It is, however, far more effective in its original state. Scandalous for its day—no opéra-comique was supposed to end tragically—*Carmen* began the trend to realism and naturalism that in Italy became known as *verismo* and in France led to the works of Bruneau (1857-1934) and Charpentier (1860-1956). Both of these composers sought to portray current social and economic problems in the plots of their operas, Bruneau finding particular inspiration in the works of Emile Zola (1840-1902).

Massenet continued the French lyrical tradition. Whereas Gounod's influence may be observed in early Bizet, in Massenet it is everywhere in evidence. Long-line melodies, guaranteed to win popular favor, give expression to the anguish of countless fallen women. Following French tradition (see Lully, Ex. 6-B), Massenet relates his recitative very closely to speech inflection (see Ex. 41). In numerous arioso sections of quasi-lyrical character, his treatment of melody anticipates Debussy. At the turn of the century, Massenet's pupil, Charpentier, capped the movement towards realism with his best known opera, *Louise,* (Ex.42), an episode from the life of a *midinette* (factory girl) in Paris. The city and its ambience prove of paramount importance to the plot, which includes among other issues, filial obligations to parents, premarital relationships among young people, and the boredom of a routine workaday existence.

40. ARIA IN REALISTIC OPERA
Carmen (1875)

A. Duet

Meilhac and Halévy
from the novel by Mérimée

Georges Bizet (1838-1875)

In this extensive excerpt from *Carmen,* we can observe how Bizet writes continuous music while at the same time incorporating several self-contained arias and duets. In the opening recitative (which is Bizet's own), Carmen, with castanets in hand, decides to dance for Don José. Retreat sounds faintly in the background (m. 29 ff.). Don José hears the bugle call, but Carmen does not notice it yet. As the retreat sounds louder and more insistently over Carmen's dancing song in the orchestra, Bizet effectively combines the two melodies (m. 53 ff.). The stunned Carmen learns that Don José intends to leave her to rejoin his company. Furiously, she taunts him (m. 71), insisting that he leave immediately. Although he implores her forgiveness, explaining that his obligations do not lessen his love for her, she continues to mock him. A fragmentary exchange between the pair leads into a short but angry duet, after which an exasperated Don José, to prove his affections, draws from his vest the flower that Carmen had given him during the first act. This action is accompanied by Carmen's Fate Motive (m. 152) in the orchestra. (Numerous recurrent motives can be isolated in this opera.) Don José then sings his Flower Song, a flowing aria without the customary symmetrical patterns. The song has a difficult *ppp* close that stymies the singer, who must decide whether to follow instructions or to violate the composer's wishes and finish *ff* to win applause.

Several times Carmen has interrupted his song, and now given a chance, she launches into her own aria in which she offers Don José a life free of cares, if he will but follow her and join the Gipsies. (Here we have a recurrence, at m. 226 ff., of the Smugglers' Song from the Quintet in the second act.) Don José almost weakens, but his conscience wins out. Desperate, he begs her to pity him, for he cannot follow her. (According to Ernest Newman, this text at m. 299 is Bizet's own; it does not appear in Meilhac-Halévy.) Don José readies himself to leave Carmen (m. 350), but he is tricked into remaining behind (finale) as the Gipsies arrive and save him from arrest by Zuniga.

The entire scene is a study in contrasts: the wanton, irrepressible nature of Carmen, who softens only to obtain her own way, and the irreproachable man of integrity, Don José, who changes almost before our eyes as the story progresses. Bizet has proven himself a master craftsman at musical characterization. Indeed, his greatest achievement rests in his ability to express the musico-dramatic situation through a combination of orchestral color and melodic line. Several features, among them the cigarette girls smoking onstage, the smugglers' den, and Carmen's violent death in front of the audience at the close of the opera, emphasize the trend to realism.

Translation

Carmen: I am going to dance in your honor, and you will see, sir, how I accompany myself in my dance. Sit down, Don José! I am starting. La, la, la. . .

Don José: [38]Wait a moment, Carmen, only a moment, stop!

Carmen: And why, if you please?

Don José: It seems to me that out there . . . Yes, that's the bugle sounding the retreat. Don't you hear it?

Carmen: Bravo, I did well! It's tiring to dance without an orchestra. [51]Long live the music that descends on us from the sky! La, la. . .

Don José: You don't understand me, Carmen. It's the retreat. I must go back to camp for the night!

Carmen: [69]To camp! For the night! I was really stupid! I'm putting myself out and taking such pains to entertain the gentleman. I was singing, and dancing, thinking (God forgive me) that I loved him even more! ta ra ra. . . [86]It's the bugle that sounds! Ta ra ta. He leaves, he's left! Back to your camp! Canary! Here, take your belt, your sabre, your helmet. Go back, boy! Return to your barracks!

Don José: It's not nice of you, Carmen, to mock me. [104]I suffer at the thought of leaving, because never, never was there a woman before you who moved me so deeply.

Carmen: Ta ra ta! [117]My God! It's the retreat. I'm going to be late! He's losing his mind. He's running! And there's his love!

Don José: And so, you don't believe I love you?

Carmen: No!

Don José: Well then, you will hear me now!

Carmen: [139]I don't want to hear anything! You'll keep them waiting.

Don José: You must listen to me, you must!

159The flower you once gave me, stayed with me in my prison. Withered and dry, its fragrance remained. And through all those hours, I shut my eyes and that fragrance intoxicated me. 172And at night I saw you. I began to curse you, to detest you, to say to myself: why did destiny let you cross my path? 182Then I accused myself of blasphemy and I felt within me only one desire, one hope, to see you again, yes, to see you again. Carmen you had only to appear, to cast a glance at me, to take possession of my soul. Oh, my Carmen, I was a slave to you. Carmen, I love you.

Carmen: 208Oh no you don't!

Don José: What are you saying?

Carmen: No, you don't love me, because if you did, you'd follow me out yonder, to the mountains. 233You would carry me on your horse and like a brave man, across the countryside, we would ride. 241Yonder to the mountains. You'd follow me if you loved me. You wouldn't depend on anyone. No officer could make you obey him. No retreat would sound to tell this lover it was time to leave! 261The open road, the wandering life with the universe your country, and you, your own master. Above all, the most rapturous prize, liberty, liberty. 277Yonder, to the mountains! . .take me!

Don José: Be quiet, Carmen, my God! 323No! I don't want to listen to you! Betray my flag, desert! That's dishonor, infamy. Not for me.

Carmen: Well then, go.

Don José: I implore you!

Carmen: No, I don't love you. I hate you. Farewell, never will I see you!

Don José: Listen to me, Carmen. All right then, let it be farewell, once and for all!

Carmen: Farewell!

40

405

*) Note: The castanet-part, printed in small notes, may be performed either in the orchestra by one of the players belonging to the latter, or on the stage by the artist singing the rôle of Carmen, in which case the rhythm may be modified at the pleasure of the artist.

donne, Qu'un peu plus___ je l'ai-mais!___ Ta ra ta ta C'est le clai-ron qui

son ne! Ta ra ta ta Il part il est par - ti! Va - t'en

(in a rage, throwing his shako at him)

donc, ca-na-ri! Tiens!___ prends ton sha-ko, ton

sa - bre, ta gi - ber - ne, Et va-t'en, mon gar-

DON JOSÉ (sadly)

çon, va-t'en! re-tourne à ta ca-ser - ne! C'est

411

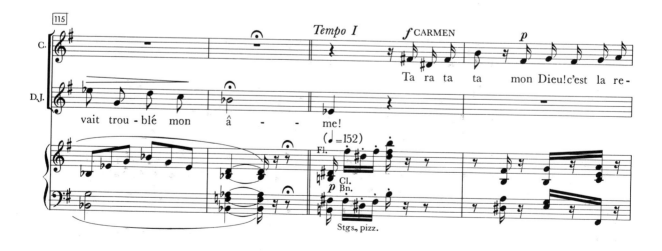

trai - te! Ta ra ta ta je vais être en re - tard! Ô mon

Dieu! ô mon Dieu!___ c'est la re - trai - te!

Je vais être en re - tard! Il perd la

tê - te. il court!___ Et voi - là son a -

414

the flower which Carmen threw at him in Act I, and shows it to Carmen.)

153

Stgs. _cresc._ _dim._ Eng. Hn.

159 _Andantino_ (♩ =69)

p con amore DON JOSÉ

D.J. La fleur que tu m'a-vais je - té - e, Dans ma pri - son___ m'é - tait res - té - e, Flé -

_pp_ W.W.

163

D.J. trie et sè - che, cet - te fleur Gar-dait tou - jours___ sa douce o - deur; Et pen -

Stgs. Cl.

167

D.J. dant des heu - res en - tiè - res, Sur mes yeux, fer-mant mes pau - piè - res, De

Eng. Hn.

171

_p_

D.J. cette o - deur___ je m'e-ni - vrais Et dans la nuit___ je te vo - yais!___ Je

Hn. Stgs. _dim._

416

*) In case the part of this duet included between A and B (page 424) is too low for the voice of the artist singing the role of Carmen, transpose a tone higher (without transition).

418

Non! je ne t'ai-me plus! Va! je te hais! a-dieu!

C. Non! je ne t'ai-me plus! Va! je te hais! a-dieu!

D.J. pri - e! É - cou-te! Car-men!

Poco ritenuto (♩=100)

mais a-dieu pour ja-mais!

C. mais a-dieu pour ja-mais!

DON JOSÉ *p* (grievingly)

Eh bien! soit... a-

CARMEN *f*

Va -

D.J. dieu!_____ a - dieu pour ja - mais!

Bizet's *Carmen* (G. Schirmer, 1895; copyright renewed 1923).

41. NARRATIVE IN FRENCH OPERA

Manon (1884)

A. Narrative, Act I

Meilhac and Gille,
after Abbé Prévost,
aided by the composer

Jules Massenet (1842-1912)

Before Manon meets her cousin, Lescaut, and tells the story of her journey, we hear her theme (mm. 1-4), followed by "conversation music" between the two young people (mm. 7-16). Notice the way Massenet's melody corresponds to the direction of speech inflection: the descent on "Lescaut" (m. 11) and the interrogatory rise on "cousin" (m. 12). Manon's hesitation is reflected in the rests in the group of triplets (m. 22). To convey her increased self-assurance, Massenet uses rapid shorter notes. The narrative commences at measure 43 on one pitch level and becomes more animated (m. 49) as Manon approaches her little refrain, "C'est mon premier voyage." The thrice repeated "pour le couvent" emphasizes her growing doubts as to her earlier intentions, while the key change (m. 57) underlines the new world she has discovered. Orchestral accompaniment, vocal line, and marvelous word-painting on "ailes" (wings) mirror Manon's enthusiasm and excitement on the trip. A slightly slower statement of her theme (m. 64) provides the needed foil for the dramatic change at measure 68. By now we have a good picture of the young and beautiful Manon. Although Massenet has used continuous music in this excerpt, the return of Manon's theme (m. 79) suggests a self-contained musical unit for the form of this example. The chorus of townsfolk that follows our excerpt shows Massenet's indebtedness to Gounod's *Faust*.

Translation

Lescaut: I imagine that this lovely child is my cousin, Manon. I am Lescaut.

Manon: You, my cousin? Kiss me!

Lescaut: Gladly, I assure you. My goodness, she's a lovely girl, a credit to our family.

Manon: Ah, my cousin, excuse me!

Lescaut: She is charming.

Manon: [28]I'm still dizzy. Ah, my cousin, excuse this emotion. I'm still dizzy. Pardon my chattering, [39]I'm on my first trip. The coach had scarcely begun to move, so much to admire with wide-open eyes! The hamlets, the woods, the plain, the travelers, young and old! Ah, my cousin, excuse me, [50]I'm on my first trip. I watched, curiously, trees quivering in the wind as we drove by. I forgot, in my delight, that I was off to the convent, to the convent, to the convent! [57]Before all those new things, don't laugh, I'll tell you, I thought for a moment I had wings! I'd fly away to paradise! Yes, my cousin. [64]Then I had a moment of sadness. I cried. I know not why. An instant later, I confess, I laughed. Ha, ha, ha! But without knowing why! Ha, ha! [74]Ah, my cousin, excuse me. I am still dizzy, still dizzy, pardon my chattering. I'm on my first trip!

41-A (Manon, who has just come out of the crowd, looks on all this hubbub with astonishment.)

Andantino (♩.=60)

430

431

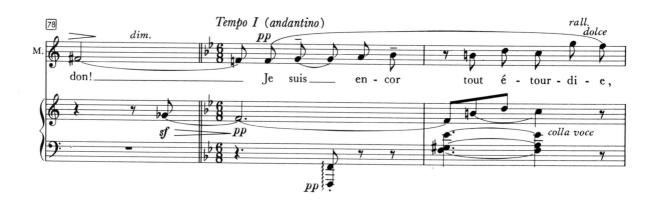

Je suis__ en - cor tout en - gour - di - e! Par - don - nez à mon ba - var - da - ge, J'en

suis à mon prem - ier voy - a - ge!

Massenet's *Manon*, ed. Carl Deis (G. Schirmer, 1940). Used by kind permission of the publisher.

B. Melodrama, Act I

In the short example of melodrama that we have included, a two-bar introduction played by the woodwinds resembles Puccini's short motives for the Bohemians. Observe that Manon's theme reappears (m. 4) as Guillot meets her.

Translation

Guillot: Accursed landlord! So, it's clear, we get no wine! What have we here? She's set my brain in a whirl. Hm. hm, miss!

Manon: That fellow's funny. My goodness!

Guillot: [10]Mademoiselle, listen to me. My name is Guillot de Morfontaine. My coffers overflow with gold, and I would give a lot to hear one word of love from your lips. Now I have finished, what have you to say?

433

(Guillot appears on the balcony of the summer-house.)

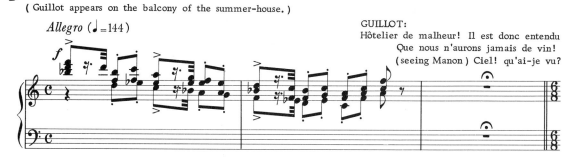

Allegro (♩=144)

GUILLOT:
Hôtelier de malheur! Il est donc entendu
Que nous n'aurons jamais de vin!
(seeing Manon) Ciel! qu'ai-je vu?

4 **Andantino** (♩.=69)

Mademoiselle! hem! hem!

a tempo

(aside) Ce qui se passe en
ma cervelle Est inoui!
MANON: (aside, laughing)
Cet homme est fort drôle,
ma foi!

GUILLOT:
Mademoiselle, écoutez-moi!
On me nomme Guillot, Guillot
de Morfontaine,
De louis d'or ma caisse est pleine,
Et j'en donnerais beaucoup pour
Obtenir de vous un seul mot
d'amour----   J'ai fini, qu'avez-vous à dire?

8 Mademoiselle.....

Massenet's *Manon,* ed. Carl Deis (G. Schirmer, 1940). Used by kind permission of the
publisher.

42. CONVERSATION MUSIC IN FRENCH OPERA

Louise (1900)

From Act I

Charpentier   Gustave Charpentier (1860-1956)

In a conversation whose musical features anticipate Debussy's style of text setting in
Pelléas et Mélisande, Louise and her father engage in the kind of commonplace dialogue
that is certainly completely removed from the unreal world of *Pelléas.* It is evening in a
Parisian worker's home. Father returns for supper. Fatigued from the long hours at his
job, he must now face the endless bickering between his wife and his daughter, Louise.
Again, rhythm and melody grow out of speech inflection.

Father: Ah, what a day!

Louise: You're tired?

Father: I feel that I'm no longer young and that the days are so long!

Louise: [13]Poor father, won't you ever take a rest?

Father: And who would keep the kettle boiling if I laid down my tools?

Mother: For thirty years you've slaved, you certainly deserve a bit of rest! [23]When you consider that there are so many loafers who spend their lives [doing nothing] . . .

. . .

Father: [6]It's been a long time since I made my choice! When you don't have an income, you must be content to work for others. . .

42 Enter Mother, bringing the soup.

donc jamais?

cheerfully

FATHER

Mother returns with the stew.

Et qui fe-rait bouillir la mar - mi - te si je quit-tais l'ou-

[18] *Largo* (♩=60)

Father serves the stew.

MOTHER

♩=64

til?

De-puis trente ans que tu t'é - chi-nes, tu au-rais bien mé-ri-

[21]

Looking in the direction of Julian's room.

Più vivo (♩=112)

angrily

té un peu de re-pos!

Quand on pen -

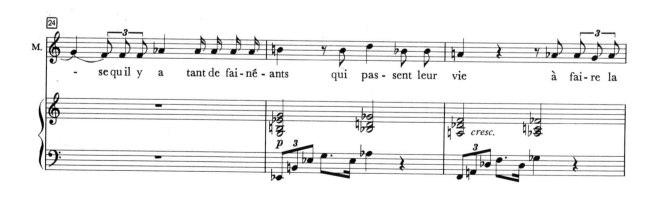

[24]

- se qu'il y a tant de fai-né - ants qui pas-sent leur vie à fai-re la

* * *

6 FATHER cheerfully

Y a long-temps que j'en ai pris mon par - ti! quand on n'a pas de ren - tes,

11

il faut se con-ten - ter d'en ga - gner pour les an - tres...

XIV
Verismo in Italian Opera
Rome, Milan, Turin
(c. 1890-1900)

In the 1880s, many French composers succumbed completely to Wagner. Either they imitated him (see the operas of Saint-Saëns, d'Indy, Bruneau, Chabrier, and Reyer) or, in their attempts to disassociate themselves, they moved in the opposite direction towards realism, which, except for Bizet's *Carmen* and Charpentier's *Louise* (see Chapter XIII) did not prove very effective. The Italians, on the other hand, embarked easily on the road to *verismo,* Italianate realism. Verdi had dealt with real people. His blood-and-thunder plots, with but slight modifications, could pass for accurate descriptions of life in numerous southern Italian villages. Two highly successful pieces in the new naturalistic (or realistic) genre, generally presented as a double bill at the opera, are one-acters: *Cavalleria rusticana* (1890) by Pietro Mascagni (1863-1945) and *I Pagliacci* (1892) by Ruggiero Leoncavallo (1858-1919). The music and the plots of both these operas are so highly charged that their effect is nothing short of sensational. Mascagni and Leoncavallo wrote other operas, but their names are inextricably linked to the two mentioned above.

Puccini, a leading exponent of verismo, belongs in a class by himself. His operas outrank those by Verdi and Wagner on the popularity lists of opera lovers the world over. Notwithstanding its appeal to amateurs, however, much of Puccini's music can pass inspection by professionals. The composer had an uncanny instinct for drama, which he combined with a highly personal musical style that is easy to recognize. Puccini's initial success came with his third opera, *Manon Lescaut* (1893), based on the same story as Massenet's earlier *Manon* (see Ex. 41). Of the twelve operas he wrote, three alone, *La Bohème, Tosca,* and *Madama Butterfly,* would place him in the forefront of Italian opera composers, with nobody—even today—to succeed him. *Turandot* (1925), the unfinished opera that his pupil Alfano completed after Puccini's death, differs in many respects from his earlier works. Conceivably, Puccini's technique might have changed had he lived longer. His melodic gift enabled him to create a kind of cellular melody that blossomed when under pressure. And in Puccini's operas these pressures mount steadily! His motives do not lend themselves to symphonic development, nor are they subjected to thematic transformation. Instead, Puccini has a unique formula that combines a high degree of melodic concentration with distinct orchestration that invariably enthralls audiences.

Puccini's scores exhibit much originality. Harmonically, he experiments with parallelism and with what Grout calls "side-slipping" of chords, the technique that Debussy used later in a number of piano pieces. (For example, in *Soirée dans Grenade,* the same chord layout appears successively on a number of different pitches.) Melodically, Puccini introduces pentatonicism, as well as fragments of the whole-tone scale, in both *Madama Butterfly* and *Turandot* to provide an element of exoticism. His vocal line is always considerate of the singer; it lies beautifully for projection and produces magical effects on listeners. His operas are essentially Italian and favor the singers, but not at the expense of the orchestra. Although he dovetails his arias, they can be extracted for concert performance. Puccini wrote little scenic music or overtures, only brief preludes and intermezzi.

43. CONVERSATION MUSIC AND DUET

La Bohème (1896)

A. Conversation Music, Act I

Giacosa and Illica
Based on a story by Henri Murger

Giacomo Puccini (1858-1924)

After a six-bar orchestral introduction (see recurrence of this theme at m. 15 ff.), the curtain rises on Act I to show the poet, Rodolfo, and the painter, Marcello, discussing the problem of how to keep warm. Librettists and composer have paid careful attention to the details of this conversation. The scene is a garret in a house on the Left Bank of Paris on Christmas Eve. Despite their physical discomfort, the gaiety of the Bohemians is apparent at the outset. Story, scenery, characters, and conversation furnish the verismo qualities of the opera. Notice how the theme associated with the Bohemians appears in the orchestra (mm. 15-16, 26-30, 35), spicing the musical texture that supports this conversation.

Translation

Marcello: He hasn't received his just income for a while now.

Rodolfo: Those silly forests, what are they doing under the snow?

Marcello: Rodolfo, I'd like to tell you a profound thought I have now. I'm cold as hell!

Rodolfo: [19] And I, Marcello, am not hiding from you that I don't believe in the sweat of the brow.

Marcello: My fingers are frozen!...as if I still had them plunged down in that great icebox that is Musetta's heart!

43-A

440

B. Duet, Act I

In the following excerpt that crowns Act I, we notice Puccini's remarkable ability to illustrate the action of the drama through music. Boy meets girl, a sick girl (see her coughing music at mm. 24-30) from the moment of their encounter. They recognize their feelings for one another (fairly rapidly, as usual in opera) and exchange mutual vows of affection. Puccini uses the short motives so characteristic of his style throughout most of the action in this scene. A chordal progression in the orchestra (mm. 44-47) is repeated five times, despite interruptions, as the young people become acquainted. Mimi leaves, but returns almost immediately because she has forgotten her

441

key. The melody to which she explains her predicament to Rodolfo is a typical Puccini love theme. The music tells us the truth (m. 75 ff.) regardless of what Mimi is saying. Rodolfo finds her key on the floor, but pockets it because he wants Mimi to stay. As he pretends to continue his search, his hand touches Mimi's. Here Puccini starts the finale (m. 155 ff.). Up to this point, we have had a fairly typical example of conversation music.

Like many Puccini arias, this one begins on a monotone (m. 157) and later bursts into song. An anticipation of Rodolfo's theme appears in the orchestral melody (mm. 158-161) flowing beneath the monotone of the singer. Puccini often states his melody this way, first in the orchestra with the soloist seemingly otherwise engaged, and later spun out by the vocalist. ("E lucevan le stelle" from *Tosca* illustrates this technique.) The orchestration of the opening of Rodolfo's aria (m. 199) is worth noting, particularly measure 207, where Puccini scores violas an octave lower than the cellos, before coming in on the strings with the complete melody. When Rodolfo finishes, he asks Mimi to tell him about herself.

Mimi begins her story in a lyrical fashion. However, Puccini reverts to a monotone (m. 232) before the actual aria gets under way. A new theme (m. 275 ff.), suggesting a parallel to Rodolfo's (m. 207 ff.), follows Mimi's principal motive. A syncopated accompaniment betrays Mimi's inner excitement. At the conclusion of the aria, she again returns to a monotone (m. 296).

The sound of the Bohemians is heard outside the window (m. 300). As they leave for the Cafe Momus, their voices die away in the distance. Puccini now makes an unexpected modulation to A major for the ravishing duet between the lovers that closes this scene and act. Again notice the peculiarly monotonous start of Rodolfo's vocal part (m. 326 ff.). The young lovers begin their duet in unison (m. 334), continue together with an incredibly luscious melody, and conclude after slight echoes (m. 356 ff.) of the earlier "Che gelida manina" (see m. 158). In this excerpt we hear continuous music, but we can detect specific points of articulation. Puccini has organized this segment of the opera into one large three-part form: first Rodolfo's aria, then Mimi's aria, and finally the duet.

Translation

Rodolfo: I'm not in the mood! Who's there?

Mimi: Excuse me.

Rodolfo: A woman!

Mimi: Please, my light's gone out.

Rodolfo: There now.

Mimi: Would you?

Rodolfo: [22] Sit down a moment.

Mimi: It's not necessary.

Rodolfo: Please come in. You're feeling ill?

Mimi: No . . . nothing.

Rodolfo: How pale!

Mimi: My breath, those stairs . . .

Rodolfo: [37] And now what can I do? I know! How sick her face looks! Feel better?

Mimi: Yes.

Rodolfo: Here it's so cold. Sit near the fire. Wait, a little wine . . .

Mimi: Thank you.

Rodolfo: To you.

Mimi: Just a little.

Rodolfo: Like this? [59] (She really is lovely!)

Mimi: Thank you. Now permit me to light my light. It's all over.

Rodolfo: In such a hurry?

Mimi: Yes. Thank you. Good evening.

Rodolfo: Good evening.

Mimi: Oh, scatterbrained me! My room key, where have I left it?

Rodolfo: [83] Don't stand in the doorway. The light is flickering in the wind.

Mimi: Oh heavens, light it again!

Rodolfo: Heavens, mine is out too!

Mimi: [98] And where can my key be?

Rodolfo: Pitch darkness!

Mimi: I'm sorry!

Rodolfo: Where can it be?

Mimi: Your neighbor is a nuisance!

Rodolfo: Why, not at all.

Mimi: Your neighbor is a nuisance.

Rodolfo: What are you saying? It seems . . .

Mimi: Search!

Rodolfo: [125] I'm searching!

Mimi: Where can it be?

Rodolfo: Ah!

Mimi: Did you find it?

Rodolfo: No!

Mimi: It seemed to me . . .

Rodolfo: [136] Honestly?

Mimi: Ah!

Rodolfo: [157] How cold your little hand is! Let me warm it. What's the good of searching? In the dark, we can't find it. Fortunately, it's a moonlit night, and here we have the moon near. Wait a minute, young lady, and I will tell you in two words who I am. Who I am and what I do, how I live. [189] Would you like that? Who am I? I am a poet. What do I do? I write. And how do I live? I live. [200] In gay poverty I squander like a lord, rhymes and hymns of love. For dreams, and chimeras, and castles in the air, I have a millionaire's soul. At times, from my safe, two thieves steal all my gems, two beautiful eyes. [211] They entered with you just now, and my usual dreams and my beautiful dreams quickly disappeared. But the theft doesn't bother me because a sweet hope has taken their place. [221] Now that you know me, you speak. Talk. Who are you? Please tell.

Mimi: Yes. They call me Mimi, but my name is Lucia. [232] My story is brief. On canvas or on silk, I embroider at home or outside. I'm contented and happy and my pastime is making lilies and roses. [240] I like those things that have such sweet magic, which speak of love, of springtime, which speak of dreams and of chimeras, those things that are named poetry. Do you understand me?

Rodolfo: Yes.

Mimi: [252] They call me Mimi. Why, I don't know. Alone, I prepare dinner by myself. I don't always go to Mass, but I do pray to the Lord. [264] I live alone, all alone, there, in a little white room. I look out on roofs and towards the sky, but when the thaw comes, the first sun is mine. The first kiss of April is mine. The first sun is mine. A rose blooms in a pot. Leaf by leaf, I spy it. So lovely is the perfume of a flower! [291] But the flowers that I make, alas, have no odor. Besides that, I wouldn't know what else to tell you. I am your neighbor, who came at the wrong time to bother you.

Schaunard: [298] Eh, Rodolfo!

Colline: Rodolfo!

Marcello: Don't you hear us? Snail!

Colline: Poetaster!

Schaunard: Damn that lazy one!

Rodolfo: [305] I'll write another three lines quickly!

Mimi: Who are they?

Rodolfo: Friends.

Schaunard: You'll hear plenty!

Marcello: What are you doing up there alone?

Rodolfo: [312] I'm not alone. We are two. Go on to Momus. Keep a place for us. We'll be there soon.

Marcello, Schaunard, Colline: Momus, Momus, Momus, let's go away tactfully.

Marcello: He found poetry!

Schaunard, Colline: Momus, Momus!

Rodolfo: Oh, sweet maiden!

Marcello: He found poetry!

Rodolfo: [327] Oh, gentle face, surrounded by moonlight's glow, in you I recognize the dream I should like to dream forever!

Mimi: [334] Ah, Love, only you command!

Rodolfo: Extreme delights already stir in my soul!

Mimi: Oh how nicely his flattery descends to my heart. You alone command, love.

Rodolfo: Extreme delights stir, love stirs in a kiss!

Mimi: [343] No please . . .

Rodolfo: You're mine!

Mimi: Your friends are awaiting you.

Rodolfo: Are you sending me away already?

Mimi: I should like to say, but I don't dare . . .

Rodolfo: Say it!

Mimi: If I came with you?

Rodolfo: What? . . . Mimi! It would be so nice to stay here. It's cold outside.

Mimi: [353] I'll be near you . . . !

Rodolfo: And on our return?

Mimi: Curious!

Rodolfo: Give me your arm, my little one . . .

Mimi: I obey, sir.

Rodolfo: What says my love?

Mimi: I love you!

Mimi, Rodolfo: Love, Love, Love!

43 - B

(Rodolfo closes the door, puts the candle down, clears a corner of the table, places on it pen and paper, then sits down and prepares to write, after having extinguished the other candle, which had remained burning.)

445

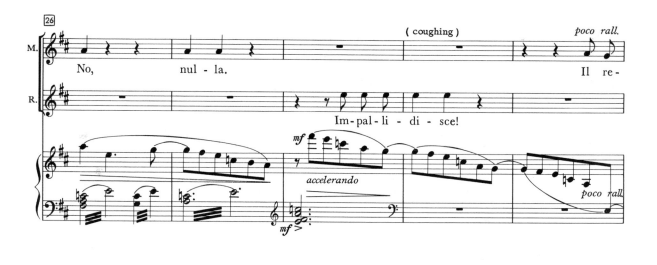

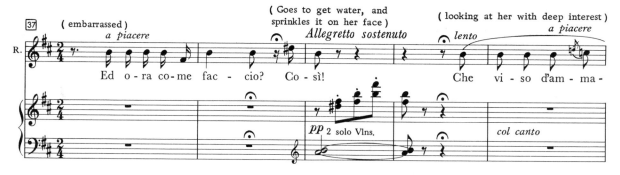

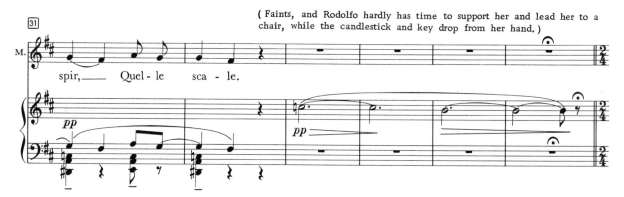

446

448

449

but, guided by Mimi's voice and movements, tries to get near her.)

Cer - co!

(Mimi stoops to the floor, continuing to search for the key; at this moment Rodolfo reaches her and as he also stoops, his hand encounters hers.)

Andantino affettuoso (♩=58)

(surprised)

Ah!

(holding Mimi's hand, with a voice full of emotion)

pp dolcissimo

Che ge - li - da ma - ni - na, se la la - sci ri - scal -

dar. Cer - car che gio - va? Al bu - io non si tro - va.

Ma per for-
tu - na è u-na not - te di lu - na,___ e qui la lu-na l'ab-

(Mimi tries to withdraw her hand.)

bia - mo vi - ci - na. A - spet-ti si-gno - ri - na, le di - rò con due pa-

ro - le chi son, chi son, e che fac - cio, co - me___

(Mimi is silent. Rodolfo releases her hand;
drawing back she finds a chair, into which
she sinks, overcome by emotion.)

vi - - vo. Vuo - - le? Chi

lor dal mio for - zie - re____ ru-ban tut-ti i gio-iel - li due la-dri gli oc-chi

bel - li. V'en-trar con voi pur o - ra, ed i miei so-gni u-sa-ti

e i bei so-gni mie-i____ to-sto si di - le - guar!___ Ma il fur-to non m'ac-

co - ra   poi - chè,____ poi - chè v'ha pre - so

454

mia è bre-ve:_____ A te-la o a se-ta ri-ca-mo in ca-sa e fuo-ri...

Son tran-quil-la e lie-ta ed è mio sva-go far gi-gli e ro-se._____ Mi

Andante calmo (♩=54)
dolcemente

piac-cion quel-le co-se che han sì dol-ce ma-lì-a, che par-la-no d'a-

mor, di pri-ma-ve-re,_____ che

par-la-no di so-gni e di chi-me-re,_____ quel-le co-se che han no-me po-e-

457

459

44. INTRODUCTORY MUSIC

Tosca (1900)

Giacosa and Illica
After the play by Sardou

Giacomo Puccini (1858-1924)

As we approach the twentieth century, we notice a tendency among opera composers to shorten their introductory music. Not only is the self-contained overture a thing of the past, but even the overture that moves right into the first scene has become a rarity. Instead, composers write a few bars of introductory music to be performed before the curtain rises, as in *Otello* (see Ex. 37), where the curtain rises on measure 4 and singers start at measure 13; or, the orchestra commences and the curtain rises immediately afterwards as in Strauss's *Elektra* (1909); or, the curtain rises *before* the orchestra begins to play, as in Strauss's *Salome* (Ex. 46). In other words, the trend is to start music and drama almost simultaneously.

One of the sharpest, most dramatic musical portraits opens *Tosca*. This distinctive harmonic progression is associated throughout the opera with Scarpia's sinister personality. Observe how Puccini insures our interest: each chord is accented, the E-major chord has a fermata over it to assure its extension, and another fermata appears at the close of measure 3. The entire passage is marked *fff* and *tutta forza*. The curtain rises at measure 4, where we hear a syncopated figure of four chords usually associated with Angelotti, the escaped political prisoner. Puccini may even have given us a foretaste of the poor fellow's end in the long chromatic descent in the bass (mm. 8-15). (Angelotti begins to sing immediately following the last bar of our printed excerpt.) William Austin, in his book on twentieth-century music, makes the salient observation that the atmosphere of *Tosca* contributes something to Strauss's *Salome* (Ex. 46), Schoenberg's *Erwartung* (Ex. 47), Berg's *Lulu* (1937), Britten's *Peter Grimes* (Ex. 50), and served as a model for Menotti's *The Consul* (1950) and Carlisle Floyd's *Susannah* (1955).

44 (At the right, the Attavanti Chapel.   A dais on the left: on it, a large picture on an easel covered by a piece of cloth.   Painter's tools lie about, also a basket.)

(Angelotti enters looking like a prisoner, emaciated, exhausted, trembling with fear, breathing heavily.)

(Surveying the scene with a rapid glance.)

XV

Early Trends
in Twentieth-Century Opera

Paris, Berlin, Prague, Boston,

London, Venice, Washington

(c. 1900-1967)

In the nineteenth century, composers became specialists. Chopin wrote no operas, and Wagner, except for a few early pieces, wrote no piano music. Meyerbeer was essentially an opera composer; Brahms announced he would sooner marry than essay an opera. He did neither. In the twentieth century, almost every composer has tried his hand at opera in one form or another, but few have succeeded in producing the equivalent of Verdi's *La Traviata,* Wagner's *Ring,* Bizet's *Carmen,* or Puccini's *La Bohème.* Although no appraisal of various trends and styles in contemporary operatic music has appeared to date, it does not seem too early to attempt a tentative assessment of the current situation.

Obviously, three of the most significant twentieth-century composers, Stravinsky, Bartók (1881-1945), and Schoenberg, are not primarily opera composers. Stravinsky's best dramatic presentations are his ballets. His short operas, *Le Rossignol* (1914) and *Mavra* (1922), and his hybrid, or quasi-operatic works such as *L'histoire du soldat* (1918), *Renard* (1922), and *Oedipus Rex* (1927) do not belong to the category of genuine opera. *The Rake's Progress* (Ex. 51), in which Stravinsky eschews later musical procedures and returns to eighteenth-century recitative and aria style, is the exception that proves the rule. Bartók's only opera, *Duke Bluebeard's Castle* (1911), seems to be among the least successful of his works. Schoenberg devoted his best efforts to instrumental music and song. During his atonal period, from which his best known piece is the song cycle (or chamber cantata) *Pierrot Lunaire* (1912), he wrote the monodrama, *Erwartung* (Ex. 47), a highly charged, exceedingly dissonant work that defies audience acceptance because of its avoidance of almost any type of thematic repetition. On this musical drama as well as on other similar dramatic works of this period, he lavished considerable care and attention. His plans and ideas for the opera *Moses und Aron* and the oratorio *Die Jakobsleiter* occupied Schoenberg for more than thirty years! Both were left incomplete at his death. Two acts, all that exist of *Moses und Aron,* have received favorable criticism; but in truth the work must be regarded as more of a tableau than a play in music.

For a genuine play in music, a return to the ideals of Monteverdi, we must look to Claude Debussy, who, in the early years of this century, recaptured for France her musical glory. Whereas the Italians dominated eighteenth-century musical style and Germans asserted themselves most vigorously in the nineteenth century, leadership reverted to France in the first quarter of the twentieth century. Although impressionism cannot be considered a movement in that Debussy did not create a "school," it did result in an opera. Impressionism in orchestral music (where it began) and in piano music (where it flourished) is almost exclusively Debussy's own province. Because of its limited properties, impressionism vanished almost as rapidly as it appeared. Operatically speaking, the significance of *Pelléas et Mélisande* (Ex. 45), Debussy's only opera, lies in its unique utilization of impressionist features: fleeting and elusive melody that disappears before it achieves complete shape; harmonic parallelism; pedal points; whole-tone scales, which, lacking a leading tone, blur the tonality; and a large orchestra with instruments used not so much for volume as for color. *Pelléas et Mélisande* has no set numbers, no chorus or ensemble, no arias, and only one musical unit that resembles a duet. The entire opera consists of different degrees of recitative that occasionally expand into arioso. The music is continuous as in Wagner's operas, and one scene moves imperceptibly into the next. Debussy uses recurrent motives whose subtle melodic profiles make them difficult to recognize even after repeated hearings. He has literally reproduced Maeterlinck's play in music, fashioning it into the musical fabric of an opera.

In Germany, Strauss in *Salome* (Ex. 46) does likewise. He sets an entire play, but within the context of a post-Wagnerian musical idiom. In his tone poems, almost all written before the turn of the century, Strauss, taking as a point of departure Wagner's harmonic palette and his technique of thematic transformation, molded the tone poem into the gigantic shapes of late nineteenth-century program music. Following his success with the tone poem, he sought to remake opera as a staged symphonic poem (see Norman Del Mar's *Richard Strauss*). In *Salome* and *Elektra*, highly compressed one-act dramas of violence, Strauss succeeds. Both of these operas anticipate the harshly dissonant German expressionist style and hence prepare the way for Berg's *Wozzeck* (Ex. 48).

Berg, the most accessible of the three expressionist composers, Schoenberg, Berg, and Webern (1883-1945), resembled Strauss in his choice of a drama of violence, Georg Büchner's *Woyzeck*, for his principal work. Although the piece is highly organized—three acts, each with five scenes, and each scene utilizing a different structural feature taken from instrumental music—Berg wrote that if he were successful, the audience would respond to none of this formal organization, but would react only to the drama. Unquestionably, he has produced a remarkable work, successful with both audiences and critics alike, and one that has probably received more performances in more cities than any other opera written after 1925.

Of American composers, George Gershwin is one who has unashamedly used jazz to his and our advantage. In *Porgy and Bess* (Ex. 49) he has fused popular, folk elements with conventional operatic techniques, and the result is highly satisfactory. Although the Italian-American composer Gian Carlo Menotti (b. 1911) sets English-language texts, his style seems more European. Both Gershwin and Menotti spoke of their need to find suitable recitative for the English language.

The British composer Benjamin Britten is among the most gifted as well as the most successful of contemporary musicians. In his remarkably personal, lyrical style, he has written more than ten operas, changing from number operas to those with continuous music, to the more functional operas, to his latest works (*Noyes Fludde* of 1958 and *Curlew River* of 1964), which show the influence, respectively, of Christian liturgical drama and the Japanese *No* plays. Our excerpt from *Peter Grimes* (Ex. 50) illustrates the effect of his exposure to film and radio music on his compositional style in opera.

Francis Poulenc, whose compositions generally exhibit the frivolous, lighthearted side of Gallic music, has also written a serious opera, and a very effective one, too, in *Les Dialogues des Carmélites* (1957), as well as the surrealist, comic opera *Les Mamelles de Tirésias* (1947), the latter to a text by the French poet, Guillaume Apollinaire (1880-1918). In our anthology he is represented by *La Voix humaine* (Ex. 52) a monodrama written for the singer Denise Duval to a text by Jean Cocteau (1889-1963). Again, economy of forces and strict adherence to text characterize this contemporary work, where the vocal line occasionally bursts forth into a real aria, although far less frequently than in either Menotti or Britten operas. Darius Milhaud (b. 1892), like Poulenc one of the original group of *Les Six,* has written large-scale choral operas, some of which Stravinsky may have had in mind when he wrote his *Oedipus Rex.* Startling new choral techniques appear in the Exhortation Scene from *Les Choéphores,* the second of the operas in Milhaud's *Orestie* trilogy (1913-1924). The trend to opera-oratorio types, very strong between 1920 and 1945, seems now to have diminished. However, the German composer Carl Orff (b. 1895), curiously disposed to using Latin texts on the one hand and fairytale subjects on the other, has also experimented with this hybrid form. Hans Werner Henze (b. 1926), another German composer, has written several successful operas, among them one based on the Manon story (Ex. 41).

Douglas Moore (1893-1969), Samuel Barber (b. 1910), and Jack Beeson (b. 1921) are American lyric composers whose works have achieved prominence. And very recently, *The Visitation* (1966) by Gunther Schuller (b. 1925), *Mourning Becomes Electra* (1967) by Marvin David Levy (b. 1932), and two works by the Argentine composer Alberto Ginastera (b. 1916), *Don Rodrigo* (1964) and *Bomarzo* (1967), have created more than a stir in international circles.

Numerous composers here and in Europe have wrestled with the special problems of opera: the aesthetic problems and the purely practical ones relating to financial considerations. Opera, full-scale opera in the nineteenth-century tradition, is costly. Rarely does a new work achieve a sufficient number of performances to justify the expenditure. Also, because of fewer performances of contemporary operas, singers are reluctant to learn new and difficult roles, which for the most part will not enter the repertory, and yet will always (because of their new and unfamiliar techniques) require months to assimilate. Then, too, today's audiences seem to prefer the works of the past. Our opera houses, unlike their counterparts in earlier days, resemble museums in their preservation and presentation of older established pieces rather than current works. Never before in the history of music has the gap between those writing and producing music and those willing to listen to it appeared so wide—or so irreconcilable. Nevertheless, we still have hopes for the future. And if attendance at opera houses in New York City is any guide, we can assert with conviction that the fabulous musical invalid known as the opera is in truth no more defunct than its counterpart, the legitimate theater.

45. IMPRESSIONIST RECITATIVE AND ARIOSO
Pelléas et Mélisande (1902)

A. Opening Scene, Act I

Maeterlinck   Claude Debussy (1862-1918)

Fortunately for posterity, Maeterlinck and Debussy were born in the same year and became intimately involved in one another's work at about the age of thirty. Maeterlinck's symbolist drama appeared in Brussels in 1892. Shortly after reading it, Debussy knew he had found the only kind of play he could set to music. (Later, he made several unsuccessful attempts at writing a libretto and music to Poe's *Fall of the House of Usher* and *The Devil in the Belfry*.) Both playwright and composer saw people as relatively helpless creatures, functioning in a preordained manner, or, as Ernest Newman described it, "[that] men and women are helpless corks on the sea of fate." There is no plot or story in the traditional sense in *Pelléas et Mélisande*. Instead, something of the pointlessness of all human endeavors is symbolically depicted by characters of whose reality we are never certain (see Joseph Kerman's brilliant essay on *Pelléas* as "sung play" in *Opera as Drama*).

Debussy used no middle man, no librettist. With suggestions from Maeterlinck, he cut and spliced where necessary and was thus able to fit the five-act play into a workable five-act opera. Some sections of Maeterlinck's text remained absolutely unaltered, despite their transplant from the play into the opera. Three hundred years after Monteverdi, Debussy achieved the goal of the originators of opera, a play set in music. The composer accepted for his libretto a text in which the author replaced traditional poetic construction with a kind of lyrical prose. The vocal line alternates between recitative and arioso; only rarely does it really blossom into song. Musically, too, Debussy veers away from traditional set forms. He seeks plastic, ever-changing shapes; he avoids clear-cut cadences; he overlaps phrases, periods, sections. He moves in parallel rather than in contrary motion, thus weakening the traditional patterns of tension and release. Streams of sound, free of the tyranny of the bar line, result from the interaction of many intricate figurations, each meticulously notated. Veiled sonorities in which individual timbres stand out, a kind of shimmering orchestration with flutes and clarinets in low registers, violins in luminous upper registers, trumpets and horns muted, and all enveloped in a gossamer web of harp, celesta, glockenspiel, muffled drum, and cymbals brushed lightly with a drum stick—these are the materials of which Debussy weaves his musical fabric. This indescribably beautiful sonority cannot be duplicated in a piano reduction.

Pelléas et Mélisande contains motives, Debussy's elusive fragments that dissolve before becoming full-fledged melodies. French melody has always had a more subtle profile than German melody and consequently seems more difficult to grasp and hold in memory. (Debussy's motives, for example, are never as easy to recognize as those by Wagner.) As Golaud approaches Mélisande for the first time, a motive from the opening bars of the opera appears in diminution in measure 1. Notice the speechlike melody with its short range and monotone recitation. Observe the manner in which the orchestra punctuates these vocal fragments (mm. 3-4). Mélisande's two brief, anxious replies go unaccompanied. The crush of minor 2nds in her melody line reflects her change of text at "Je me jette à l'eau!" The recurrence of the opening motive is harmonized with parallel 5ths and octaves (m.16) emphasizing the loneliness of the characters.

Translation

Golaud: Why are you weeping? Don't be afraid, you've nothing to fear. Why do you cry here, all alone?

Mélisande: Don't touch me, Don't touch me or I'll throw myself in the water!

Golaud: I'll not touch you. [15] Look, I shall stay here, next to this tree. Don't be afraid.

45-A

Debussy's *Pelléas et Mélisande* (By permission of Durand & Cie, Editeurs-propriétaires à Paris).

B. Blindman's Well, Act II, Scene i

Mélisande, now Golaud's wife, sits beside a well in the park. Pelléas is nearby. Violins and, occasionally, flutes imitate the rustling of leaves and the rippling of water in the seemingly tranquil atmosphere (see sixteenth notes in mm. 1-4, and m. 80). Another motive in the vocal part at "Prenez garde" (m. 7) darts in and out of the texture (see eighth notes in treble staff of accompaniment at mm. 12, 14, and 81). The music here seems to mirror the flickering, unsteady reflections in the water. Notice the water figure (m. 9) where Mélisande wants to dip her hands in the water. Her hands hurt (see the tritone in the bass staff of the accompaniment at mm. 10-11). The warning motive (from m. 7) returns as Pelléas tells Mélisande to guard lest her hair fall into the water. "Didn't Golaud find you at a well?" he asks. And Golaud's second motive appears in the bass (mm. 25 and 27) just as it had appeared at the opening of the opera. Starting at measure 37, the ring motive (top voice with double stems) recurs in either one or the other staff of the accompaniment (in both staves at mm. 52-53, 56-57). It shows a familial resemblance to Golaud's motive from measure 25. Mélisande begins to play with the ring Golaud gave her. She drops it and it falls into the well. What will she tell Golaud, she asks Pelléas. The truth, he says, only the truth. A variant of the ring motive sounds again (top voice of accompaniment) as they go out.

Translation

Mélisande: I am going to lie down on the marble. I should like to see the bottom of the well.

Pelléas: It's never been seen. It is perhaps as deep as the sea.

Mélisande: If something bright were shining below, perhaps one could then see it.
Pelléas: Don't lean over like that.

Mélisande: I'd like to touch the water. . .

Pelléas: Be careful not to slip. . .I'm going to take hold of your hand.

Mélisande: [8]No, no, I'd like to dip both hands. . .It seems my hands are not well today.

Pelléas: Be careful, Mélisande! Your hair. . .

Mélisande: I can't, I can't reach it.

Pelléas: [18]Your locks have fallen into the water. . .

Mélisande: Yes, they are longer than my arms. . .they are longer even than I. . .

Pelléas: Wasn't it beside a well that he found you?

Mélisande: Yes. . .

Pelléas: What did he say to you?

Mélisande: Nothing, I don't remember any more.

Pelléas: [22]Was he very close to you?

Mélisande: Yes, he wanted to kiss me.

Pelléas: And you didn't want him to?

Mélisande: No.

Pelléas: Why didn't you want him to?

Mélisande: Oh, oh, I saw something passing by there at the bottom. . .

Pelléas: [34]Be careful! You will fall! What are you playing with?

Mélisande: With the ring he gave me.

Pelléas: Don't play that way above such deep water.

Mélisande: [40]My hands don't shake. . .

Pelléas: How it shines in the sun! Don't throw it so high in the air! It's fallen!

Mélisande: It's fallen into the water!

Pelléas: Where is it?

Mélisande: [47]I don't see it sinking.

Pelléas: I think I see it shine.

Mélisande: My ring?

Pelléas: Yes, yes, over there. . .

Mélisande: Oh, oh! It's so far from us! No, no. That's not it. It's lost, lost. [58]Only a big circle remains on the water! What are we going to do now?

Pelléas: There's no need of being so distressed about a ring. It's nothing. Perhaps we'll find it. If not, we'll find another one of them for you.

Mélisande: [67]No, no. We will never find it, nor will we ever find any other! I thought I had it in my hands, nevertheless. . .I had already closed my hands and it fell in spite of everything. . .I threw it too high, in the sun's rays.

Pelléas: Come, we'll return another day. Come, it's time. They'll be coming to find us. The clock struck twelve noon just as the ring fell.

Mélisande: [78]What are we going to tell Golaud if he asks where it is?

Pelléas: The truth, the truth.

480

481

Debussy's *Pelléas et Mélisande* (By permission of Durand & Cie, Editeurs-propriétaires à Paris).

C. Act III, scene ii

At the climax of the opera in Act III, Pelléas comes to tell Mélisande he will leave the next day. As he calls to her from beneath her tower window, Debussy begins the most ravishing music of the entire opera. "Reach out your hand so that I may kiss it farewell," Pelléas tells her. He reaches up and she stretches down, but they do not quite touch. Suddenly her hair tumbles down, enveloping him. The intensity of the music matches that of the text (mm. 19-24). Parallel 5ths flow beneath the clarinet melody (mm. 28-31). Then Debussy sets the same melody at measure 30 (in diminution in the vocal part) and again in measure 36 and measure 40 (in the treble staff of the accompaniment). In Debussy's music, this constant repetition of short motives at higher and lower pitch levels displays a refreshing use of the sequence. For the deliriously beautiful passage at measures 54-60, Debussy has written alternately two against three as if to simulate the fluttering of a captured bird.

Translation

Mélisande: I can't lean out any farther.

Pelléas: My lips cannot reach your hand.

Mélisande: [3]I can't lean out any farther. It's all I can do not to fall! Oh, oh, my hair is falling down the tower!

Pelléas: Oh, oh, what's this? Your hair. Your hair is falling down on me. All your tresses. All your beautiful locks have fallen down from the tower. [19]I have them in my hand. I hold them in my mouth. I have them in my arms. I put them all round my neck. . .No more tonight will I open my hands!

Mélisande: [26]Let me go, let me go. You'll make me fall.

Pelléas: No, no. I have never seen hair like yours,, Mélisande. [34]Look, look, they come from so high up and they overflow down to my heart. They have even flooded my knees. And they are gentle, gentle as if they have fallen from heaven. [45]I can't even see the heavens for your tresses. Do you see, see? I can hardly hold them all in both hands. Some of them fall as far as the boughs of the willow. [54]They seem like birds in my hands, and they love me. They love me more than you do!

Mélisande: Let me go, let me go!

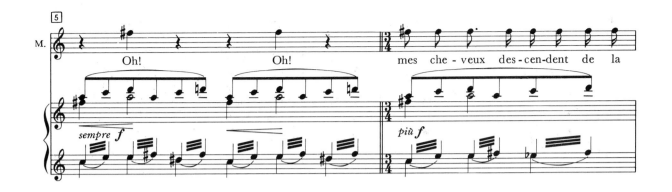

(While thus leaning out her hair suddenly turns over and envelops Pélleas.)

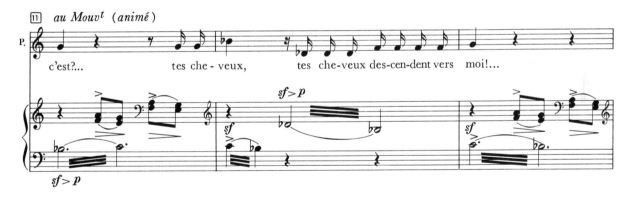

Debussy's *Pelléas et Mélisande* (By permission of Durand & Cie, Editeurs-propriétaires à Paris).

D. Act V, scene i

Golaud had killed Pelléas and wounded Mélisande when he encountered them in their first (and what would have been their last) embrace. Mélisande, who has given birth to a child, lies dying. Golaud questions her, persistently seeking evidence that she has been unfaithful to him. His obstinacy is reflected in a recurrent motive (mm. 2-5, 8-10). As he continues to demand the truth, the truth at the moment of death, Mélisande asks who is going to die. Is it she? The Mélisande motive from the opening of the opera drifts into the texture at measure 17. Mélisande dies, and Golaud will never know the truth.

Translation

Mélisande: No, no, we were not guilty. Why are you asking me all this?

Golaud: Mélisande, tell me the truth for the love of God!

Mélisande: Why should what I have said not be the truth?

Golaud: [10] Don't lie like that at the moment of death.

Mélisande: Who is going to die? Is it I?

Golaud: You, you and I. I, as well, after you. [18] And we must have the truth. Now at last, we must have the truth. Do you hear? Tell me all! I'll forgive all!

Mélisande: Why am I going to die?. . .

489

45-D

490

Debussy's *Pelléas et Mélisande* (By permission of Durand & Cie, Editeurs-propriétaires à Paris).

46. POST-WAGNERIAN VOCALISM

Salome (1905)

Wilde play
in a translation by Hedwig Lachmann

Richard Strauss (1864-1949)

In the last dozen years of the nineteenth century, Strauss produced the majority of the tone poems with which his name is generally associated. He brings some of the same instrumental and formal techniques to his opera, *Salome*. A large orchestra provides continuity for a multi-sectional work, which is unified principally by its extra-musical program, the story, but also through thematic recurrence in the post-Wagnerian manner. Although faced with seemingly insoluble performance problems before its initial production in Dresden, the highly original *Salome* achieved instant success with audiences. Many music critics disagreed with popular opinion, however, and condemned the work for various reasons, such as its prose (instead of poetic) libretto. In order to give himself more room for musical illumination of Lachmann's splendid translation from Wilde's original French text, the composer compressed or deleted several passages. By thus tightening the textual material, Strauss obtained a more heightened expression of the drama. As in the later expressionist opera, *Wozzeck* (Ex. 48), the changing colors of the moon, a vital ingredient of the stage setting, reflect the course of the action and the personality of the individuals caught in the plot.

Using appropriate music to intensify the theatrical effects, Strauss has been able to increase the horror of the final outcome. The audience recognizes the evil inherent in Salome shortly after her first appearance on stage, when her insatiable demands foretell the ensuing disaster. Salome, a willful, spoiled child—Strauss has called for a sixteen-year old with the voice of an Isolde and the body of a graceful nymph—insists on seeing Jokanaan, whose admonitions she has heard sounding forth from the cistern, where he has been imprisoned by her stepfather, Herod. Salome has prevailed on Narraboth, the young Syrian guard, already enamored of her, to disobey Herod's orders and bring her the prisoner. As the soldiers go to fetch Jokanaan, the orchestra plays a moving instrumental interlude of which we have included the last thirteen bars. One of the prophet's motives appears in measures 2-6; another, his main motive, emerges at measure 13 ff. and measure 25 ff. in the accompaniment. The music reflects Jokanaan's persistent questions, here concerning the whereabouts of Herod.

Translation

Jokanaan: Where is he, whose cup is filled with sin? Where is he, who, wrapped in a silver robe, will one day die in front of all the people? [24] Bid him come forward that he may hear the voice of him who cries aloud in the houses of kings and in the wilderness.

46-A   *Breit* (♩=♩ *des* ¾ *Metr.* ♩=76)

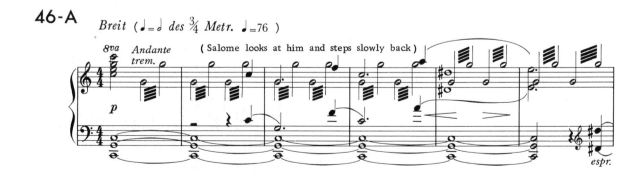

der in der Wü-ste und in den Häu-sern der Kö - ni-ge ge-

kün - det hat.

B. Scene iii

Salome finds the prophet frightening and fascinating at the same time. Narraboth's warnings (mm. 2-4) go unheeded as Salome continues to stare at Jokanaan. Before our eyes, the young Salome is transformed into a lustful woman. She begins her monologue, a quasi-set piece of three verses that begins at measure 5. Strauss's music envelops the text in luxurious and sensual wrappings. Salome alternately praises and rejects different parts of Jokanaan's physical presence. First his body! She wants to touch his white body. We can sense the fantastic release afforded the listener by the long-delayed resolution to a B-major chord at measure 6. As Salome concludes her first stanza (measure 47), Jokanaan replies in what has become his customary style: "Zurück Tochter Babylons." He will hearken only to the word of the Lord. Scorned, Salome retorts venomously–his body is hideous (m. 63 ff.). She weakens, however, and renews her efforts (second stanza, not reprinted here), this time describing his hair. "Daughter of Sodom" is his answer, and Salome turns on him once again, comparing his hair to a crown of thorns, to serpents writhing round his neck.

Translation

Narraboth: Princess, I implore you. Go inside.

Salome: Jokanaan, I am amorous of your body! Jokanaan, your body is white as the lilies of a field never touched by a sickle. [19]Your body is white as the snows on the hills of Judaea. The roses in the garden of the Queen of Arabia are not so white as your body. [28]Neither the roses in the garden of the Queen, nor the feet of the dawn as it lights on the leaves, nor the breast of the moon on the ocean, nothing in the world is so white as your body. Let me touch your body.

Jokanaan: Stand back, Daughter of Babylon! Evil came into the world through woman. Don't speak to me. [55]I will not listen to you. I shall hearken only unto the voice of the Lord, my God.

Salome: Your body is horrible. It is like. . .

46-B

C. scene iii (cont.)

Finally, in her third stanza, Salome sighs with utmost passion. It is his mouth that she desires most. And as she describes it vividly in words, Strauss supports her text with a fittingly luscious accompaniment (mm. 1-25). Jokanaan must let her kiss his mouth, she cries (mm. 25-30). "Never!" he shouts. Salome's persistence is manifest in the repeated notes of the vocal part doubled in the orchestra (m. 35).

Translation

Salome: Your mouth is redder than the feet of the men who tread the wine, stamping in the winepress. It is redder than the feet of the doves who dwell in the temples. [10] Your mouth is like a coral branch in the twilight of the sea; like purple in the mines of Moab, the purple of kings. Nothing in the world is so red as your mouth. Let me kiss it, your mouth.

Jokanaan: [31] Never, Daughter of Babylon! Daughter of Sodom, never!

Salome: I want to kiss your mouth, Jokanaan.

500

D. scene iii (cont.)

Unwilling to take no for an answer, Salome continues to plead despairingly (m. 1), and after Jokanaan has cursed both her and her mother, Herodias, with greater urgency (m. 16), Strauss reflects this increased tension with frequent chromaticisms. Jokanaan is equally obdurate in his rejections of Salome's advances; his tenacity is emphasized by the use of the same type of melodic reiteration that Salome sings earlier (see Ex. 46-C, m. 35). Notice his vocal line at measures 21, 30-31, and 37-39.

Translation

Salome: Let me kiss your mouth, Jokanaan.

Jokanaan: [6]Be thou accursed, daughter of an incestuous mother. Be thou accursed.

Salome: [16]Let me kiss your mouth, Jokanaan.

Jokanaan: I will not look at you. Thou art accursed, Salome. Thou art [accursed.]

46-D

molto accelerando

33

J.

Du bist ver -

sfz

Strauss, *Salome*. Copyright assigned to Boosey & Hawkes Music Publishers Ltd. Reprinted by permission of Boosey & Hawkes, Inc.

E. scene iv

Although the music flows uninterruptedly throughout the single act of the opera, Strauss has divided the action into four scenes, with the orchestra continuing to play while the characters enter and exit. The drama builds to a climax in the third scene where Salome sees Jokanaan for the first time. In the middle of the fourth and final scene, after Salome performs the "Dance of the Seven Veils," she asks that Herod give her the head of Jokanaan as her reward. Horrified, the king offers her anything else in his kingdom, everything he has, but Salome, encouraged by her mother in this desire, will not be diverted. Her insistence is reflected in the use of the same melodic phrase she had used earlier with Jokanaan when she implored him first to let her touch his body, etc. (Ex. 46-B). Her wish granted, Salome sings to the head before her as Strauss reuses most of the themes associated with her and with the prophet. Notice the repeated notes at measures 14, 18-19, 35-36, 40-41. Another one of Salome's principal motives appears at measures 6-7 in the accompaniment and recurs throughout this excerpt. As the orchestra repeats the earlier passionate utterance of Salome (m. 48; see m. 19 in Ex. 46-B), Strauss makes one final comment on her personality with an abrupt clash of two keys at measure 49 (see * in the score below). The dissonance is shattering, a fitting climax to the act.

Strauss had been experimenting with the power of music to reflect various verbal and psychological concepts, as Mann has indicated in his excellent analyses of the operas. He achieved a resounding success with this work, in which musical characterization, orchestral sonority, and dramatic expression are combined with excellent results.

Translation

Herod: Something terrible will happen.

Salome: Ah, I have kissed your mouth, Jokanaan. Ah, I have kissed it, your mouth. [19]There was a bitter taste on your lips. Was it the taste of blood? No, but perhaps this is the taste of love...[31]They say that the taste of love is bitter...But what of that? What of that? I have kissed your mouth, Jokanaan. I have kissed it, your mouth.

Herod: This woman must be killed!

46-E

HEROD

Es wird Schreck - li - ches ge - schehn.

cresc.

8va

ff

ff

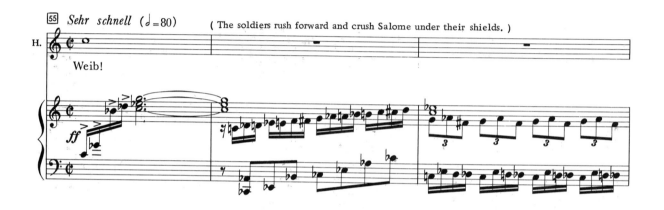

47. EXPRESSIONIST MONODRAMA

Erwartung (1909) *

Pappenheim
with suggestions by the composer   Arnold Schoenberg (1874-1951)

A complex, tightly-knit example of Schoenberg's early style, *Erwartung* (Expectation) was written in two weeks and requires about thirty minutes for performance. In his notes for the German premiere at Wiesbaden in 1928 (on a double bill with Busoni's *Turandot*), Paul Bekker noted the dramatic and musical links between this work and *Tristan*, but he also foresaw the importance of *Erwartung* for the future.

In 1913, Schoenberg wrote to the singer Marie Gutheil-Schoder (1874-1935) that the vocal part of his new work was conceived for her, and he asked her to consider the role despite its difficulty. In a letter to the Intendant (director) of the Berlin opera, the composer gives exceptionally precise performance instructions. He indicates, for example, that he is aware of the insufficient time he has allowed for the three scene changes. He knows these transformations must be managed without bringing the curtain down, and he suggests how this may be accomplished. For the fourth scene, another problem arises. The audience should be able to see the house in the background, while the forest must no longer be visible. Therefore, Schoenberg decides to send along a model with two revolving discs that he has made himself, hoping that this construction might be duplicated for the production.

Schoenberg had considered every detail of the composition. In a discussion of chords of six or more notes in his *Harmonielehre* (*Treatise on Harmony,* 1911), he describes a chord of eleven different notes and almost as many timbres, which he included in *Erwartung.* He explains that whereas the wide spacing of these notes softens the dissonance, the chord will still provide the required effect. In a few measures, Schoenberg has distilled the essence of pages of Wagner and Strauss. The zig-zag line of the vocal writing and even the personality of the woman, here seen searching for her lover who has left her for another, might be contrasted with the elegant young woman in Poulenc's *La Voix humaine* (Ex. 52). Mahler used to give every part in his scores a different dynamic marking in order to achieve his total effect. Schoenberg solved the problem otherwise, through the use of H and N (see mm. 2, 4, 7-8, etc.) to indicate *Hauptstimme* and *Nebenstimme* (principal part and subordinate part). Even so, except for measures 7, 11, and 45, every bar has at least one dynamic indication.

Our excerpt starts with scene iii, where the Woman continues looking for her lover in what is musically and textually an interlude before the fourth and final scene, the climax of the piece. Notice that Schoenberg has not left enough time for the *Verwandlung* (scene change) at measures 25-35. And as the fourth scene begins, we must be able to see the cottage in the rear of the stage with only traces of the forest at stage front. For here, near the home of the other woman, is where she will find the body of her lover.

For many years, all critical analysis of *Erwartung* centered on its apparently athematic or non-repetitive construction. The work's unity supposedly derived from the text alone. Recently, however, Herbert H. Buchanan (in JAMS, 1967) presented some logical arguments against this theory. In "A Key to Schoenberg's *Erwartung*," he lists three musical units as the basis of the "motivic material which provides cohesion throughout the primarily non-repetitive [piece]." Buchanan cites a textual and musical quotation from one of the composer's earlier works, the song "Am Wegrand," Op. 6, No. 6 (1905), which appears at a crucial point in the work (m. 411) at the start of the final climax, and he shows its significance in the unification of the whole piece. Buchanan also indicates Schoenberg's use of intervallic relationships, particularly the major-minor third intervallic cell, as well as a secondary theme from the same "Am Wegrand," all of which work to supply the essential unity.

---

*1924 in the Table of Contents refers to the date of the first performance.

Scene III. *(Path remains in darkness. To the side of the path, a wide, bright border. Moonlight falls on a glade of trees. Beyond, high grasses and ferns, large yellow toadstools. The Woman steps out of the darkness.)*

Woman: There comes a light! Oh, only the moon. How good. . .Something black is dancing there. . .A hundred hands. . .Don't be stupid. . .it's the shadows. [9]Oh, how your shadows fall on the white walls. . .But you must leave so soon. . .Are you calling? And is it so long until evening? But the shadow crawls. . .Still! [17]Yellow, wide eyes, popping as if on stems. . .How it stares. . .No animal, dear God, no animal. I'm so afraid. Darling, my darling, help me. . .

Scene IV. *(Moonlit, wide street coming out of the forest at right. Meadows and fields [yellow and green strips alternately]. A bit towards the left, the street disappears again in the gloom of clumps of tall trees. To the extreme left, one sees the street deserted. Beyond, there is also a path extending downward from a house. In it, all windows have dark, drawn shutters. A balcony out of white stone. The Woman enters slowly, exhausted. Her dress is torn, her hair dishevelled. Bloody scratches on her face and hands.)*

Woman: [36]He is not here either. Along the entire road no living thing and no sound. . .The wide, bleached fields are without breath, as if dead. Not a blade is stirring. . . [43]But always the city. . .and this pale moon. . .no cloud, not the shadow of a nightbird's wing in the heaven. . .

47

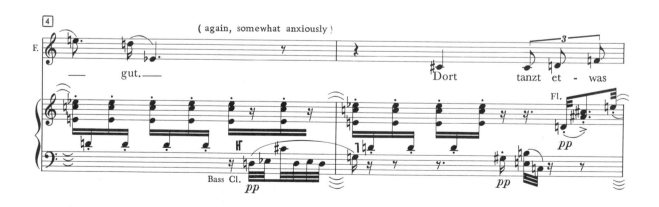

Schoenberg's *Erwartung,* piano reduction by Edward Steuermann (Universal, 1922). Used by permission of Belmont Music Publishers.

48. EXPRESSIONIST SPRECHSTIMME AND ARIA

Wozzeck (1925)

A. Act I, scene i

Berg
after Büchner

Alban Berg (1885-1935)

Berg, like Debussy and Strauss, set an entire play to music. And today, almost half a century after its completion, *Wozzeck* remains a landmark of contemporary opera. Berg writes that he did not intend to provoke operatic reforms through *Wozzeck*; rather, he was concerned with the Büchner drama as a social document and hoped that through his music he might strengthen the impact of the play on future audiences. Despite his avowed intentions, however, several of the techniques that Berg essayed in *Wozzeck* were soon appropriated by other composers, for example, *Sprechstimme,* a kind of recitative midway between speech and song, which Schoenberg applied earlier in *Pierrot Lunaire* (1912), and the use of instrumental forms as a means of operatic organization, a technique employed recently by Alberto Ginastera in *Bomarzo* (Ex. 53).

Wozzeck consists of fifteen scenes that the composer has divided equally into three acts of five scenes each. Each scene is a self-contained unit, based on instrumental forms such as suite, rhapsody, or sonata (see the following outline by Willi Reich, Berg's pupil). The music is continuous through scene changes. Indeed, one hears the full sonority of the large orchestra only during these interludes. Otherwise, it is used sparingly. In accordance with Berg's wishes, the complex musical organization of the opera does not, and should not, reveal itself to the audience, whose response to the opera must derive solely from the drama. Although the music demands prolonged and intensive analysis, we shall have to content ourselves with a superficial view of the

514

scheme of the work as indicated by the composer and a glance at some of the notational problems as they appear in the score. With regard to the text, George Perle, who is currently writing a book on the Berg operas, states that "with few exceptions, the only changes Berg made in the text of the individual scenes are such as would occur to a composer in the actual course of composition." Perle also attributes Berg's order of scenes to a 1919 publication of the Büchner play edited by Paul Landau (who first published this edition in 1909).

ACT I

Five Character Sketches

Scene 1. Suite (Ex. 48-A)

Scene 2. Rhapsody

Scene 3. Military March and Cradle Song (Ex. 48-B)

Scene 4. Passacaglia

Scene 5. Andante Affetuoso

ACT II

Symphony in Five Movements

Scene 1. Sonata-Form

Scene 2. Fantasie and Fugue (Ex. 48-C)

Scene 3. Largo (Ex. 48-D)

Scene 4. Scherzo (Ex. 48-E)

Scene 5. Rondo Martiale

ACT III

Six Inventions

Scene 1. Invention on a Theme (Variations and Fugue)

Scene 2. Invention on a Tone (Ex. 48-F)

Scene 3. Invention on a Rhythm

Scene 4. Invention on a Six-note Chord (Ex. 48-G)

Instrumental Interlude. Invention on a Key (d minor)

Scene 5. Invention on a Persistent Rhythm (Perpetuum Mobile)

Except possibly for *Bomarzo* (Ex. 53), no excerpt in our anthology displays comparable intricacies of notation (see below). Frequent changes of tempo, meter, texture, dynamics, and range coupled with the exceedingly complex harmonic and melodic progressions present extraordinary problems to the performers. Tempo changes often relate proportionally to one another (notice the metronome markings at mm. 10 and 21). The composer, always compulsive in his habits, has notated very precise performance instructions and supplied every note with its own accidental. Berg also used the previously cited H and N (see p. 509) that Schoenberg employs in *Erwartung* (Ex. 47) to indicate principal and subsidiary lines. Berg contrasts the sections of the work by means of differing instrumentation. Our first excerpt from the Suite (I, i) features a rhythmic motive associated with the words "Jawohl, Herr Hauptmann" at measures 5-6 and 23-25. An even more significant musico-textual theme that appears frequently in the course of the opera is the expression "Wir arme Leut' " (Us poor people") to the notes

wir ar - me Leut'

The jagged vocal line, typical of Berg's style throughout this opera, appears here in the interrogation of the poor soldier Wozzeck by the sadistic Captain (Hauptmann). Notice the word-painting on "wind" at measures 25-28. To underline the sent-entious and moralistic remarks of the Captain (m. 10 ff.), Berg has accompanied the vocal line with a sentimental viola cadenza.

Translation

Captain: No longer see the mill-wheel, I'll become melancholy.

Wozzeck: Yes sir, Captain.

Captain: [7]Wozzeck, he always looks so harassed. A good man doesn't act that way. A good man who has a good conscience does everything slowly. [18]Do say something Wozzeck. How's the weather today?

Wozzeck: Very bad, sir, Captain. Wind!

Captain: I feel it already. . .

48-A

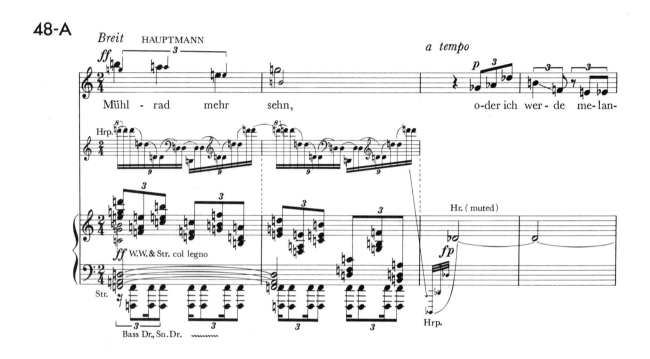

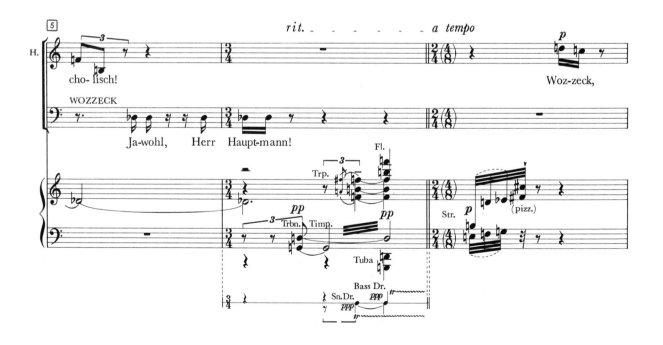

Etwas langsamer (♩=circa 48-54), aber sehr frei

Er sieht immer so ver- hetzt aus!   Ein   gu - ter Mensch tut das nicht.

sehr frei, quasi Cadenz

Solo Vla.   6

sentimental

Wieder im Takt

Ein gu - ter Mensch, der sein gu - tes Ge - wis - sen hat,   tut al -

(Solo Vla.)

poco f

- les lang - sam...

4 Hrn.

Tub.

Basses

(p)

(Solo Vla.)

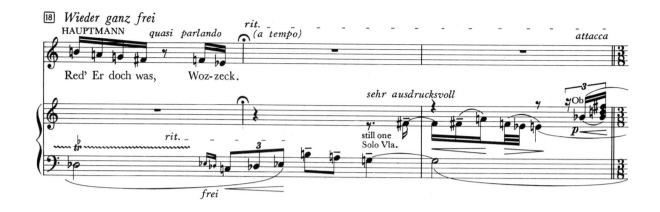

HAUPTMANN

Berg's *Wozzeck,* piano arrangement by Fritz Heinrich Klein (Universal, 1931, 1958). Used by permission.

B. Marie's Lullaby, Act I, scene iii

In Marie's Lullaby, we can observe Berg's solution to the problem of song in opera (cf. Mozart's solution in Ex. 19). Fully conscious of the need for "introducing passages in the style of popular music, and of thus establishing in my operas a relationship between art-music and popular music," he explains that "to everything that musically fell within the popular sphere [he gave] an easily perceptible primitive character" (cf. Berg's views on *Wozzeck,* printed on p. 261 ff. in the Appendix of Hans Redlich's *Alban Berg*). The means Berg used include symmetrical, balanced phrases (notice the two-bar introduction followed by 4 + 4 in $\frac{6}{8}$, 4 + 4 in $\frac{3}{4}$, and each phrase group repeated); intervals of a fourth, which suggest a quasi-tonal, though non-triadic harmony; melodies based on whole-tone scales in contrast to the diminished and augmented intervals that characterize the vocal line in other sections of the opera. Furthermore, the Lullaby includes nonsense syllables, universally understood, even by the unsophisticated. In this excerpt, Berg calls for a chamber orchestra (differentiating the texture from the surrounding material), and also, as if to emphasize Marie's loneliness, empty 5ths at measure 43 ff. (We might compare Verdi's use of the same interval in the Willow Song in *Otello,* Ex. 37-B).

Translation

Marie: Hush-a-bye, baby! Young lady, what are you about to start? You've a small child, but no spouse. [7]Why bother about it now! I'll sing the whole night long: Hush-a-bye, baby, my darling son, nobody cares, ne'er a one. [19]Hansel, saddle your horses now. Feed them enough and to spare. No oats to eat today. No water to drink today. [27]Nothing but wine shall it be! Nothing but wine shall it be!

48-B

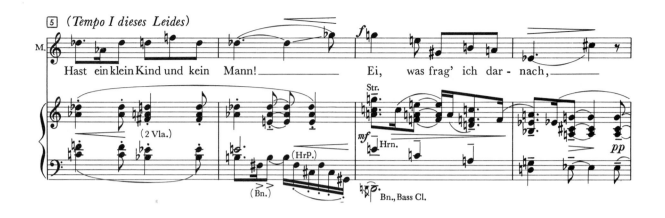

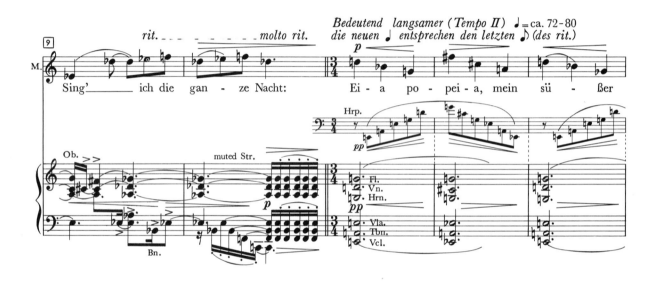

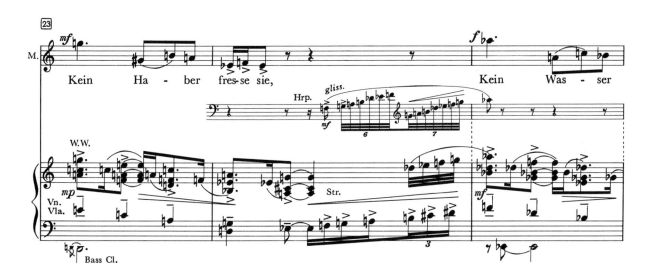

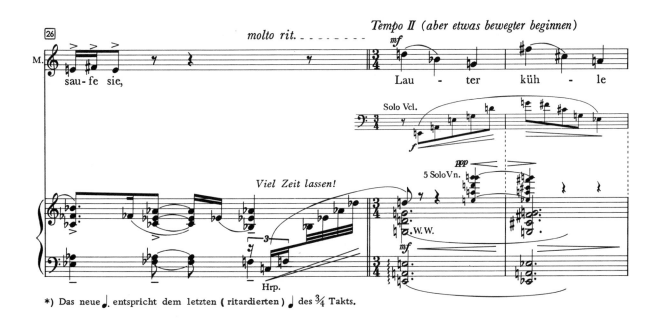

*) Das neue ♩. entspricht dem letzten (ritardierten) ♩ des ¾ Takts.

Berg's *Wozzeck*, piano arrangement by Fritz Heinrich Klein (Universal, 1931, 1958). Used by permission.

C. Conversation, Act II, scene ii

In the following conversation (a segment of the Fantasie and Fugue from the second act), the Captain and the Doctor begin their relentless verbal attack on Wozzeck. Here they start to taunt him about the promiscuity of his mistress, Marie. We hear first the Captain's theme (m. 1) as it appeared at the very opening of the opera. Berg deliberately gives the Captain a jagged vocal line in a choppy rhythm (observe the roots of this style in m. 54 of Ex. 46-E), while setting Wozzeck's part as a conjunct melody (of even eighth notes) that begins to skip as the soldier becomes increasingly agitated. Berg includes one of Wozzeck's motives (from II, i) as the soldier comments that the earth is hot as hell to some people; the Doctor's motive appears at measures 11-12 in the vocal part. Notice that in these measures the tritone pierces all three voice parts. We might compare this conversation with its counterpart in Puccini's *La Bohème* (Ex. 43-A).

Translation

Captain: Incidentally, a pair of lips! Oh, I, too, once knew the meaning of love! But fellow, you're white as chalk!

Wozzeck: Captain, I'm just a poor devil! I've got nothing in this world! If you're joking, sir. . .

Captain: [9]Joke! I? That you. . .a joke, man?

Wozzeck: Captain, to some the earth is hot as hell, and hell is so cold beside it.

Doctor: [11]Your pulse, Wozzeck! Short, hard, arhythmic! Facial muscles stiff, taut, eyes fixed.

Captain: Man, do you want to shoot yourself? He's piercing me with his eyes! [13]I mean well by you, for you're a good fellow, Wozzeck, a good fellow!

Wozzeck: Captain, it's quite likely. . .for men, it's quite likely. . .Good God! You could delight in hanging yourself! Then you'd know just where you stood!

48-C

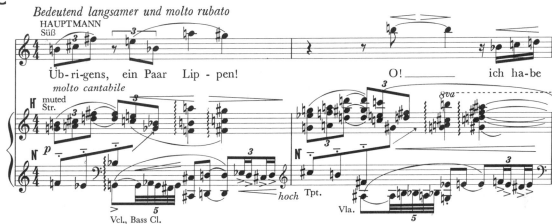

Berg's *Wozzeck,* piano arrangement by Fritz Heinrich Klein (Universal, 1931, 1958). Used by permission.

D. Marie and Wozzeck, Act II, scene iii

Berg allows only seven bars for this scene change into the slow movement (Largo) of the symphony, which is the structural form of this section of the opera. A chamber orchestra of fifteen instruments (modeled on Schoenberg's Chamber Symphony, No. 1, Op. 9) accompanies this confrontation between Marie and Franz Wozzeck. (Notice that here Marie uses his first name.) In the preface to the orchestral score, Berg defines *Sprechstimme* as a kind of rhythmic declamation, for the performance of which the foreward to Schoenberg's *Pierrot Lunaire* and the score of *Die glückliche Hand* should be consulted. In Berg's shortened preface these instructions appear:

> The melodies in the vocal part which are distinguished by special notes are not to be sung. The performer has the task of changing them into a spoken melody while taking into account the pitch of the notes. This is achieved by:
>
> 1. adhering very precisely to the rhythm (and note values), allowing no more freedom than in normal singing:
>
> 2. being aware of the difference between singing and speaking voices: in singing the performer stays on the note without changes; in speaking he strikes the note but leaves it immediately by rising or falling in pitch, but always bringing out the relative pitches of the notes.
>
> The performer must take great care not to fall into a singing manner of speaking. This is not what the composer intends; nor does he desire a realistic, natural manner of speaking. On the contrary, the difference between ordinary speech and speech that can be used in music should be clear. On the other hand there should be no suggestion of singing.[1]

Notice the notation for *Sprechstimme* beginning at measure 12.

Translation

Marie: Good day, Franz.

Wozzeck: I see nothing! I see nothing! Oh, one should see. One should be able to sieze it with one's fingers!

Marie: What's the matter, Franz?

Wozzeck: [16]Is that you, Marie? A sin so great that the stench could drive the angels from heaven! But you have a rosy mouth, a rosy mouth. No blister on it?

Marie: [21]You're raving, Franz. I'm frightened.

Wozzeck: You're beautiful as sin. But can mortal sin be so fair, Marie. There! Did he stand there? Like this?

Marie: [26]I can't forbid people their right of way. . .

Wozzeck: Devil! Did he stand there?

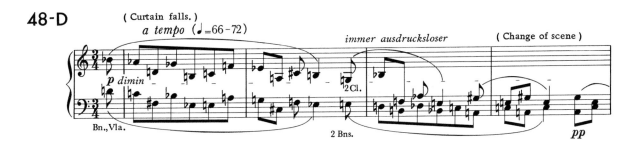

[1] From the full score, Universal Edition, A. Kalmus translation.

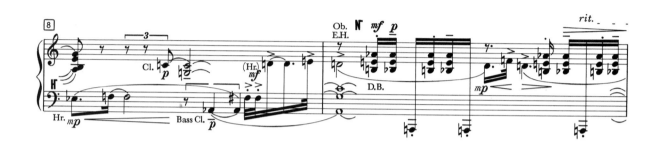

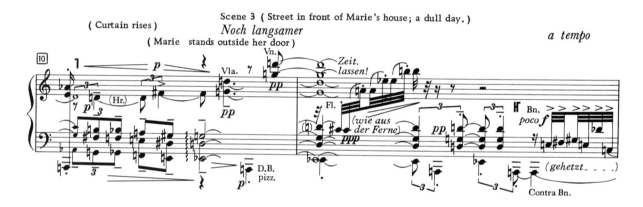

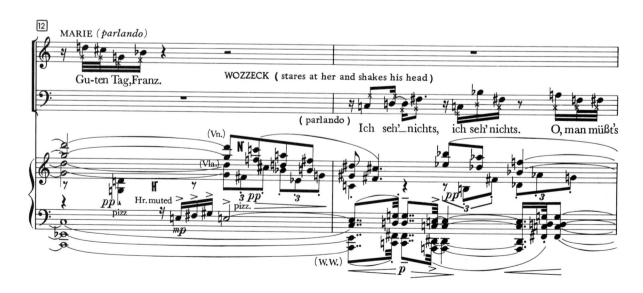

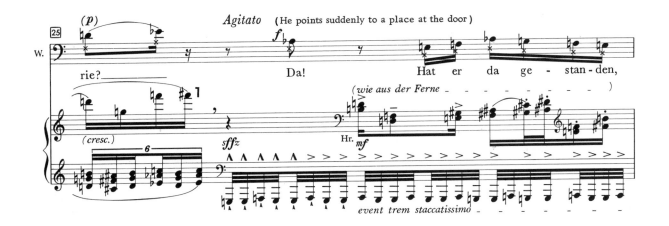

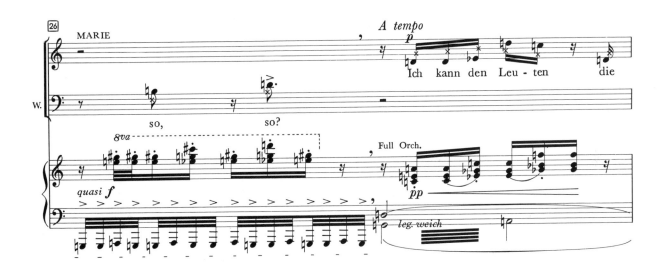

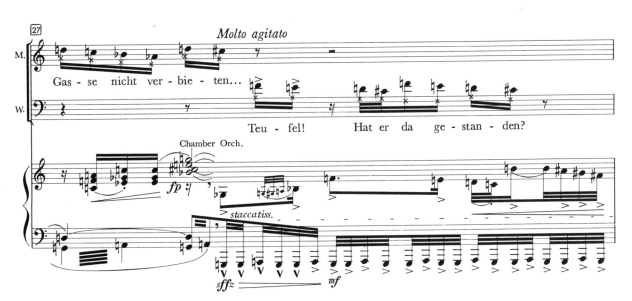

Berg's *Wozzeck,* piano arrangement by Fritz Heinrich Klein (Universal, 1931, 1958). Used by permission.

E. Hunters' Chorus, Act II, scene iv.

A hunters' chorus at the tavern comprises the second trio of the scherzo of the five-movement symphony (which forms the second act). By means of the irregular meter and erratic harmony of their song, Berg portrays the disorderly clientele at the tavern. Again, the set piece grows naturally out of the dramatic situation (cf. comment on Lullaby, Ex. 48-B).

Translation

Chorus: A hunter from the south was riding through a shady grove! Hallee, Hallo! Oh happy is the hunter's life from morning unto night! Hallee, Hallo!

Andres: [9] Oh, daughter, dearest daughter, what thought you my love, when [flirting] with the coachman. . .

48-E

Berg's *Wozzeck*, piano arrangement by Fritz Heinrich Klein (Universal, 1931, 1958). Used by permission.

F. The Murder Scene, Act III, scene ii

Six inventions provide the musical substructure of Act III (see outline, p. 515). For the accompaniment, Berg again chooses a transparent texture, whose thinner instrumentation contrasts sharply with the density of the very short orchestral interlude that follows (mm. 12-26). Our excerpt opens and closes on the note B, which is sustained as a pedal point throughout the entire scene and culminates in a huge orchestral crescendo, thus justifying Berg's title: "Invention on a Tone." Notice the ominous tritone in Wozzeck's opening vocal melody (m. 3), and also observe the significant stage direction (m. 2). Berg, who believed that an operatic composer must also be a stage director, paid particular attention to extra-musical details. During this scene, in good performances of the opera, the color of the moon will change to a fiery red at the moment of the murder.

Translation

Wozzeck: Nothing!

Marie: How red is the rising moon!

Wozzeck: Like a blood-red iron!

Marie: [6]Why do you tremble? What do you want?

Wozzeck: If not I, Marie, then none other!

Marie: Help!

Wozzeck: Dead!

48-F

Berg's *Wozzeck*, piano arrangement by Fritz Heinrich Klein (Universal, 1931,1958). Used by permission.

G. Wozzeck's death, Act III, scene iv

Ironically, or perhaps typically for Berg, in the scene that is most accessible dramatically—the one in which music and drama combine to produce several moments of the utmost tension in the audience—Berg has written the most intricate pattern of melodic/harmonic structural relationships. This scene, "The Invention on a Six-Note Chord" (hexachord), will disclose the design of its tightly woven musical fabric only to those willing to devote hours to separating the threads. A vertical set (hexachord) forms the underpinning of the scene. This is not the only verticalized set that the composer includes in *Wozzeck*, but it is unusual in its components. George Perle (see his superb article, "The Musical Language of Wozzeck", in *Music Forum*, Vol. 1) describes this set as "a five-note segment of the cycle of 5ths plus one odd note." Perle (see his Ex. 68-B) piles the notes vertically as a chord and also arranges them melodically, calling them by their enharmonic equivalents (see below).

Obviously, there are times when melodic/harmonic uses are not always distinct from one another (see m. 4 and mm. 8-9). However, we can indicate at least two melodic uses of the set readily visible in the voice parts of the aforementioned measures. Actually, Berg has used the hexachord as

(1) a chord: either in the original disposition or, more typically, rearranged at the original level [which cannot be found in this excerpt] or transposed [numerous examples are contained within our excerpt]; or

(2) melodically: as a "trope" in Josef Hauer's sense of the term, that is, an unordered pitch collection with specific intervallic content, but no assigned sequence at the original level or transposed.

Translation

Wozzeck: I don't find it. But I must wash myself. I'm bloody. Here's a spot, and there another.
  [5]Woe! Woe! I'm washing myself with blood! The water is blood. . . Blood. . .

48-G

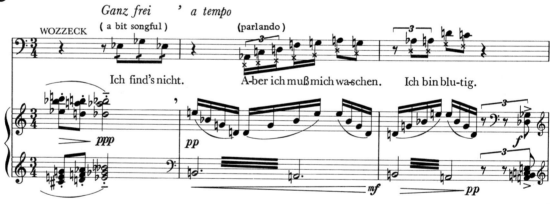

538

Berg's *Wozzeck,* piano arrangement by Fritz Heinrich Klein (Universal, 1931, 1958). Used by permission.

49. FOLK OPERA

Porgy and Bess (1935)

A. Recitative, Act I

Du Bose Heyward
Ira Gershwin

George Gershwin (1898-1937)

Porgy and Bess was George Gershwin's last major work. Earlier in his career, he had written numerous Broadway shows and pieces for piano and orchestra. Unlike Milhaud or Copland, both of whom approached American popular music as an exotic element with which to spice their art music, Gershwin was "doing what comes naturally." Because of his prior experience in the musical theater, where separate pieces or numbers were the norm, most of the arias, choruses, and ensembles in *Porgy and Bess* are similarly complete and self-contained units. This does not imply that Gershwin never wrote continuous music. At times, he did. As a matter of record, he seems to have been perfectly aware of traditional as well as contemporary techniques of text setting. He uses both types of recitative, spoken dialogue, and on occasion, a kind of *Sprechstimme* (compare Ex. 48). Our first excerpt illustrates a section of continuous music with measures 1-2 and 9 in accompanied recitative that contrasts with the quasi-*Sprechstimme* at measure 7. In a statement quoted in David Ewen's biography of him, Gershwin comments that he tried to make his recitatives correspond as closely as possible to Negro speech inflection. With regard to the songs, Gershwin said: "I have written songs for *Porgy and Bess.* . . . But songs are entirely within the operatic tradition."

Armed with an excellent story, which was fashioned into a fine libretto through the collaboration of Du Bose Heyward, author of the original story, and Ira Gershwin, the composer's brother, Gershwin produced a singular work, an exciting contemporary, three-act folk opera with singable tunes that remained with audiences after the curtain fell. Hardly a man writing today can best that record.

49-A

*) Symbols indicate direction of voice and approximate pitch.

B. The Buzzard's Song

The Buzzard's Song is one of the least known numbers from the opera, perhaps as a result of its atypical form. Closer to the traditional aria than to the popular song, the piece is shaped into an ABA' design.

When Mr. Archdale arrives, he first scolds Frazier for selling fake divorces and then tells Porgy that he has arranged for Peter's release from jail. As Archdale leaves, Porgy notices a buzzard flying overhead. Comments from Porgy, the chorus, and then Archdale precede the beginning of the song (m. 14). Notice the trill in the treble (m. 3) and the chromatic scales in the bass (mm. 7-8) that Gershwin uses to create the eerie atmosphere of the supernatural (compare Ex. 30). For similar reasons, the composer incorporates the ominous sound of the tritone in the bass at measures 3-5 and at outlying points of the first chord in measure 6 (G-C♯). The vocal part consists of an essentially conjunct melody with leaps at measure 20 (later at m. 63) and at measure 27 (later at m. 70) to underline the text. The first verse ends at measure 30. Four sinister-sounding bars lead to the middle section—a few bars of reiterated notes followed by a declamatory interlude at measures 42-52—and a snippet of *Sprechstimme* provides a transition into the last verse, which then begins at measure 57. Cross relations (A against A♭), 9ths, and a recurrent chromatic sextuplet in the accompaniment set the mood of the piece, which concludes with the chorus's echoing a portion of Porgy's last phrase (m. 70 ff.). The text offers a sample of the kind of dialect that appears throughout the opera. Gershwin deleted this song after the Boston opening in an effort to shorten Porgy's exhausting role. It was reinstated in 1952, when an all-Negro company took *Porgy and Bess* to Europe on a spectacularly successful tour. In a highly laudatory review of the opera after its first Berlin performance, H. H. Stuckenschmidt, the eminent musical journalist, author of a biography of Schoenberg, and one of the foremost spokesmen for modern music, wrote:

"Is it an opera? Certainly not if we measure it with the same yardstick as we use for Wagner and Debussy. . . . Neither music drama nor lyric drama, *Porgy and Bess* must be compared instead with the great folk operas, the Singspiel or the early buffa. On every score, it comes out on top![1]

[1] H. H. Stuckenschmidt's *Oper in dieser Zeit* (Hannover, Germany: Friedrich Verlag, 1964), p. 72.

Ha, ha, ha, ha, ha! Ha! _____ Buz-zard, on yo' way!

Ole age, what is you a - ny - how,

nut - tin' but be - in' lone - ly. _____

Pack yo' things an' fly from here, _____

Car - ry grief an' pain._____ Dere's two folks liv - in'

in dis shel - ter Eat - in', sleep - in', sing - in', pray - in'.

Ain' no such thing___ as lone - li - ness.___ An' Por - gy's young a -

Grave

gain._____

50. RECITATIVE AND ARIA IN TRADITIONAL OPERA
Peter Grimes (1945)

A. Act II, scene i

Slater
after Crabbe

Benjamin Britten (b. 1913)

With few exceptions, all of Benjamin Britten's compositions include the human voice. Britten, an exceptionally prolific composer, established himself in the front rank of contemporary musicians with his early opera *Peter Grimes*, commissioned by the Koussevitsky Foundation. For his subject, Britten selected *The Borough*, a poem by the eighteenth-century writer George Crabbe, in which the story of Peter Grimes is told through a sequence of twenty-four letters. The composer brought the material to Montagu Slater, who made the necessary changes that included updating the action to the early nineteenth century, eliminating the heroic couplets of the original and substituting a more modern text, and compressing the material into a libretto of three acts of two scenes each. Britten then added an opening prologue (no overture) to acquaint the audience with events that had occurred earlier. (Compare Ex. 2-A and Ex. 51-B.) With his obvious theatrical flair, Britten, who had already worked in radio and films, seems to have added an extra dimension to music for opera. For example, he experimented with the use of music at different levels—foreground, background, and intermediate—to produce what White, his biographer, calls "cross-fading." This feature proves particularly helpful for scenes in which overlapping actions call for music on several levels. (Mozart and Berg wrote for two or more groups of players simultaneously. Here, however, Britten arranges these sounds as if using a radio engineer's mixing panel.)

Britten expressed himself in favor of continuous music, but he also recognized the need for set numbers where the libretto demanded them. To achieve continuous music, Britten links the prologue and each of the scenes within each act by means of orchestral interludes. With regard to set numbers, our first excerpt shows how they grow naturally out of the drama. Ellen, the widowed school mistress, and Peter's new apprentice are sitting on the beach when she discovers a bruise on the boy's body. While the faint, but distinct sound of the church service filters through from offstage, Ellen starts questioning Peter about the boy (m. 2). Her aria begins at measure 5; Peter's interjections (mm. 6-7 and m. 14) reflect his embittered personality. The musical phrase of Peter's last cry (mm. 26-27), after he has struck Ellen, becomes a principal motive for the balance of the opera. Other characters in the following section (m. 31 ff.) derive their musical material from this phrase, and their cynical "Grimes is at his exercise!" reaches a climax at the conclusion of our example. The melody of this phrase appears in augmentation as the ground bass of the passacaglia interlude that follows this scene.

50-A

552

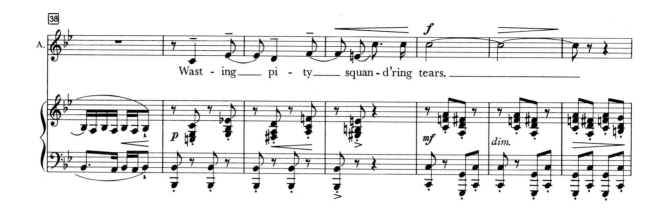

(poco meno _ _ _ _ _ _ _ _ _ _ _ _ _ _ _ _)   (The service is over and

Par - son, law - yer,   all___ at   prayers!___

Par - son, law - yer,   all___ at   prayers!___

Par - son, law - yer,   all___ at   prayers!___   Now___

people gradually collect outside the church door.)

Now_____ the church pa - rade be-gins.

Now_____ the church pa - rade be-gins.

the church pa - rade be-gins.

Fresh be - gin - ning___ for___ fresh sins.___

Fresh be - gin - ning___ for___ fresh sins.___

Fresh be - gin - ning___ for___ fresh sins.___

557

Britten, *Peter Grimes.* Copyright 1945 by Boosey and Hawkes, Ltd. Reprinted by permission of Boosey and Hawkes, Inc.

B. Prologue

The English language is notoriously difficult to set to music. Because he has proven himself to be among the most gifted in his endeavors in this direction, we might note Britten's comments on recitative.

> Good recitative should transform the natural intonations and rhythms of everyday speech into memorable musical phrases (as with Purcell), but in more stylized music the composer should not deliberately avoid unnatural stresses if the prosody demand them, nor be afraid of a high-handed treatment of words, which may need prolongation beyond their common speech length or a speed of delivery that would be impossible in conversation.[2]

Our excerpt contains two different types of recitative: accompanied recitative (mm. 2-3), and unaccompanied recitative that is also *senza misura* (free, without strict rhythmic values). Notice the dotted vertical lines, which the composer placed there to give the singer an idea of the pace and accent of the declamation.

[2] Eric Walter White, *Benjamin Britten: A Sketch of His Life and Works,* 2nd. ed. (London: Boosey & Hawkes, 1954), p. 109.

Peter____ we shall re-store your name____ warmed by the

new es-teem that you will find.

f energico

Un-til the Bo-rough hate...

Britten, *Peter Grimes.* Copyright 1945 by Boosey and Hawkes, Ltd. Reprinted by permission of Boosey and Hawkes, Inc.

51. RECITATIVE, ARIA, AND ENSEMBLE IN NEO-CLASSICAL OPERA
The Rake's Progress (1951)

Auden and Kallman

Igor Stravinsky (b. 1882)

It would seem that *The Rake's Progress* represents the culmination of Stravinsky's neo-classical compositions. Although he had previously set Russian, French, and Latin texts, this was Stravinsky's first major work in English. As such, Robert Craft tells us, "He was very concerned with singability, with vowel sounds in vocal ranges, with the effect of words on vocal quality and the other way around." [3] He wanted every word to be heard. Stravinsky believes that music drama and opera are two very different things, and he has devoted his efforts to the latter. Certainly in *The Rake's Progress* we have a bona fide Mozartian opera buffa with secco and accompanied recitatives usually with prose texts, and arias, duets, choruses, and ensembles generally with verse texts. There are three acts of three scenes each, and an Epilogue. Each scene is complete in itself.

In our excerpt, Tom Rakewell has just expressed a wish for money. Nick Shadow appears with the news of Tom's inheritance. He presents his news in secco recitative and continues (our excerpt) in an aria. In the following Quartet (m. 40 ff.), Tom delights in his good luck and thanks Nick for the news; Nick, in turn, thanks him because he (Nick) has found a new master; Anne, Tom's fiancee, and Truelove, her father, thank God for Tom's good fortune. Notice the imitative entries on "Be thanked" set to a descending 9th. Observe also the allegorical implications in the last names of the characters.

51-A (Tom rushes into the house, and Nick reaches over the garden gate, unlatches it, enters the garden and walks forward. Tom reenters from the house with Anne and Trulove.)

(♩ = 96)

mf

(*col 8va ad lib.*)

[3] Robert Craft, "A Personal Preface" in *The Score,* XX (June, 1957).

560

The fate-ful end of quest-ion-ing   Here by   A new

and grate-ful mas-ter's side____ Be   thanked, and as my For-tune and my guide__

____ Re - main, con - firm, de - ny _____

NICK

Be   thanked, for mas-ter-less

Stravinsky, *The Rake's Progress*. Copyright 1949, 1950, 1951 by Boosey & Hawkes, Inc.
Reprinted by permission.

B. scene ii

Before the close of the first scene, Nick turns to the audience and says: "The Progress of a Rake begins!" We might compare the opening words of La Musica in the Prologue from Monteverdi's *Orfeo* (Ex. 2-A) and note the similar intentions of the two composers: to explain to the audience the action that follows. The curtain falls, and when it rises again after an orchestral introduction (m. 1-60), we are in Mother Goose's Brothel (inspired of course by Hogarth's picture). The bouncy chorus of the Whores and Roaring Boys sounds like a combination of C major and e minor. The casual listener senses something awry, out of focus. Boys and girls sing alternately and then together. Notice the syncopation (m. 65 and m. 71), the irregular phrasing (m. 79-80), and the modulation to B major at measures 27-28. Stravinsky seems to have written this piece with tongue in cheek.

51-B Mother Goose's Brothel, London. (At a table, downstage right, sit Tom, Nick and Mother Goose drinking. Backstage left a Cuckoo Clock...... Whores, Roaring Boys.)

571

ROARING BOYS

Tenors

With air com-man-ding and wea-pon han-dy We rove in a band

Basses

through the streets at night, Our on - ly no-tion to make com - mo - tion

And find oc - ca-sion to pro-voke a fight, to pro-voke a fight.

WHORES
Sopranos

In tri - umph glo-ri-ous with tro-phies cu-ri-ous We re - turn vic -

Altos

to - ri-ous from Love's cam - paigns; No troops more prac-tised

ROARING BOYS

WHORES

With dar - ting glan-ces and bold ad - van - ces We o - pen fire u-pon

young and old; Sur - prised by rap-ture, their hearts are

cap - tured, And in - to our laps they pour their gold.

Stravinsky, *The Rake's Progress.* Copyright 1949, 1950, 1951 by Boosey & Hawkes, Inc.
Reprinted by permission.

52. ARIOSO IN FRENCH MONODRAMA

La Voix humaine (1958)

A. Opening

Cocteau   Francis Poulenc (1899-1963)

Because a monodrama makes singular demands on a performer, it poses certain
problems for its creator as well. We have seen how carefully Schoenberg approached the
issue in *Erwartung* (Ex. 47). Certainly Poulenc, too, concerned himself with the
difficulties of having only one person on stage throughout the duration of the piece, of
engaging this character in a telephone conversation of which the audience hears only
half (and must be able to surmise the other portion), of pacing the part with a sense of
the physical limitations of the singer. Yet somehow or other a chasm separates these
two works. Possibly the differences between them reflect their different national origins.
Schoenberg's Frau is Woman, earthy German woman. Her experience is traumatic. We

are deeply shaken even before the curtain falls. Poulenc's Madame has feelings; she suffers, and despite its being easier to identify with her than with the Frau, her anguish seems superficial by comparison. Poulenc's music does her justice. It portrays a tight, restrained, tense, but also chic and elegant Parisienne, with all that the word Parisienne implies.

The piece opens with a short orchestral introduction. The composer's choice of intervals (the cross relation and the tritone in the first three bars), sporadic rests, and frequent tempo changes suggest the woman's uncertainty. Madame is awaiting a call from her lover, and her anxiety mounts each time the phone rings and it is not he. Poulenc, possessed of an excellent sense of prosody, has wisely left her voice part unaccompanied so that we hear her words clearly. The orchestra simply punctuates her phrases. Notice that the orchestral tissue is far more transparent than in the Schoenberg piece.

Translation

Madame: Hello, hello.   But no, Madame. This is a party line. Hang up. [24] You're on with one
   of your party-liners. But Madame, get off the line. Hello, operator! Oh, no, this is not...

52-A

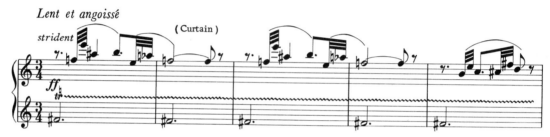

Madame has been disconnected and asks the operator to re-dial her lover's apartment. Here she finds Joseph, his houseman, but Monsieur is not at home. "Of course!" she quickly replies, concealing her embarrassment. "Tonight is not his night home. How stupid of me!" The long pause at measure 24 highlights the next section where her lover finally calls (m. 29 ff.). The tritone still appears in the orchestra, but Madame sounds more animated, less irritated. She is in control of herself, concerned with keeping up appearances. Later on, we find one of the few genuine lyrical effusions, as Madame reminisces with her lover about their past shared experiences. Most of the monodrama, however, is set in an arioso style, halfway between recitative and aria. Notice that the orchestra, too, is subdued, mostly *piano,* the *fortissimo* at measure 25 stressing Madame's anxiety. At no time does the orchestra obscure the vocal part. We might also mention here that this monodrama is not divided into scenes, as *Erwartung* is. Poulenc reduces dynamics and density of texture on occasion to give the illusion of the start of a new section, but he has not indicated separate scenes as Schoenberg has done.

Translation

Hello, Operator, he's calling me back. . .All right, Hello! Autueil 0477? Hello! It's you, Joseph?. . .It's Madame. . .Someone has disconnected us, Monsieur and I. . .Not there?. . .Yes, yes. . .he's not coming home tonight. . .[13]Really, how stupid of me! Monsieur must have telephoned me from a restaurant. We were disconnected so I re-dialed his number. Excuse me Joseph. . .Thank you. Good night, Joseph. [29]Hello, ah! chéri! It's you? We were cut off. . .No, no I was waiting. Someone rang, I picked up the receiver, but there was nobody on the line. . .Undoubtedly. . .Of course. [36]You're sleepy? It was kind of you to have called, very kind. . .No, I am here. What?

Forgive me, it's silly, Nothing, nothing, there's nothing wrong. [43]I swear to you there's nothing wrong. It's the same. Not at all. You're mistaken. Only, you understand, they talk, this talk. . .Listen to me, my love. I have never lied to you. Yes, I know, I know. I believe you. [53]I'm sure of it. . .No, it's not that, it's because I just lied to you. . .

52-B

583

C. Conclusion of the Act

At the close of the monodrama, notice that the pitch of Madame's voice is higher (mm. 1-2). Observe her desperate cry at measure 4, and the *fff,* one of the few in the score, as the distraught woman loses her composure and gives in completely to her emotions. Poulenc, a born melodist, has made minimal use of extended lyricism in this 45-minute tragedy. The composer created the part for Denise Duval, who had sung the leading roles in Poulenc's two earlier operas, *Les Mamelles de Tirésias* and *Les Dialogues des Carmélites.* In the score he gives the following precise instructions for the presentation of the piece:

1. The solo role of *La Voix humaine* must be played by a young and elegant woman. This is not a matter of an aging woman whose lover has abandoned her.
2. All fermata depend on the performer. These rests are very important and the conductor and singer should decide in advance on the exact amount of time for each pause.
3. Vocal passages without accompaniment must be in free tempo. Move rapidly from anguish to repose and vice versa throughout the piece.
4. The entire work should be bathed in the sensuality of the orchestra.

Translation

Hang up! Hang up, quickly! I love you, I love you, I love you. . .love you. . .

52-C

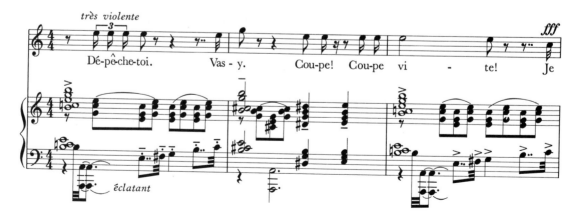

Poulenc's *La Voix humaine.* © 1959 by Editions Ricordi, Paris. By permission of the Publisher. All Rights Reserved.

53. RECITATIVE, ARIA, AND CHORUS IN SERIAL OPERA
Bomarzo (1967)

Láinez   Alberto Ginastera (b. 1916)

Like many of his contemporaries, Ginastera, the leading Argentine composer, concerns himself very much with different styles of recitative. In *Don Rodrigo* (1964), for example, a note affixed to the score suggests that in this work the singer employ spoken and sung language as well as its diverse combinations. To differentiate between the various types of recitative, the following instructions are given:

I. Speech with prosodic rhythm: Rodrigo

II. Speech with musical rhythm:

Rod-ri - go

In those cases where the pitch may be high, medium, or low, it will be indicated accordingly:

III. Speech with relative pitch:

Rod-ri - go

IV. Speech-Song:

Rod-ri - go

V. Singing:

Rod-ri - go

In passages in recitative, the figuration indicates the relative speed of the syllables:

Rod-ri - go   to   Rod-ri - go

In *Bomarzo,* his newest opera, which has had fantastic success in the United States, Ginastera has given the chorus a most unusual role. Seated with the orchestral players, at times it performs traditionally, commenting on the action. At other times, Ginastera directs the chorus to hum a "labial glissando" moving up and down an interval of a whole tone (m. 12), to whisper (*susurrar*) the name "Bomarzo" (m. 5ff.), and to utter the following consonants, L J G K P N, *senza voce* (m. 15) to suggest the stone monsters in Bomarzo's garden attempting to speak. All of these sounds contribute to the weird, unnatural atmosphere that Ginastera seeks. (See Ex. 53-A.)

Pier Francesco, the Duke of Bomarzo, is about to die. Between the time he has swallowed poison and the time it begins to take effect, a period of approximately fifteen seconds, the events of his life pass before him and the audience in rapid review. Of course, we are not dealing with real time, nor for that matter do we know what is real and what is illusion at any time during the opera; rather, it is the interplay of reality and fantasy that enchants us for the duration of the fifteen scenes of the music drama. Ginastera places equal emphasis on music and drama, and although he shows clearly the influence of Debussy and Berg, we find a unique quality to his music that cannot be described apart from the actual aural and visual sensation of the opera itself.

Our excerpts include two different styles of recitative by the chorus, as well as an extraordinary example of style stratification: a medieval antiphon, *O Rex gloriae,* Example 53-B, in a twentieth-century harmonization (in the full score). Finally, the composer has permitted us to reprint a portion of an aria, the "Rituel del círcolo mágico" (Rite of the Magic Circle) taken from the scene known as "El Horoscopo" (The Horoscope). Here the singer is requested to sing in microtones, pitches that lie between the semitones on the piano keyboard. Whereas string players and trombonists can play these notes without too much difficulty, singers must practice this technique rigorously before they can achieve the intonation with confidence. Observe the notation of these pitches (marked by the editor with an *) in our third excerpt (Ex. 53-C).

In this last excerpt of our anthology, we should like to quote Ginastera's most informative comments in a recent interview (*The New York Times,* February 14, 1968). In Argentina, it had been charged that *Bomarzo* is obsessed with sex and violence. Ginastera agreed and said that, in addition to these two essential building blocks, a third, hallucination, also plays an important role in the construction of Bomarzo. "Any good opera must have these or similar dramatic qualities," he said. "*Salome* is sex. *Tosca* is violence. *Boris Godunov* is hallucination. And *Wozzeck* is all three together." So, too, is *Bomarzo.*

Happily, excerpts from each of the operas Ginastera mentioned appear in our anthology. Ginastera's statement supports our conviction that a successful opera composer still seeks, in the preparation of an opera, to combine the same ingredients that have been utilized by his predecessors throughout the history of the genre.

53-A

(Each singer in the Chorus must utter the guttural sounds
of these consonants senza voce and with free discontinuous rhythm.)

587

53-B

53-C

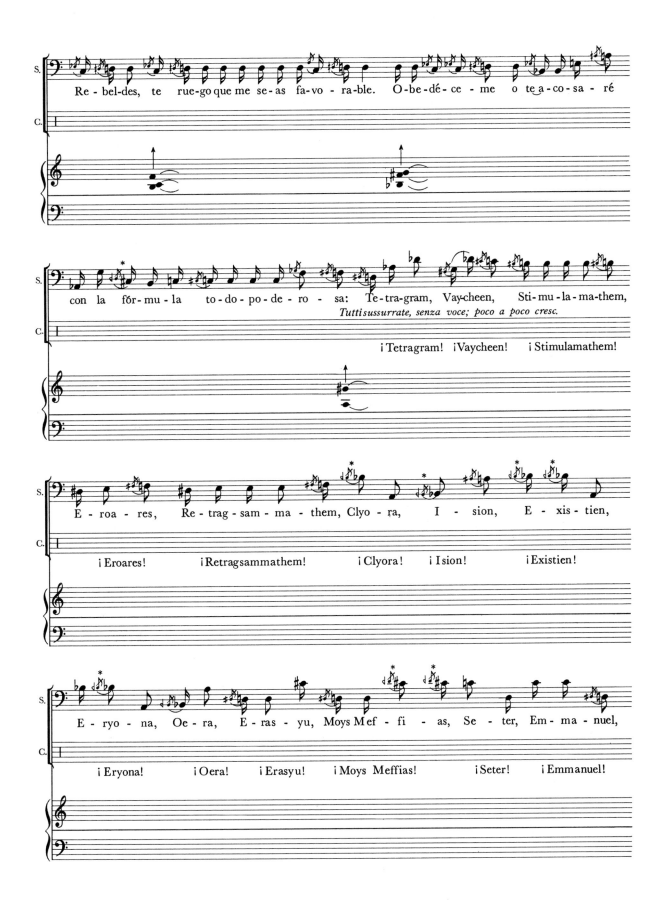

591

Ginastera, *Bomarzo*. Copyright 1967 by Boosey & Hawkes, Inc. Reprinted by permission.

BIBLIOGRAPHY

From the vast literature on opera, we have indicated a selection of reference works. Books of general interest are listed first, followed by books, monographs, and biographies that provide information on more specific topics. All but two of the items are in English. Exceptionally informative works are printed in capitals; asterisks precede titles of paperbacks.

General Works

Grout, Donald J., A SHORT HISTORY OF OPERA, 2nd ed. 2 vols. New York: Columbia University Press, 1965. Absolutely the best, most informative history of opera, with an extensive bibliography of close to 200 pages. This book is in a class by itself.

Kinsky, Georg, *History of Music in Pictures.* Dover reprint of English edition, New York: 1951. Useful for background material and iconographic data. The original German edition (1929) has the best plates.

Lang, Paul Henry, *Music in Western Civilization.* New York: W. W. Norton & Company, Inc., 1941. Excellent to fill in social and historical background.

Rosenthal, Harold, and John Warrack, eds., CONCISE OXFORD DICTIONARY OF OPERA. London: Oxford University Press, 1964. Small but useful compilation of material for the layman.

Weisstein, Ulrich, ed., *The Essence of Opera.* New York: The Free Press, 1964. Annotated compilation of material on opera written by composers, librettists, critics, etc., translated and arranged in historical sequence.

Operatic Premieres

Lowenberg, Alfred, ANNALS OF OPERA, rev. ed. by Frank Walker. Geneva: Societas Bibliographica, 1955. Yearly record of opera productions from 1597 to 1940. Much information presented here that is unavailable elsewhere. Most importantly, dates of performances.

*Mattfeld, Julius, *A Handbook of Operatic Premieres,* 1731-1962. Detroit: Studies in Music Bibliography, 1963. Nearly 2000 operas and related works listed alphabetically by title of opera. Also contains composers' index.

Opera Plots

*Fellner, Rudolph, *Opera Themes and Plots.* New York: Simon and Schuster, 1958. Synopses and musical examples from 32 operas.

*Newman, Ernest, *Stores of Great Operas* 2 vols. New York: Vintage Books, Inc., 1958. Absolutely the best of its kind. Most informative material on operas and backgrounds of the compositions. The material of these books is taken from Newman's *Stories of Famous Operas* and from his *More Stories of Famous Operas* (see also Newman's *Seventeen Famous Operas*). Occasionally the same opera is discussed in more than one collection, but then Mr. Newman provides us with additional information.

*Simon, Henry W., *100 Great Operas and their Stories*, rev. ed. New York: Doubleday & Company, Inc., 1960. Contains largest number of plots, covering most of the operas in the current repertory here and abroad.

*Carse, Adam, *The History of Orchestration.* Dover reprint, 1964.

*Dent, Edward, *Opera* Baltimore: Penguin Books, Inc., 1940. Good introduction to operatic history.

*Kerman, Joseph, *Opera as Drama.* New York: Vintage Books, Inc., 1956. Excellent essays on specific operas.

I. *Early Baroque Opera*

Bukofzer, Manfred, MUSIC IN THE BAROQUE ERA. New York: W. W. Norton & Company, Inc., 1947. Probably the best background material for this chapter. Scholarly, but readable.

Ewen, David, "The Early Opera and Oratorio" in *Pioneers in Music.* New York: Thomas Y. Crowell Company, 1940.

Rolland, Romain, "The Beginnings of Opera" in *Some Musicians of Former Days* translated by Mary Blaiklock. London: Kegan Paul, Trench, Trubner & Co. Ltd., 1915.

Schrade, Leo, *Monteverdi, Creator of Modern Music.* New York: W. W. Norton & Company, Inc., 1950.

Sonneck, O. G., "A Description of Alessandro Striggio and Francesco Corteccia's Intermedi *Psyche and Amor*" included in *Miscellaneous Studies.* New York: The Macmillan Company, 1921.

*Wellesz, Egon, "The Beginning of Baroque in Music" in *Essays on Opera.* Translated by Patricia Kean. London: Dennis Dobson Ltd., 1950.

See also facsimile editions of Cavalieri's *Rappresentatione di anima e di corpo* of 1600 (Farnborough, Hants., England: Gregg Press reprint, 1967), Peri's *Le Musiche sopra Euridice* of 1601 (Rome: Reale Accademia d'Italia, 1934), and Monteverdi's *Orfeo* of 1607 (Augsburg: B. Filser, 1927).

II. *Middle Baroque*

Demuth, Norman, *French Opera: its Development to the Revolution.* London: The Artemis Press, 1963.

Dent, Edward, *Foundations of English Opera.* Cambridge, England: The University Press, 1928.

Rolland, Romain, "The First Opera Played in Paris" and "Notes on Lully" in *Some Musicians of Former Days.*

Worsthorne, Simon, VENETIAN OPERA IN THE SEVENTEENTH CENTURY. London: Oxford University Press, 1954. One of the best in English on this period.

*Wellesz, Egon, ESSAYS ON OPERA. Several good essays on seventeenth-century opera.

See also facsimile of Monteverdi's manuscript of *L'incoronazione di Poppea,* prepared by Giacomo Benvenuti (Milan: Fratelli Bocca, 1938).

III. *Late Baroque Opera*

Dent, Edward, "The Operas" in *Handel: A Symposium.* Edited by Gerald Abraham. London: Oxford University Press, 1954.

————*Alessandro Scarlatti,* 2nd printing with preface by Frank Walker. London: Edward Arnold, Ltd., 1960.

Girdlestone, Cuthbert, *Rameau.* London: Cassell, 1957. For those who read French, Masson's *L'opéra de Rameau* (Paris: H. Laurens, 1930) is superb.

Lang, Paul Henry, *George Frideric Handel*. New York: W. W. Norton & Company, Inc., 1966. Good material on operas.

See also The Baroque Theater: A Cultural History of the 17th and 18th Centuries by Margarete Baur-Heinhold. Translated by Mary Whittall. New York: McGraw-Hill Book Company, 1967.

IV. *Opera in the Early Classical Period*

Einstein, Alfred, *Gluck*. Translated by Eric Blom. New York: E. P. Dutton & Co., Inc., 1936.

Howard, Patricia, *Gluck and the Birth of Modern Opera*. London: St. Martin's, 1963. Excellent discussion of Gluck's techniques of composition.

Mueller von Asow, Hedwig, and E. H. Mueller von Asow, *The Collected Correspondence and Papers of Christoph Willibald Gluck*. New York: Random House, 1962. Very informative.

Rolland, Romain, "Metastasio, the Forerunner of Gluck" in *A Musical Tour Through the Land of the Past*. Translated by Bernard Miall. New York: Holt, Rinehart & Winston, Inc., 1922.

Sitwell, Sacheverell, "The Castrati, and Others" in *Baroque and Rococo*. New York: G. P. Putnam's Sons, 1967.

V. *Eighteenth-Century Comic Opera*

Cooper, Martin, *Opéra-Comique*. New York: Chanticleer Press, 1949.

Gagey, Edmond, *Ballad Opera*. New York: Columbia University Press, 1937.

Kidson, Frank, *The Beggar's Opera*. Cambridge, England: The University Press, 1922.

Strunk, Oliver, ed., *Source Readings in Music History*. New York: W. W. Norton & Company, Inc., 1950. See particularly Ch. XIV for operatic rivalry in France. (This book has been reprinted in several paperback volumes.)

See also facsimile of *Beggar's Opera* in edition by Louis Kronenberger and Max Goberman. New York: Argonaut Books, 1961.

VI. *Synthesis of Buffa and Seria*

*Blom, Eric. ed., *Mozart's Letters*. England: Penguin Books, 1956. A selection from *The __ Letters of Mozart and His Family* by Emily Anderson. Excellent. (See also her *The Letters of Mozart and His Family,* 2 vols.; 2nd ed. prepared by A. H. King and M. Carolam, New York: St. Martin's, 1966.)

*Broder, Nathan, ed., *The Great Operas of Mozart*. New York: W. W. Norton & Company, Inc., 1962. Background and libretti with translations of five principal Mozart operas.

*Dent, Edward, *Mozart's Operas,* 2nd ed. London: Oxford University Press, 1947. First-rate.

Deutsch, Otto Erich, *Mozart: A Documentary Biography*. Translated by Eric Blom, Peter Branscombe, and Jeremy Noble. Stanford, Calif.: Stanford University Press, 1965. A new approach to biography: the documents tell the story.

Hughes, Patrick (Spike), *Famous Mozart Operas*. New York: The Citadel Press, 1958. Excellent guide to the same five that Broder discusses (see above), but no libretti.

VII. Nineteenth-Century French Opera Before Wagner

Arvin, Neil Cole, *Eugène Scribe and the French Theatre.* New York: Benjamin Blom reprint, 1967.

Crosten, William L., *French Grand Opera: An Art and a Business.* New York: King's Crown Press, 1948.

Longyear, R. Morgan, "Notes on Rescue Opera" in *The Musical Quarterly*, vol. 45 (January 1959).

VIII. Nineteenth-Century Italian Opera Before Wagner

Ashbrook, William, *Donizetti.* London: Cassell, 1965.

Michotte, Edmond, *Souvenirs personnels, La Visite de R. Wagner a Rossini* (Passy, 1860) and *Souvenirs: Une Soirée chez Rossini à Beau-Séjour* (Passy 1858). Annotated and translated by Herbert Weinstock. Chicago: University of Chicago Press, 1968.

Weinstock, Herbert, *Rossini.* New York: Alfred A. Knopf, 1968. Readable, but does not contain too much new material. Francis Toye's *Rossini,* New York: W. W. Norton & Company, Inc., 1963, paperback, is better value, but a bit dry.

See also the facsimile of Bellini's *Norma,* 2 vols. Rome: Reale Accademia d'Italia, 1935.

IX. Nineteenth-Century German Opera Before Wagner

Abraham, Gerald, *Slavonic and Romantic Music.* New York: St. Martin's, 1968. A collection of essays. Material on Weber and other German romantics.

Warrack, John, *Carl Maria von Weber.* London: Hamish Hamilton, 1968. Fine biography and the only one in English. Good discussion of the operas.

See also facsimile of score of Weber's *Der Freischütz,* Berlin: privately printed, 1942, and Strunk's *Source Readings,* Ch. XVIII.

X. Wagner's Operas

Donington, Robert, *Wagner's "Ring" and Its Symbols.* London: Faber and Faber, 1963. Psychological concepts examined by a musicologist.

Hall, Gertrude, *The Wagnerian Romances.* New York: Alfred A. Knopf, 1907. Excellent despite its title. One of the earliest English discussions of the principal operas.

*Newman, Ernest, *Wagner as Man and Artist.* New York: Vintage Books, Inc., 1952.

———— *The Wagner Operas.* New York: Alfred A. Knopf, 1949. Excellent, in a class by itself.

———— *The Life of Richard Wagner,* 4 vols. New York: Alfred A. Knopf, 1933-1946. Excellent not only for information on Wagner, but also for the social and musical life of this period in German history.

Robb, Stewart, *Richard Wagner's "The Ring of the Nibelung."* New York: E. P. Dutton & Co., Inc. 1960. Fine English translation of the texts of the *Ring* operas; also contains superb introductory notes by Edward Downes.

———— *Richard Wagner's "Tristan and Isolde."* New York: E. P. Dutton & Co., Inc., 1965. Same treatment (as above) for *Tristan und Isolde,* but German original included here.

Skelton, Geoffrey, *Wagner at Bayreuth.* London: Barrie & Rockliff, 1965.

Stein, Jack, *Richard Wagner and the Synthesis of the Arts.* Detroit: Wayne State University Press, 1960. An absorbing study by a professor of Germanic languages who often writes about music.

*White, Chappell, *An Introduction to the Life and Works of Richard Wagner.* New York: Prentice-Hall, Inc., 1967. Basic material covered.

Zuckerman, Elliott, *The First Hundred Years of Wagner's "Tristan."* New York: Columbia University Press, 1962. Excellent monograph by a sociologist.

See also the many fine facsimiles of Wagner's operas.

XI. Late-Nineteenth-Century Italian Opera

Hughes, Spike, *Famous Verdi Operas.* London: Robert Hale, 1968. Excellent discussions of twelve operas, more than are generally found elsewhere. No libretti.

Hussey, Dyneley, *Verdi.* London: J. M. Dent, 1948. Excellent and readable.

Martin, George, *Verdi: His Music, Life and Times.* New York: Dodd, Mead & Co., 1963. Fine drawings.

Walker, Frank, *The Man Verdi.* New York: Alfred A. Knopf, 1962. New information and very fine.

*Weaver, William, *Verdi's Librettos.* New York: Anchor, 1963. Five Verdi operas in good translations; also has original libretti. (Francis Toye's *Verdi* of 1931 is now available in paperback, but still rather dry.)

XII. Nationalism in Opera

Abraham, Gerald, "The Genesis of *The Bartered Bride*" in *Music and Letters,* vol. 28 (January 1947).

Calvocoressi, M. D., *Mussogorsky.* London: J. M. Dent, 1946.

Leyda, Jay, and S. Bertensson, *The Mussorgsky Reader.* New York: W. W. Norton & Company, Inc., 1947.

Newmarch, Rosa, *The Russian Opera.* London: Herbert Jenkins Limited, 1914.

XIII. Realism in French Opera

Curtiss, Mina, *Bizet and His World.* New York: Alfred A. Knopf, 1958. Excellent book by a non-musician.

Dean, Winton, *Bizet.* New York: Collier Books reprint, 1962. See other articles on *Carmen* by this author.

XIV. Verismo in Italian Opera

Carner, Mosco, *Puccini: A Critical Biography.* London: Gerald Duckworth & Co., Ltd., 1958. Excellent.

*Hughes, Patrick (Spike), *Famous Puccini Operas.* New York: The Citadel Press, 1962. See his Mozart and Verdi books.

*Weaver, William, *Puccini Librettos.* New York: Anchor, 1966. Five Puccini operas in good translations; also has original language.

XV. Early Trends in Twentieth-Century Opera

Del Mar, Norman, *Richard Strauss: A Critical Commentary on His Life and Works.* 2 vols. London: Chilton Book Company, 1962, 1969.

Ewen, David, *Journey to Greatness.* New York: Holt, Rinehart & Winston, Inc., 1956. Biography of Gershwin.

Kerman, Joseph, "Opera as Sung Play" in *Opera as Drama.* Excellent discussion of Debussy's *Pelléas et Mélisande.* Those who read French might also consider one of the earliest analyses of the opera by Debussy's friend and classmate, Maurice Emmanuel.

Lederman, Minna, ed., *Stravinsky in the Theatre.* New York: Pellegrini & Cudahy, 1949. Beautiful edition on fine paper. Includes articles on Stravinsky by contemporary artists who worked with him in different genres.

Lockspeiser, Edward, *Debussy: His Life and Mind.* 2 vols. London: Cassell, 1962-1965. Excellent and most informative, but no musical examples.

Mann, William, *Richard Strauss: A Critical Study of the Operas.* London: Cassell, 1964. Detailed analyses of the operas.

Redlich, Hans, *Alban Berg: the Man and His Music.* London: John Calder, 1957. Includes reprints of Berg's lectures.

Reich, Willi, *Alban Berg.* Translated by Cornelius Cardew. London: Thames and Hudson, 1965. Very readable.

Rufer, Joseph, *The Works of Arnold Schoenberg.* Translated by Dika Newlin. Glencoe: The Free Press, 1963. A catalogue of his compositions, writings, paintings, all most informative.

Stein, Erwin, ed., *Arnold Schoenberg: Letters.* Translated by Eithne Wilkins and Ernst Kaiser. New York: St. Martin's, 1965. Fascinating account of his activities and ideas by Schoenberg himself in his letters.

White, Eric Walter, *Benjamin Britten: A Sketch of His Life and Works,* 2nd ed. London: Boosey and Hawkes, Limited, 1954.

_____Stravinsky: *The Composer and His Works.* Berkeley and Los Angeles: University of California, 1966. Helpful on all dramatic works.

Wörner, Karl H., *Schoenberg's "Moses and Aaron."* Translated by Paul Hamburger. London: Faber and Faber, 1963. Excellent monograph. Original libretto and translation included.

Currently, one of the few books offering a survey of twentieth-century opera is H. H. Stückenschmidt's *Oper in dieser Zeit* (Hannover: Friedrich Verlag, 1964), which consists of a series of reviews of operas seen and criticised by this eminent musical journalist since 1925.

Index